D1807597

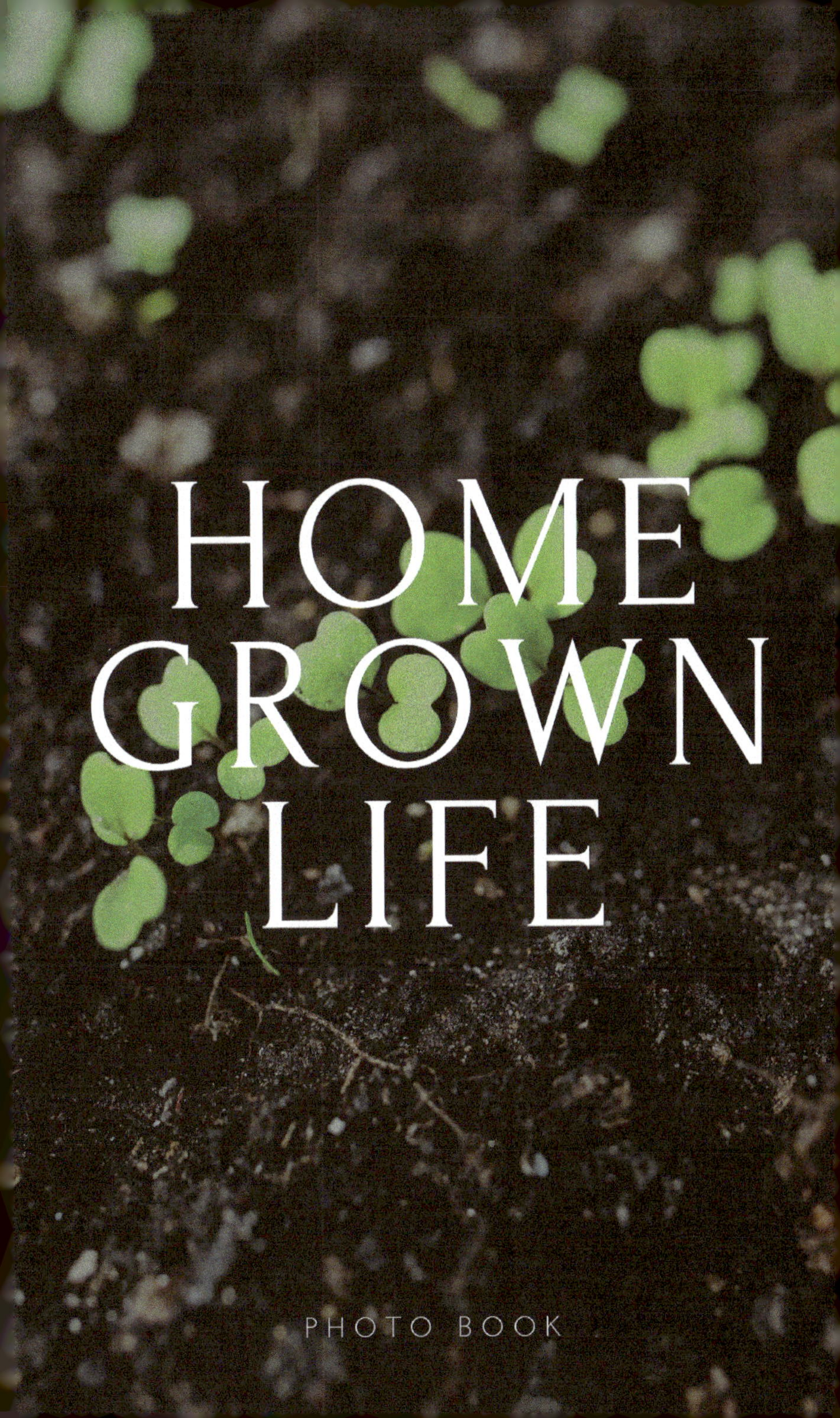

HOME GROWN LIFE

PHOTO BOOK

HOME GROWN
LIFE

"Love is the **flower** you've got to let grow."

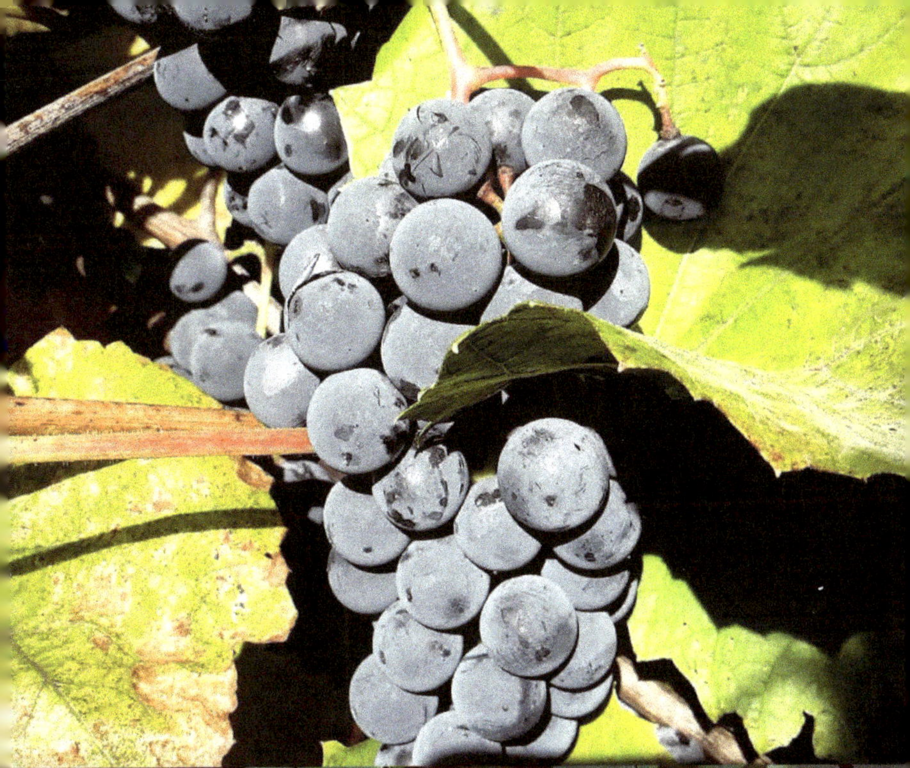

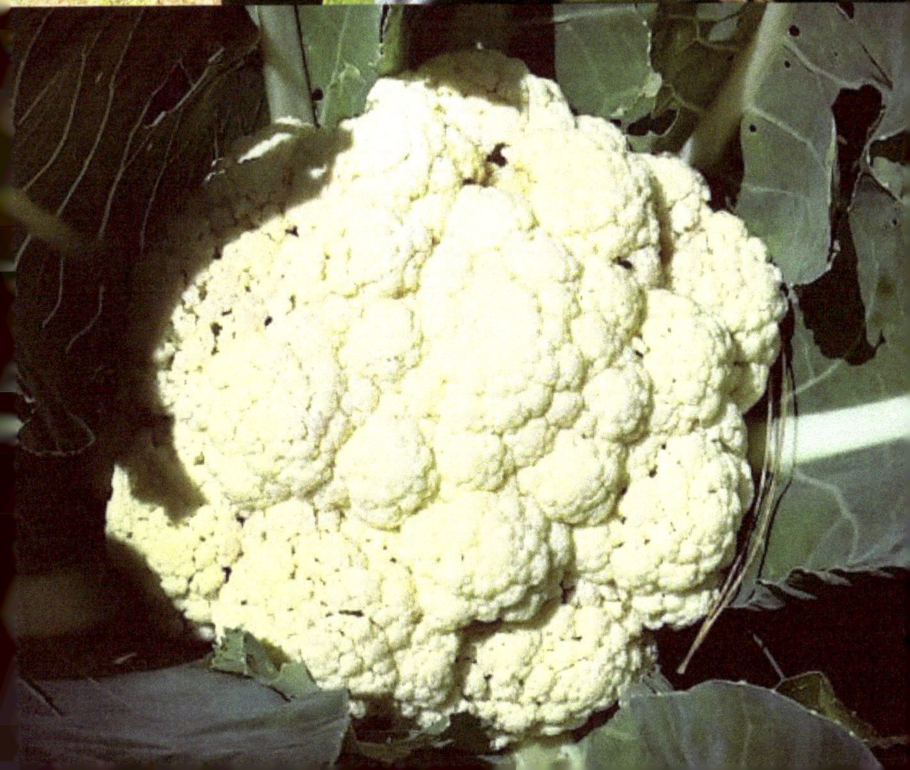

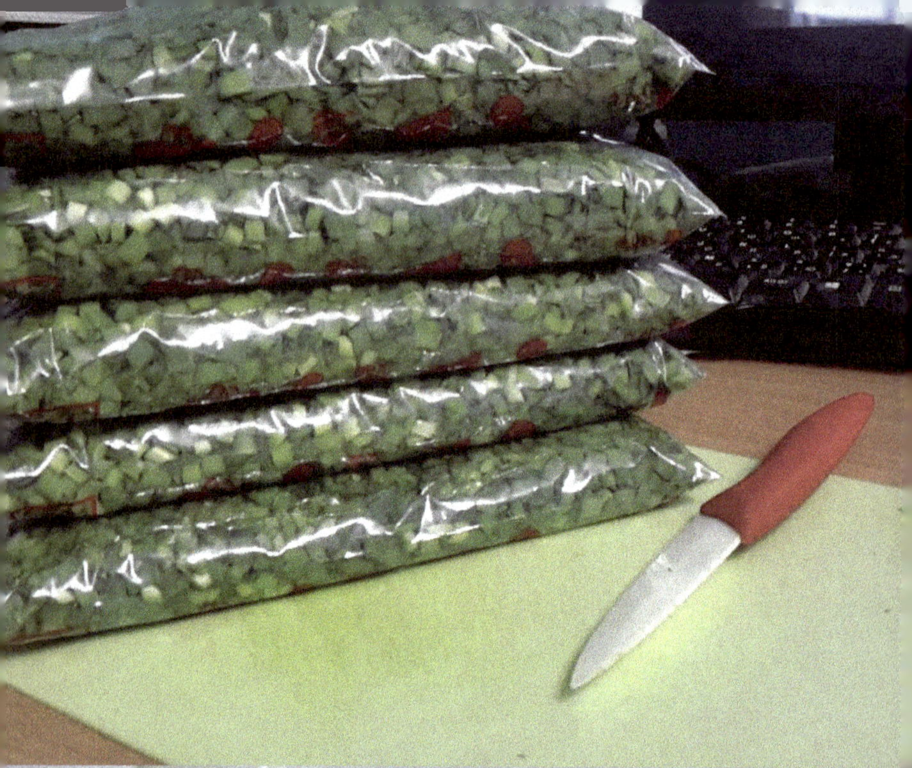

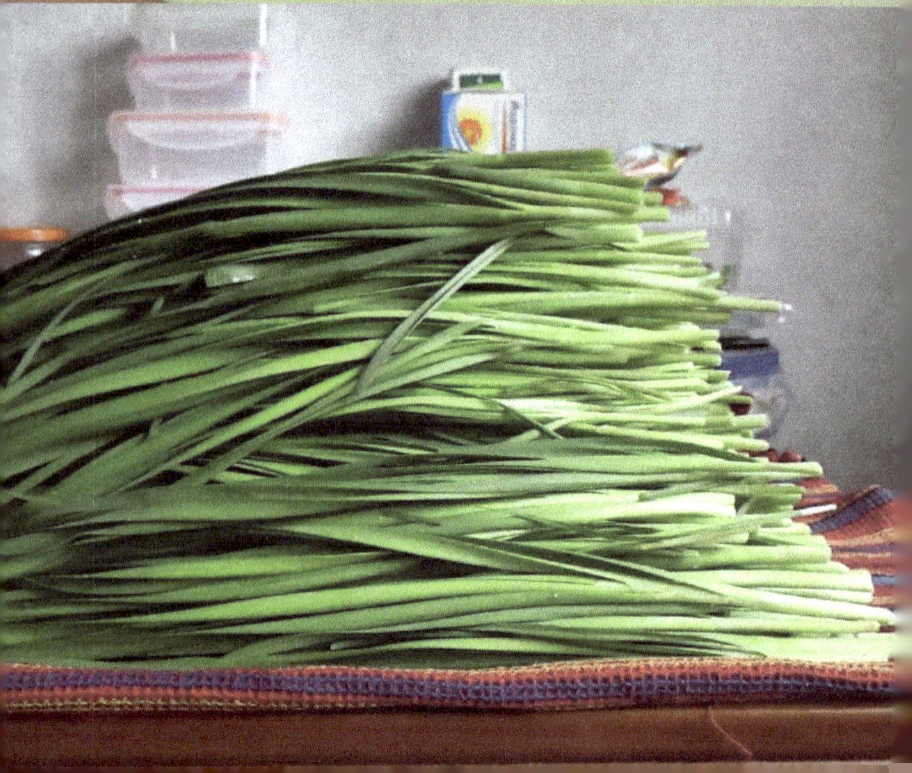

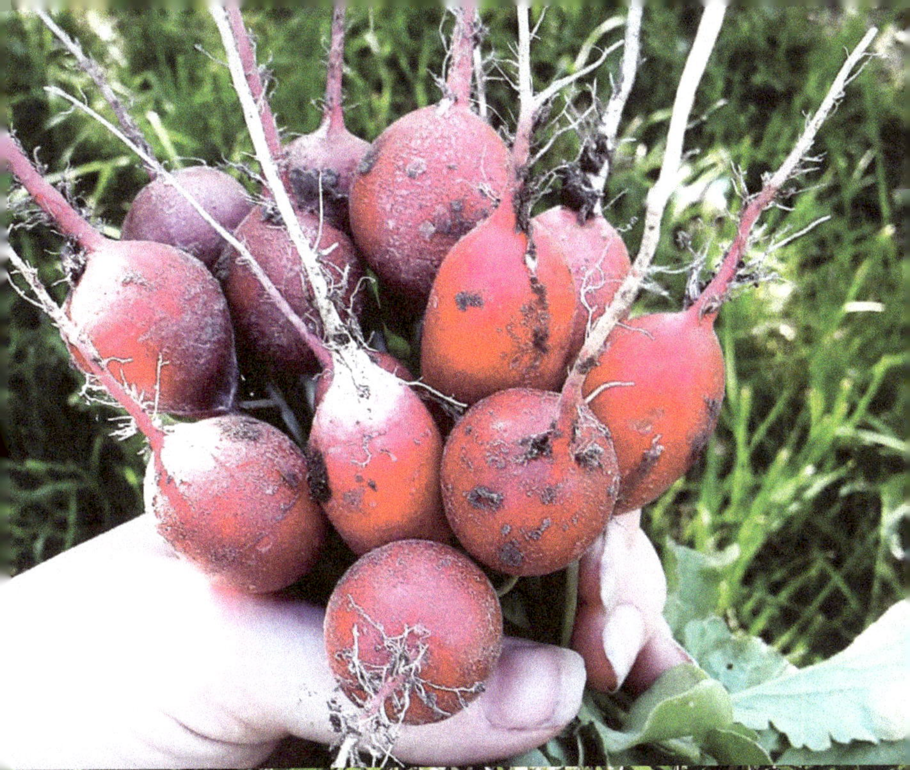

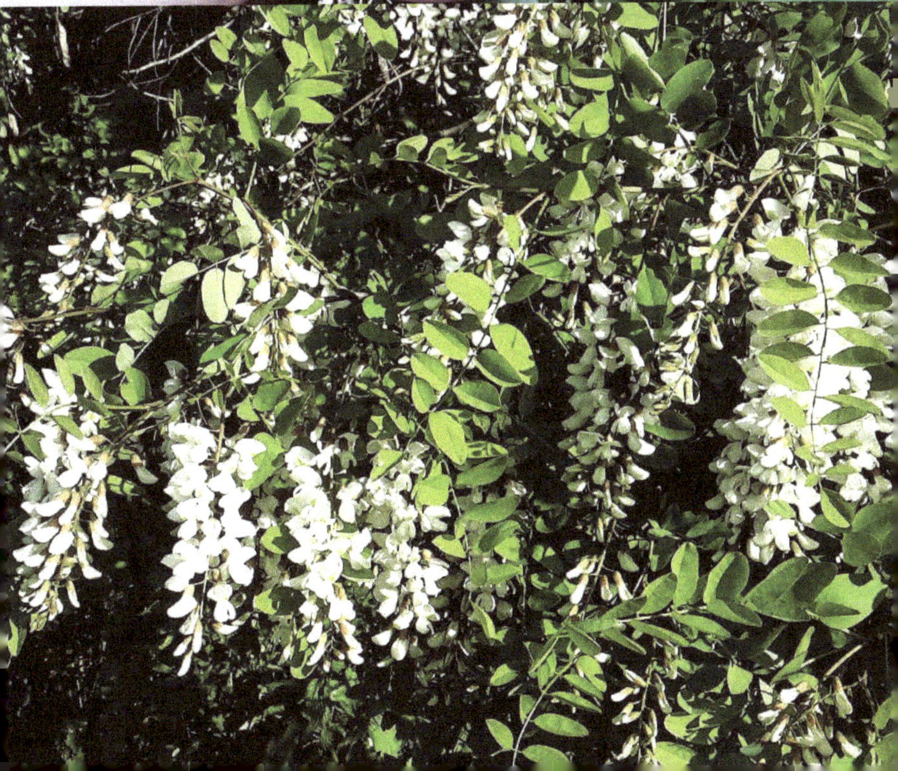

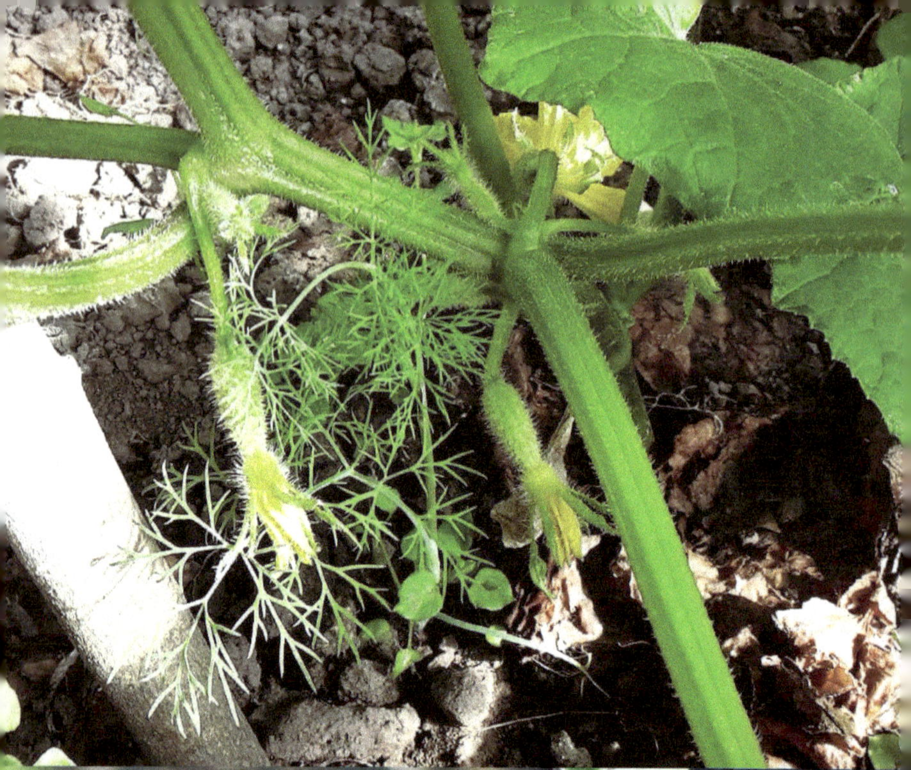

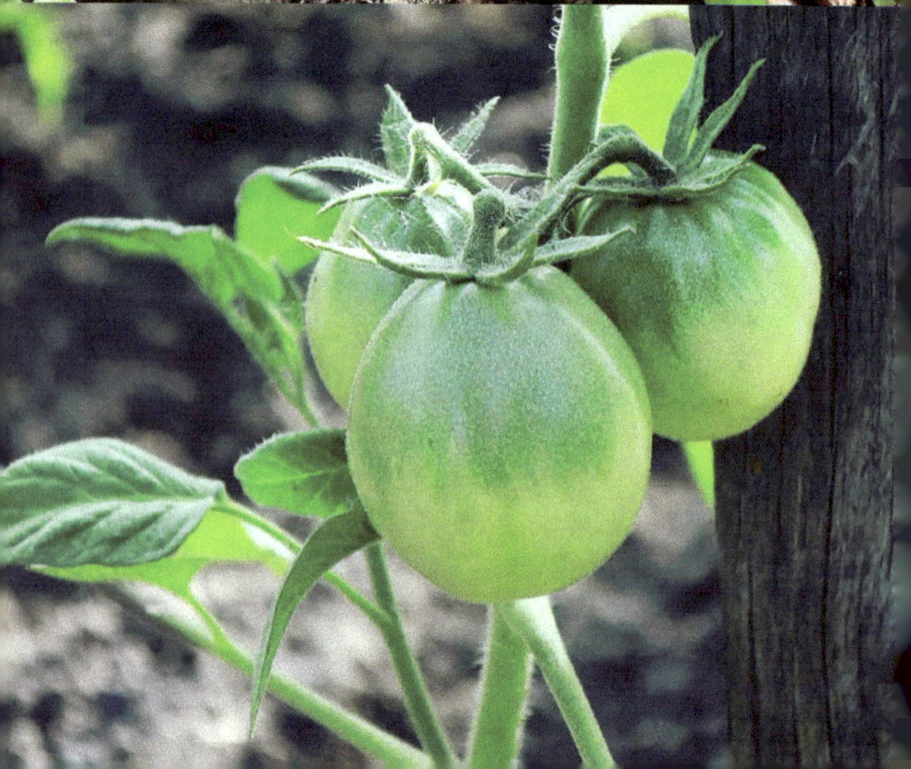

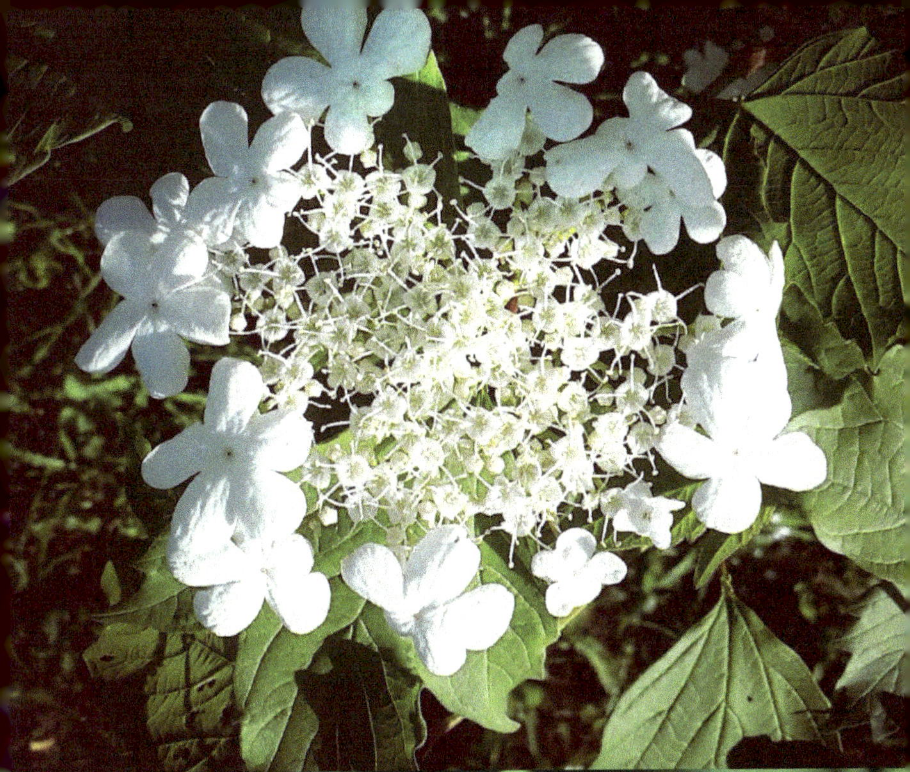

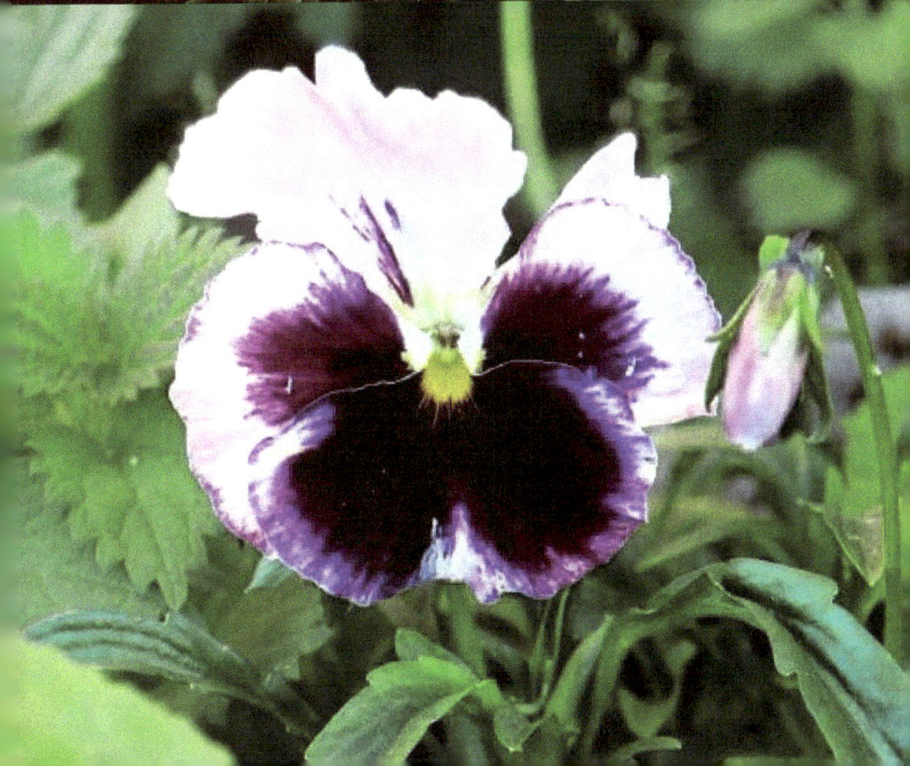

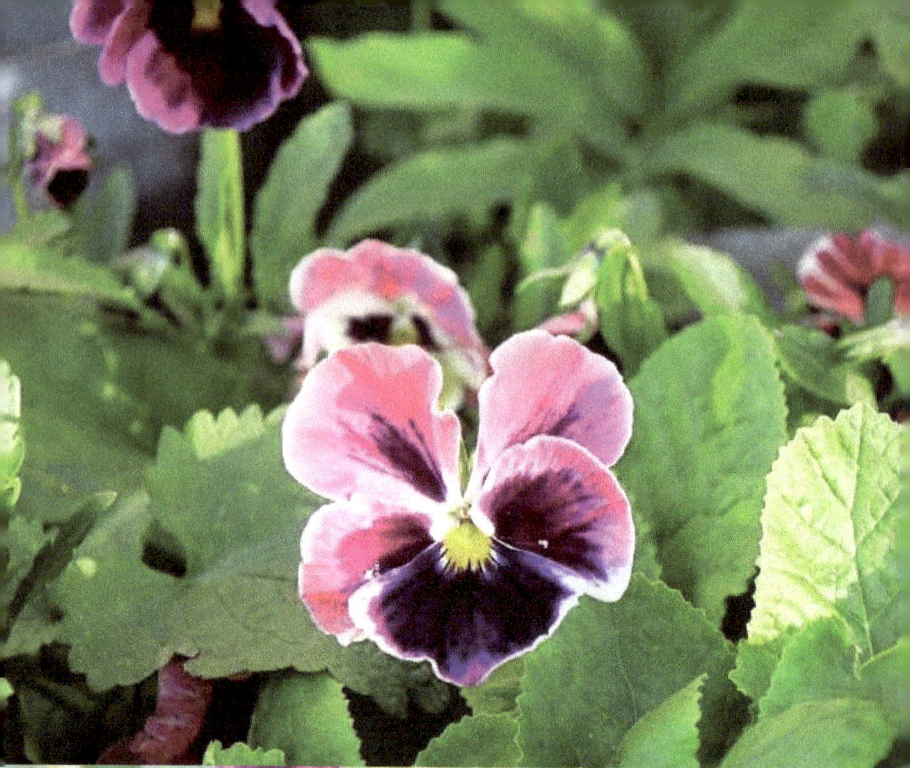
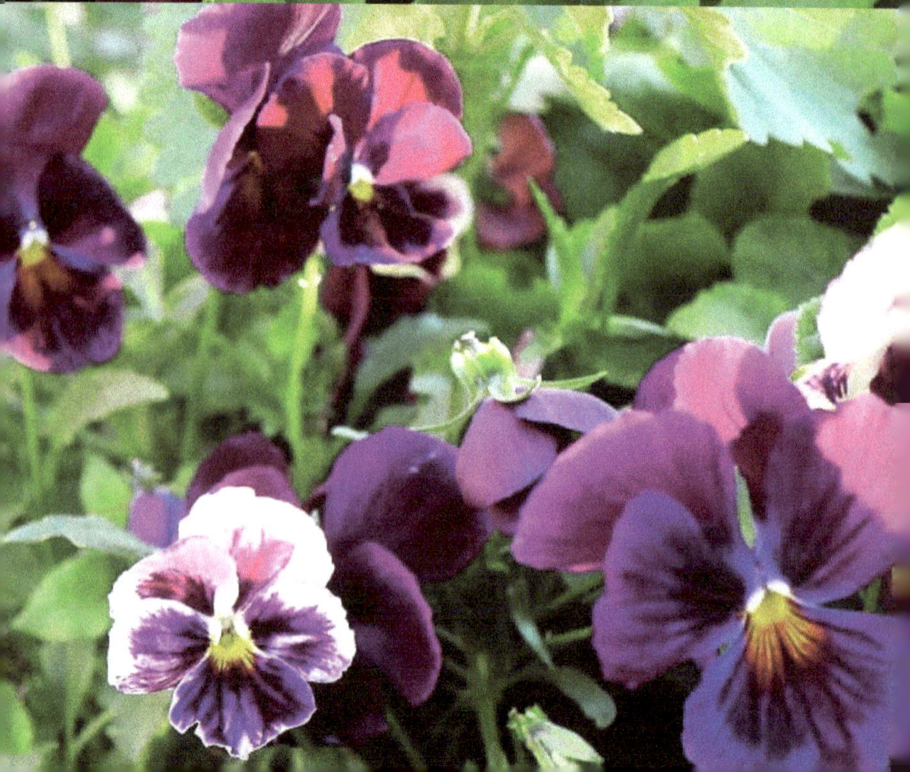

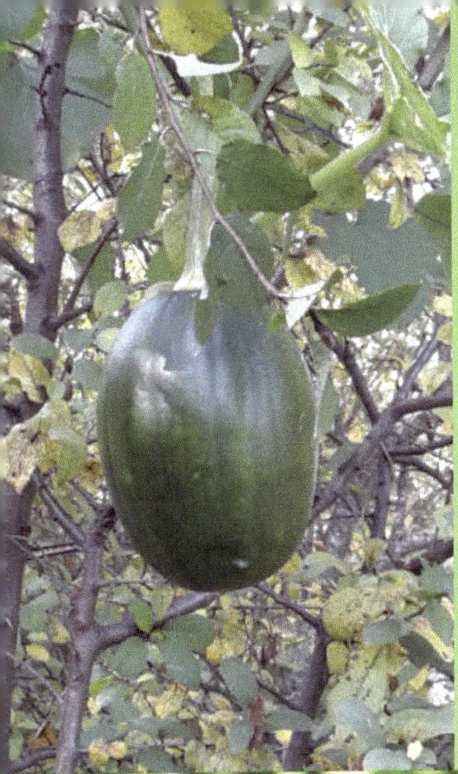
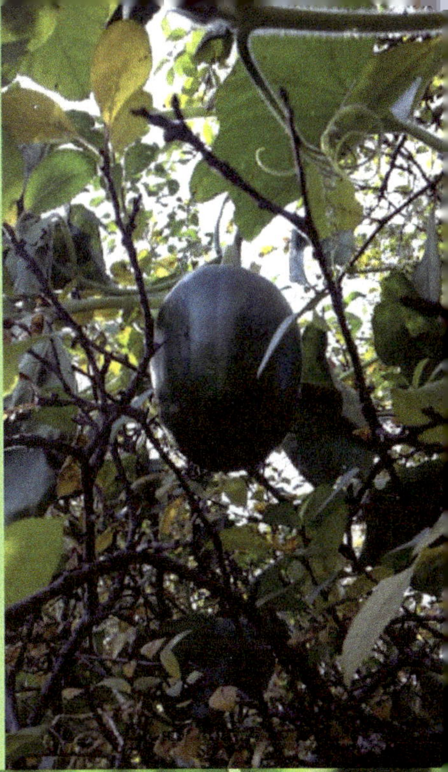
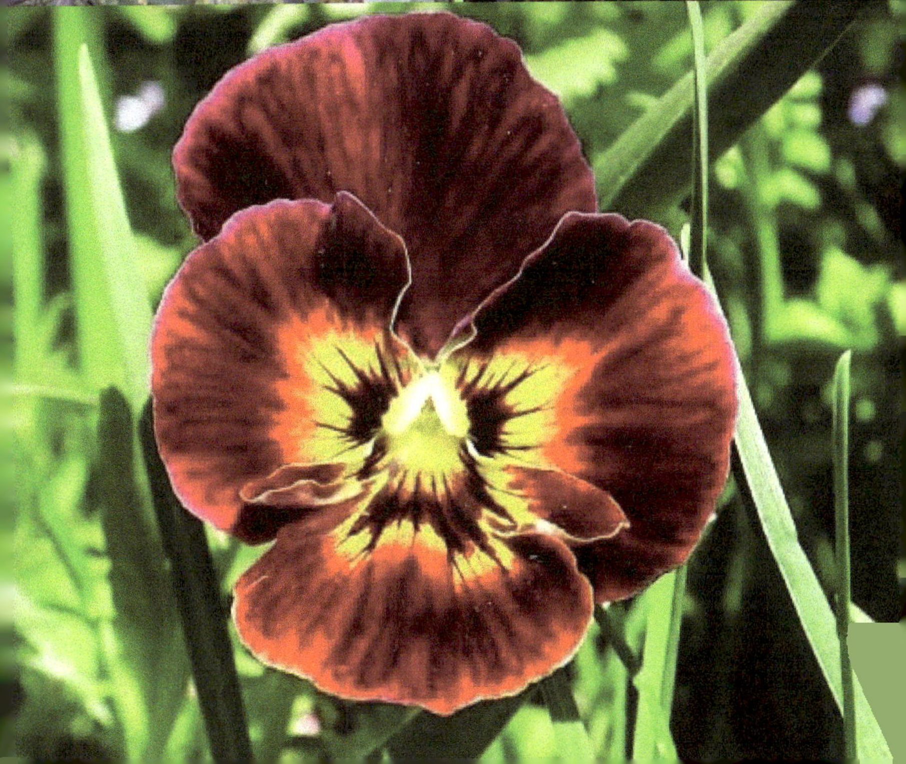

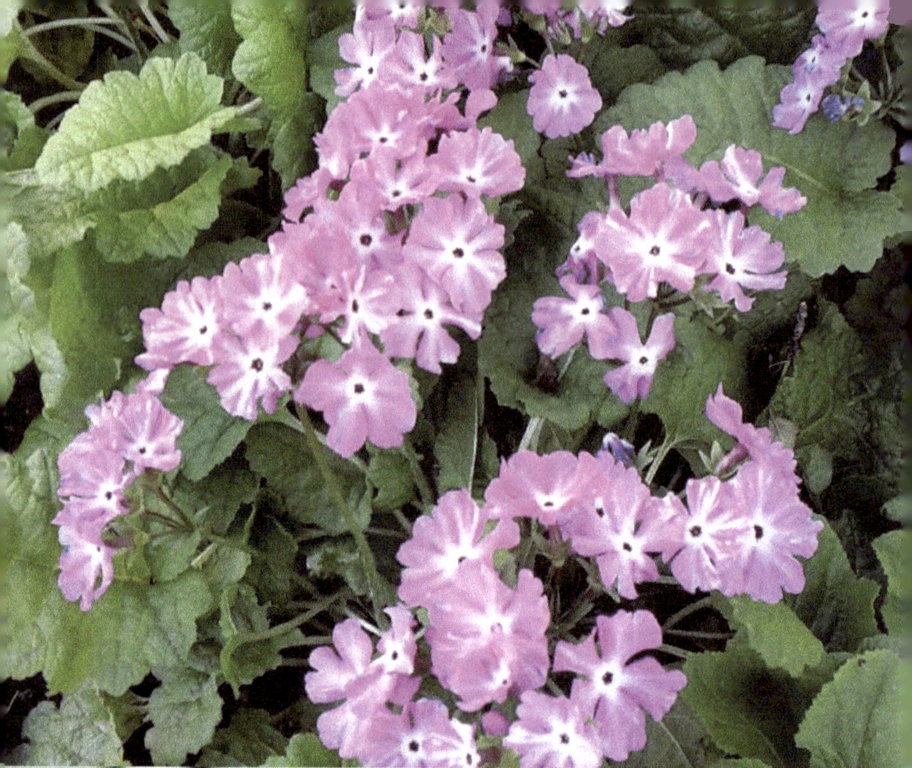

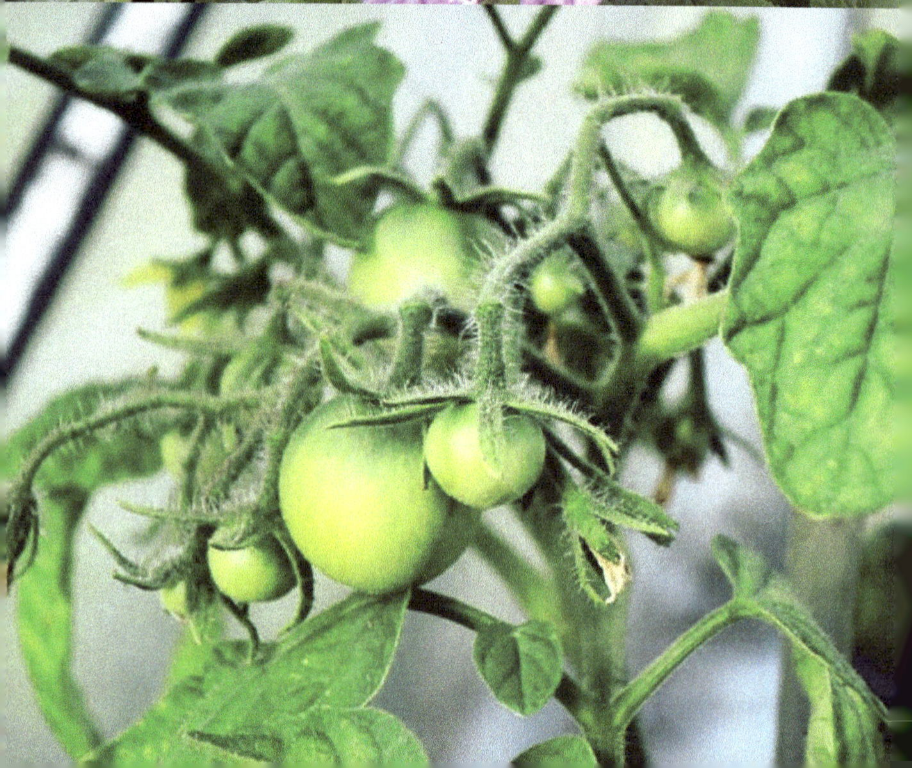

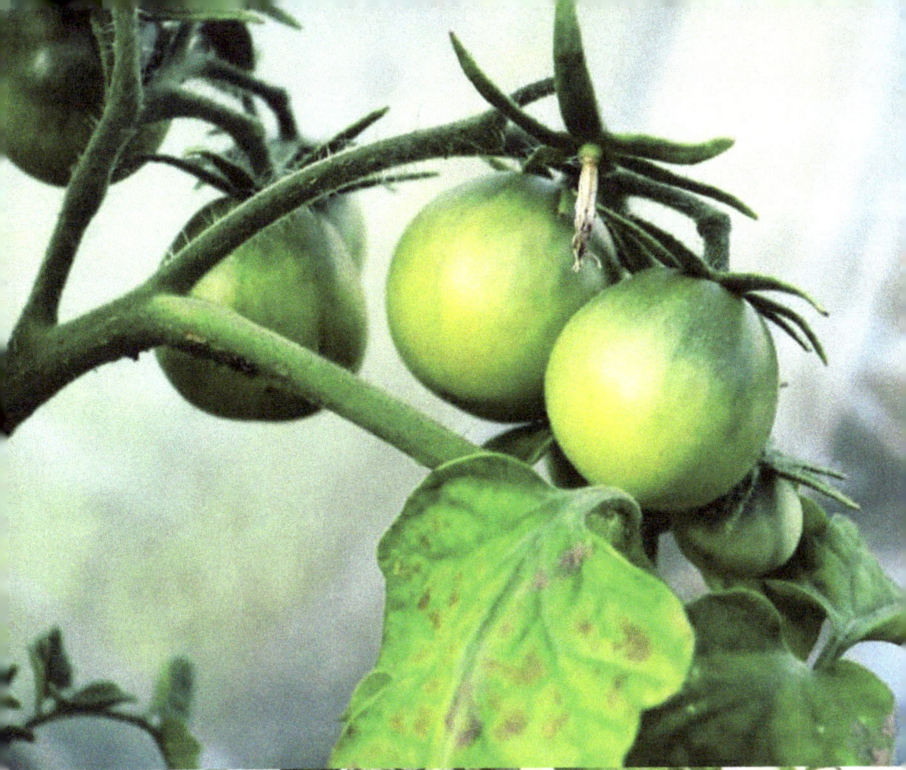

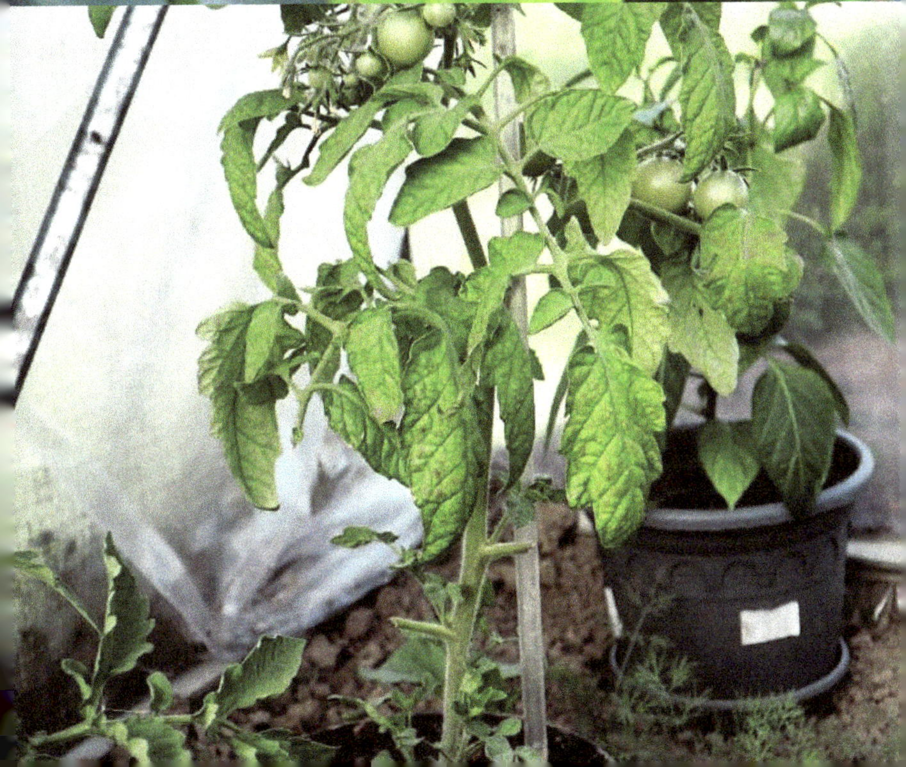

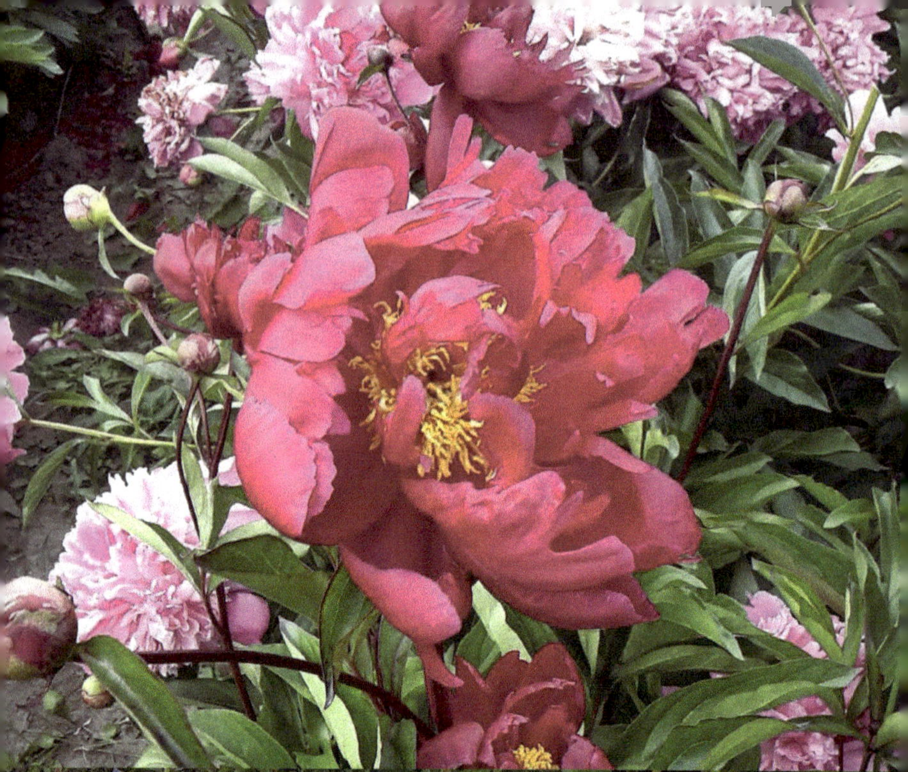

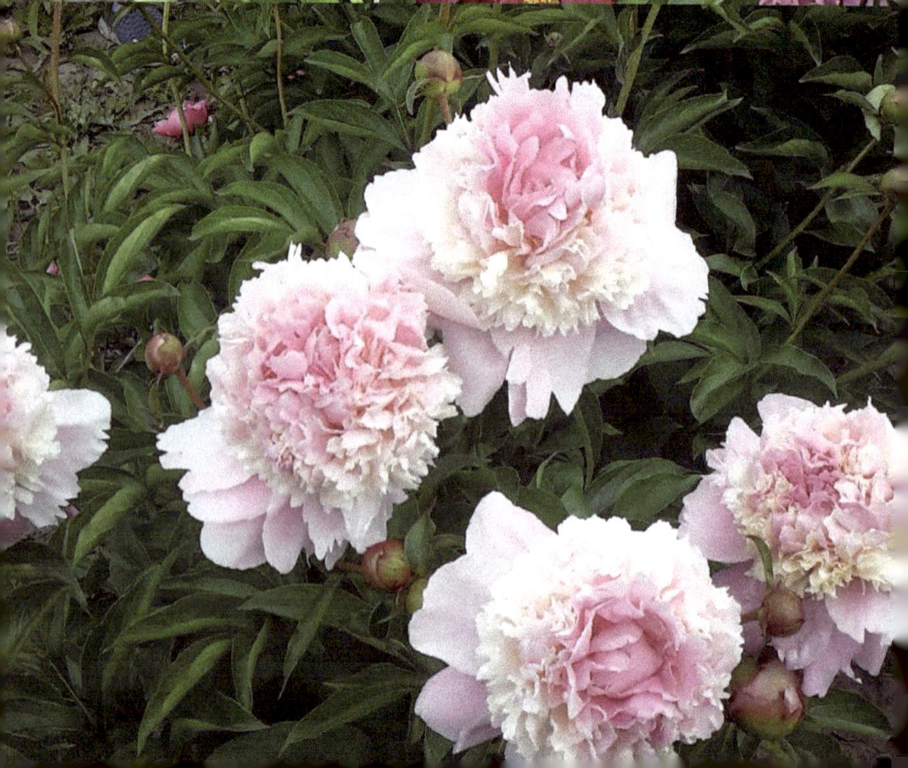

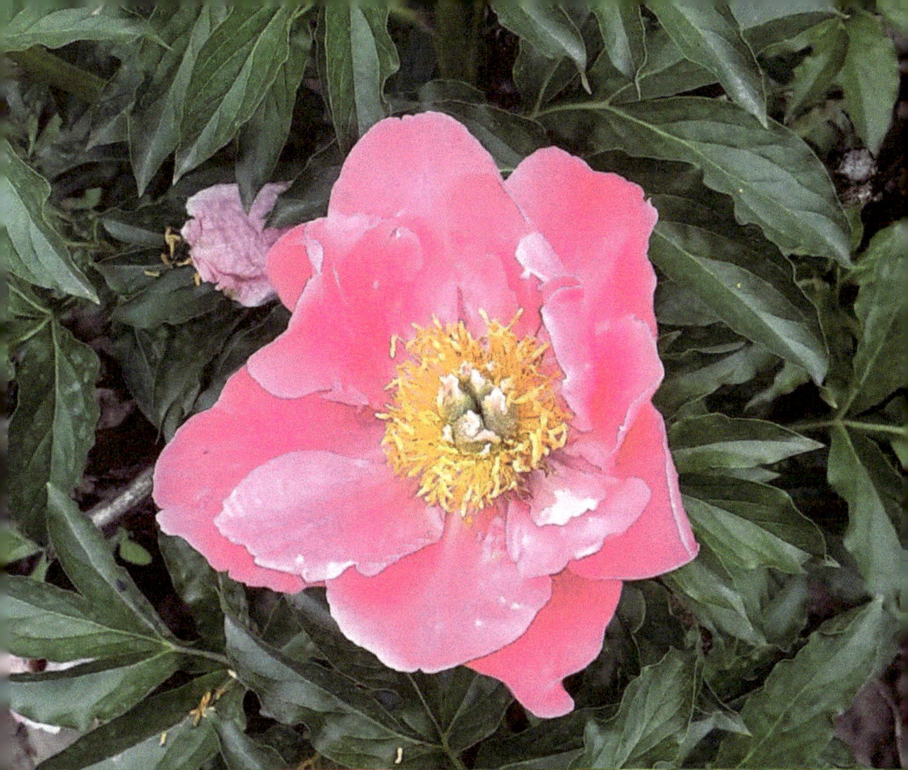

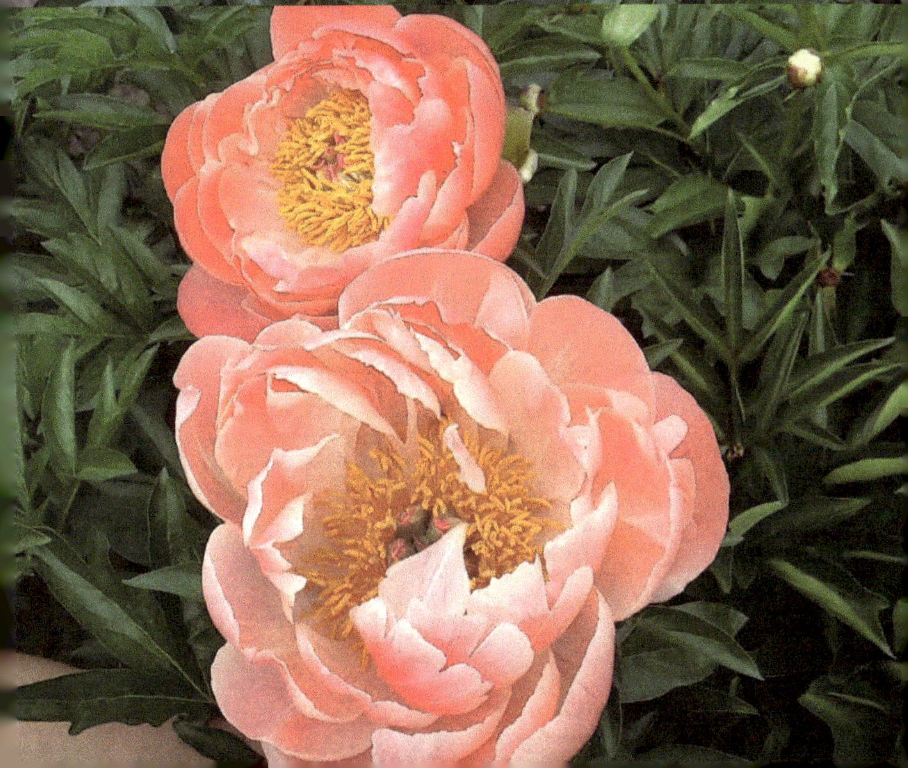

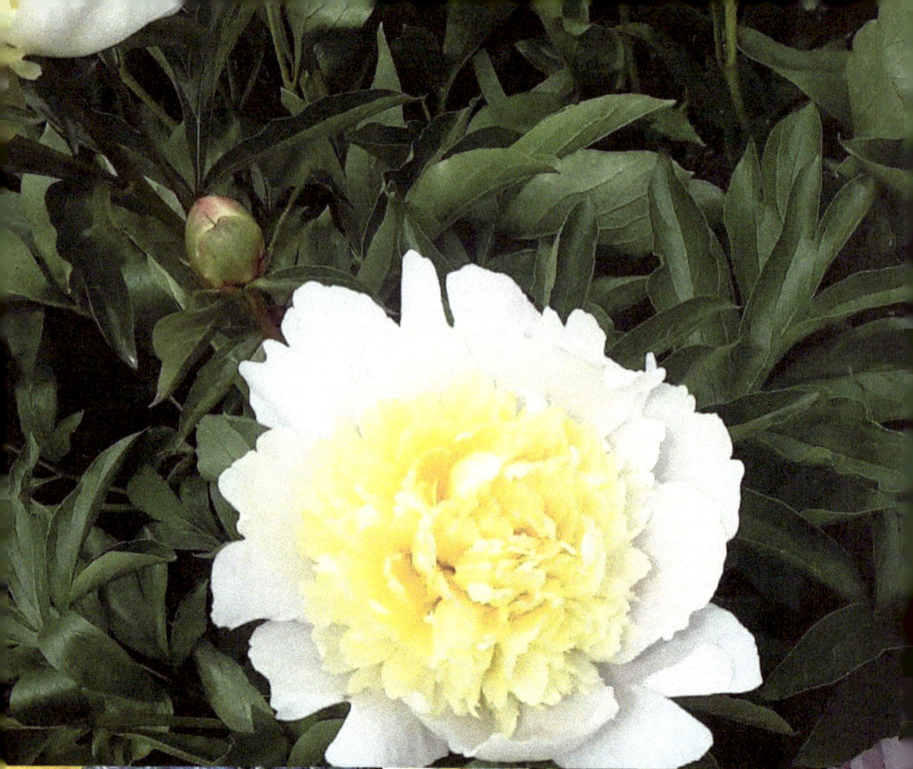
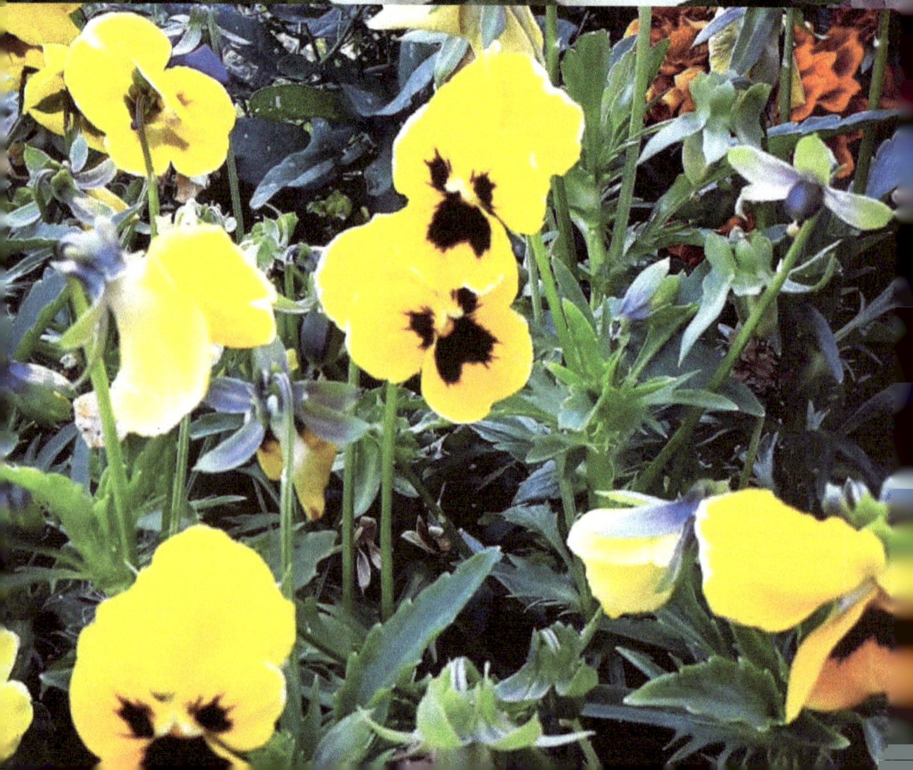

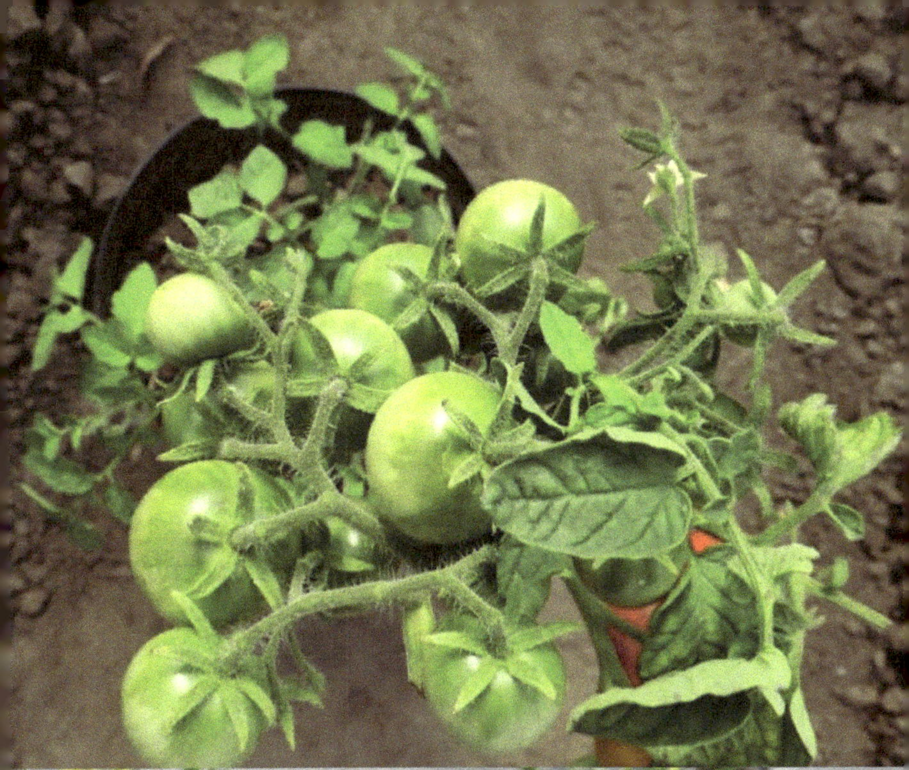
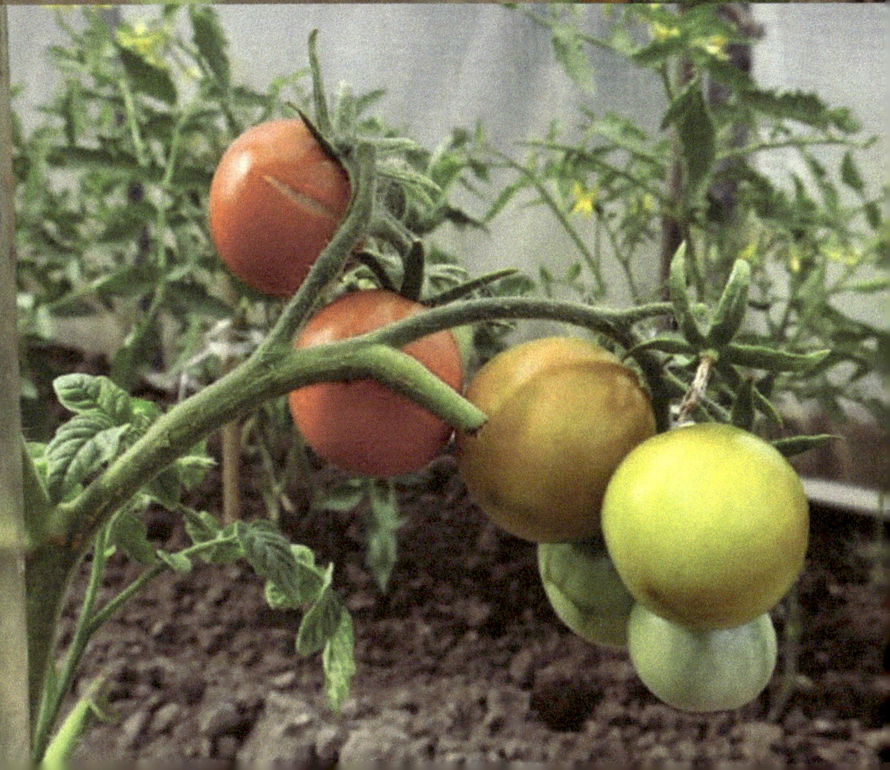

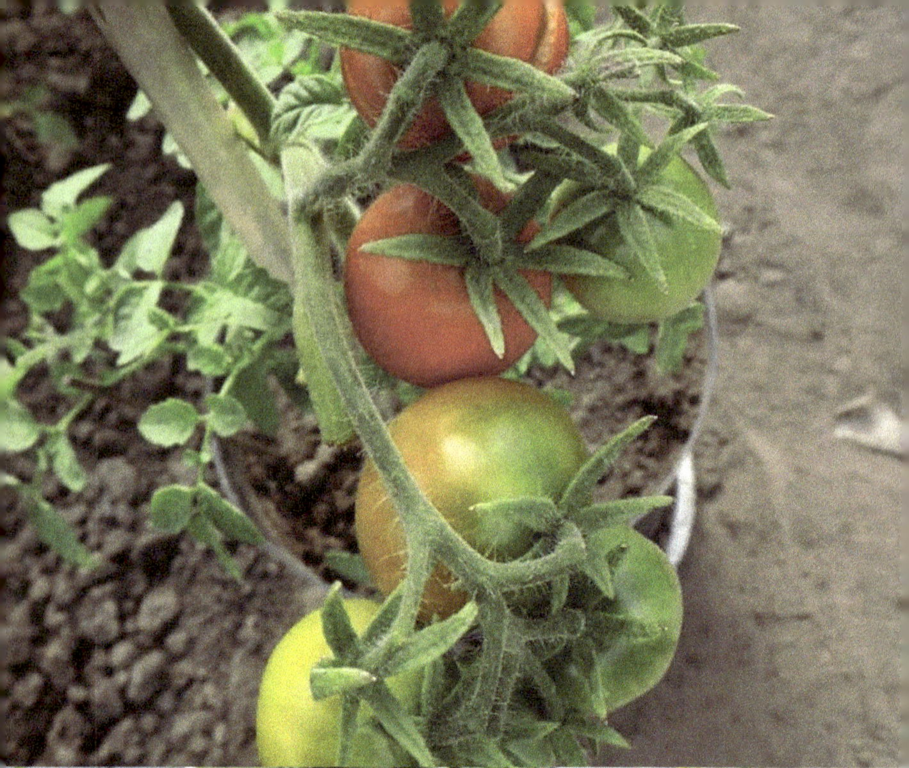

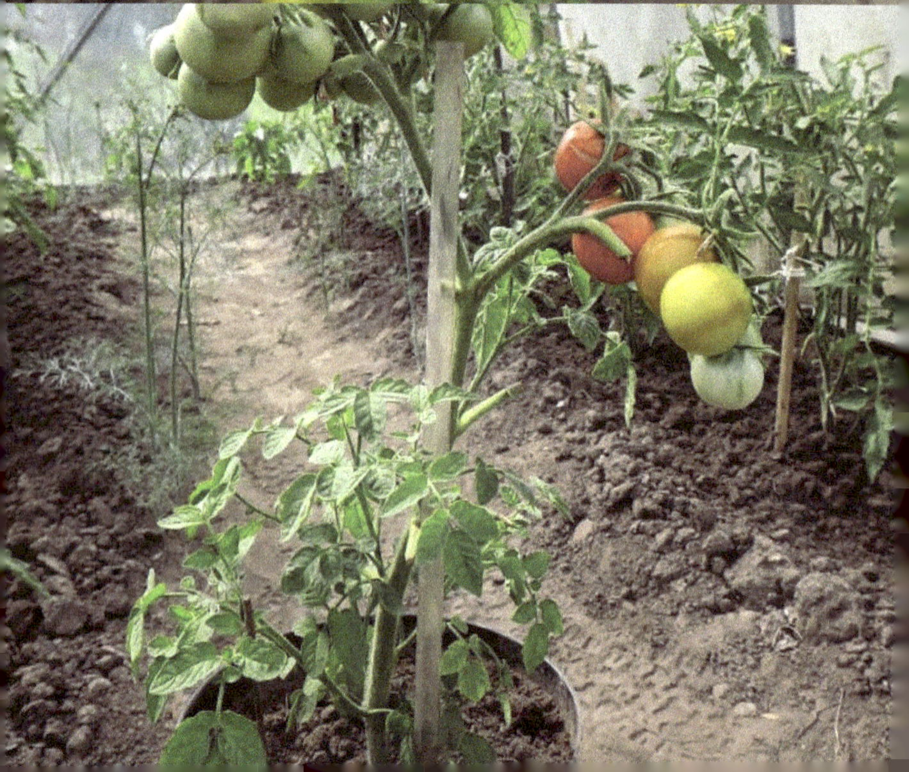

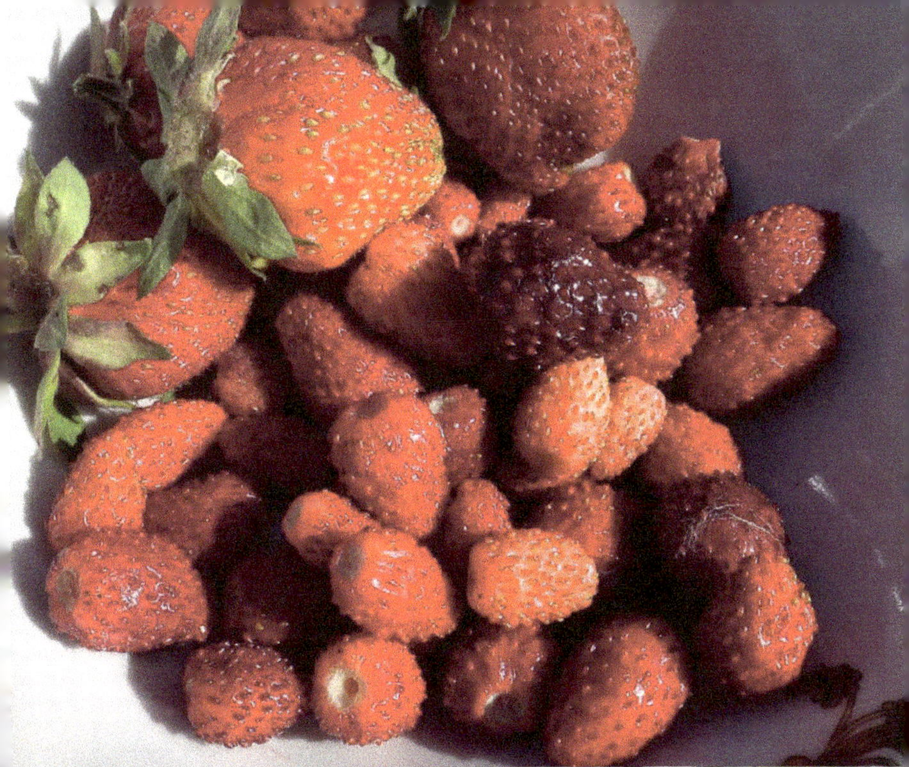

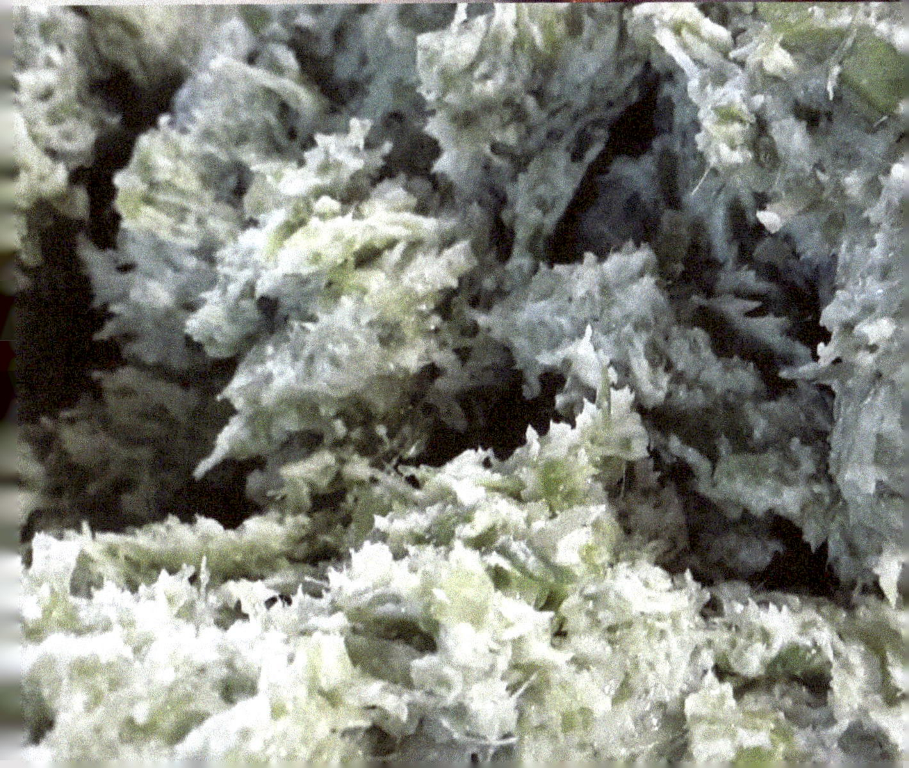

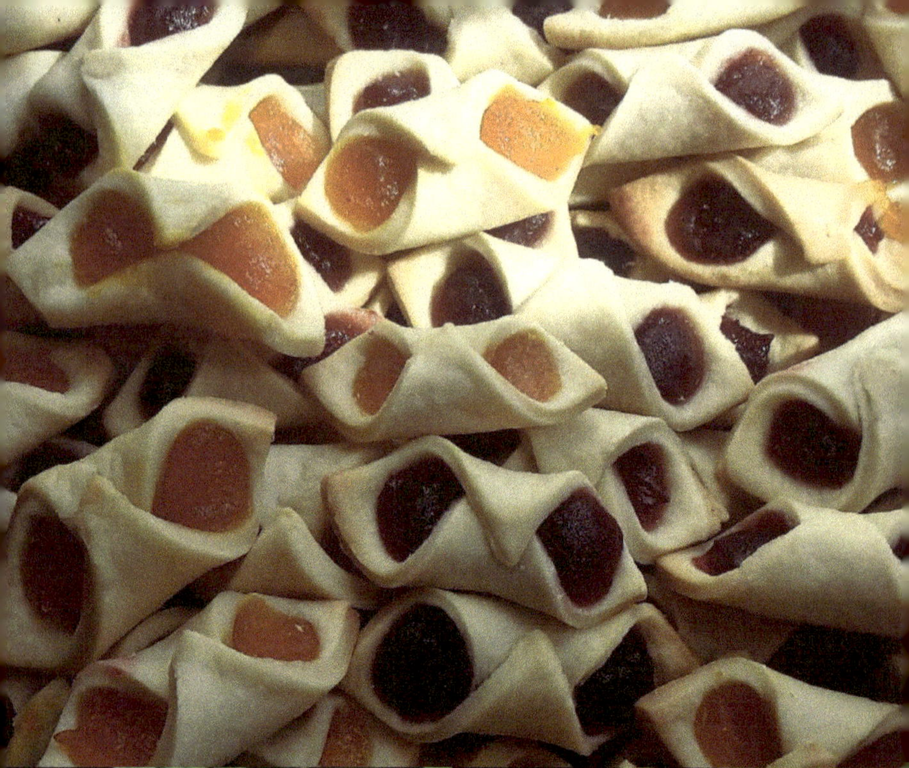

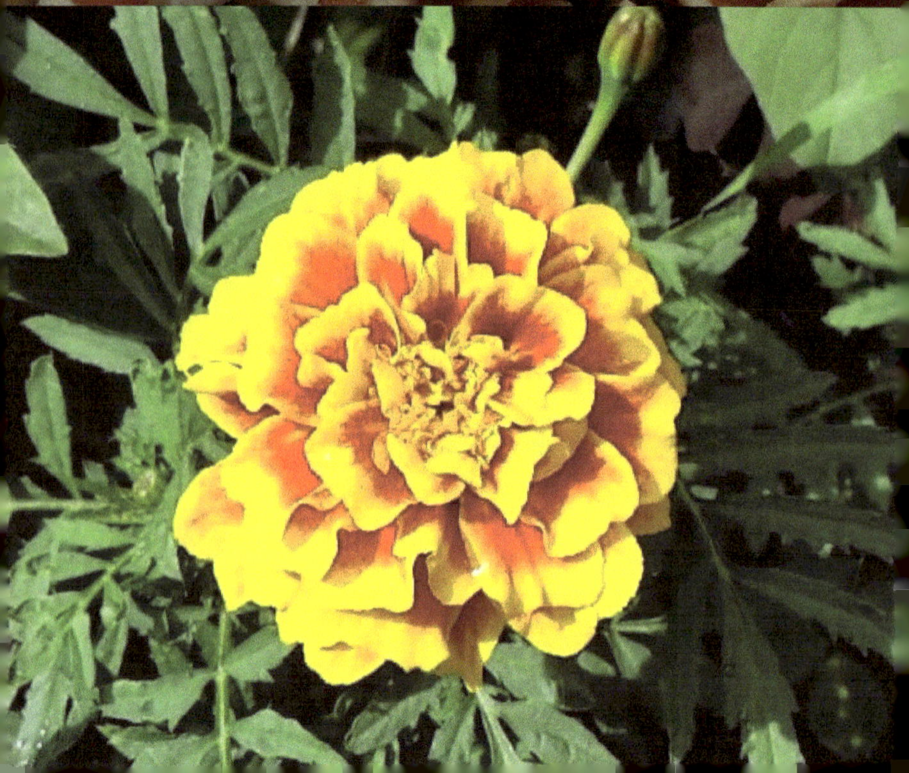

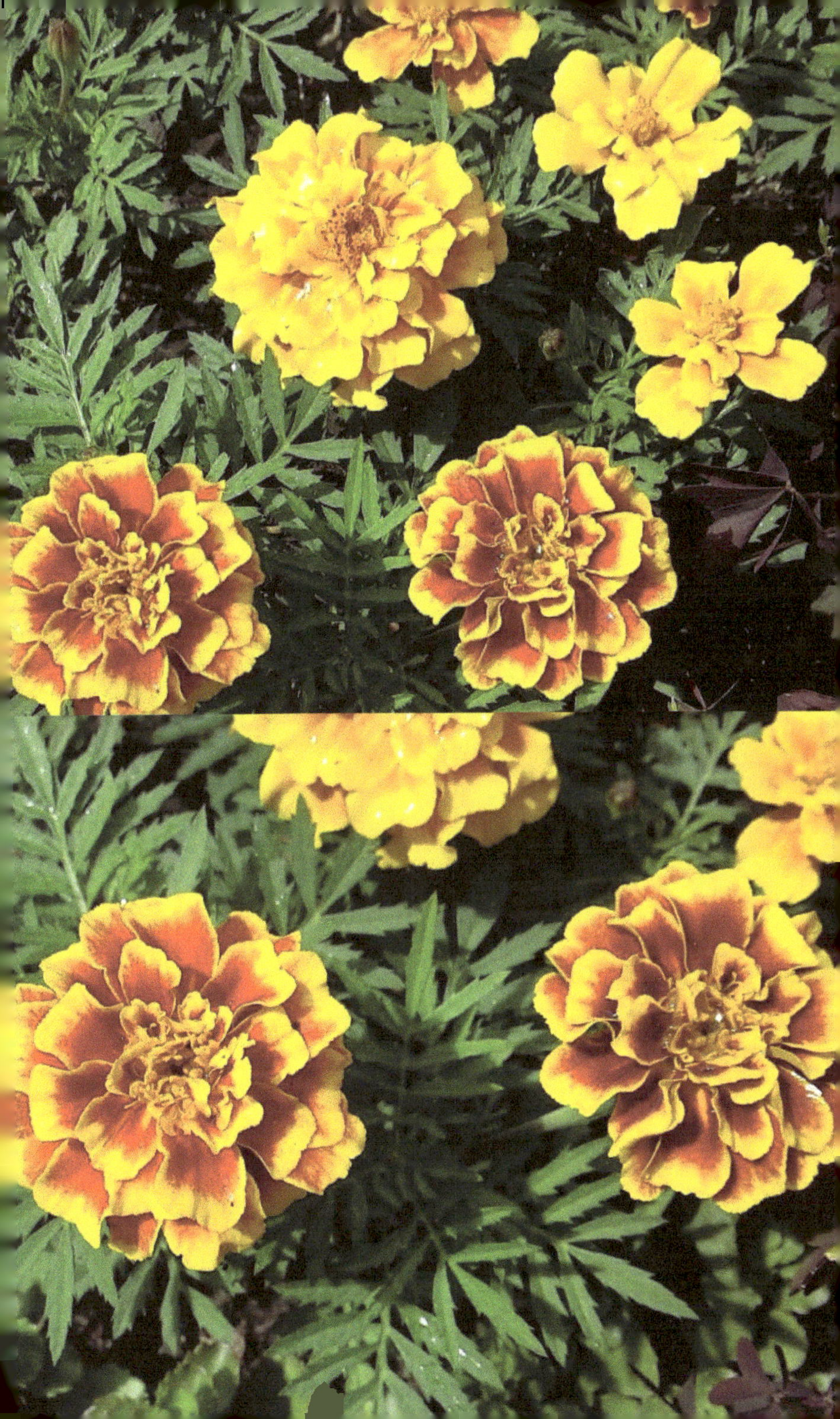

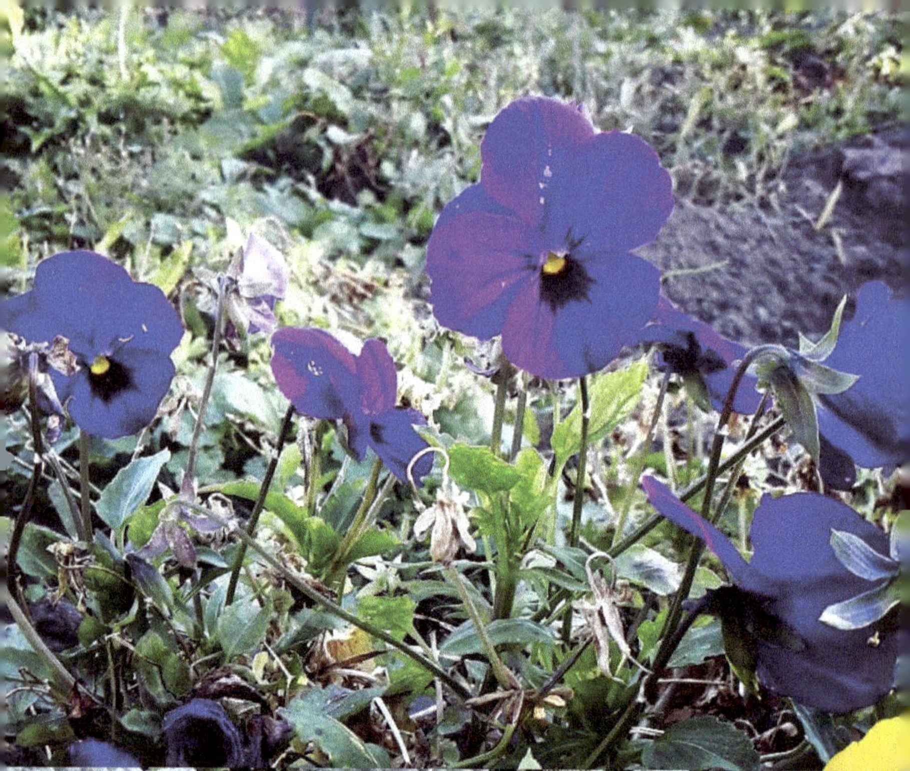

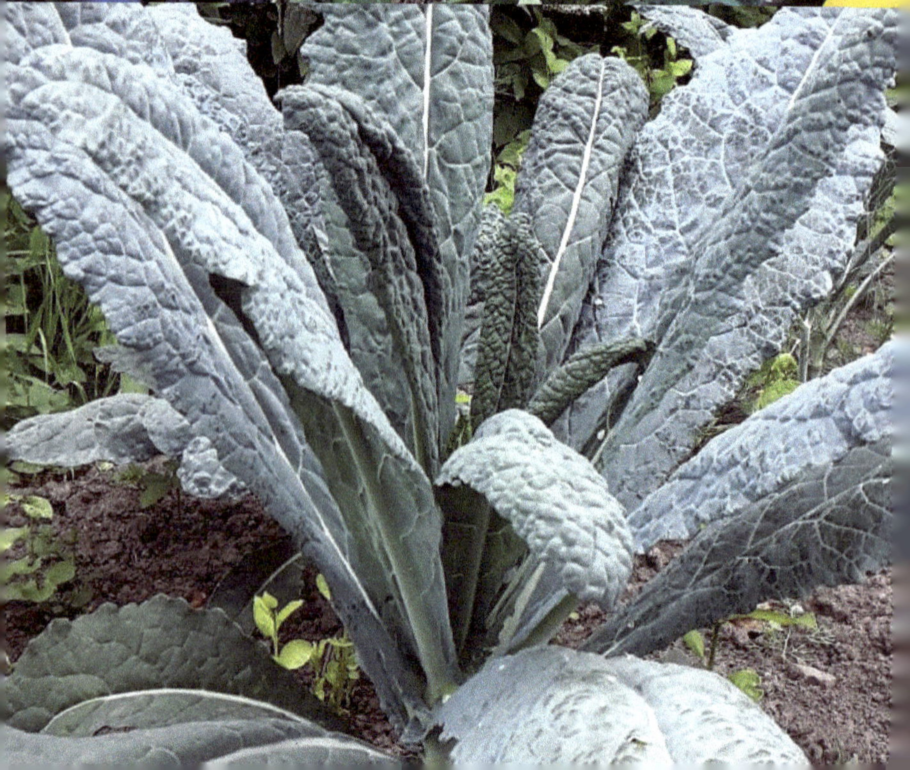

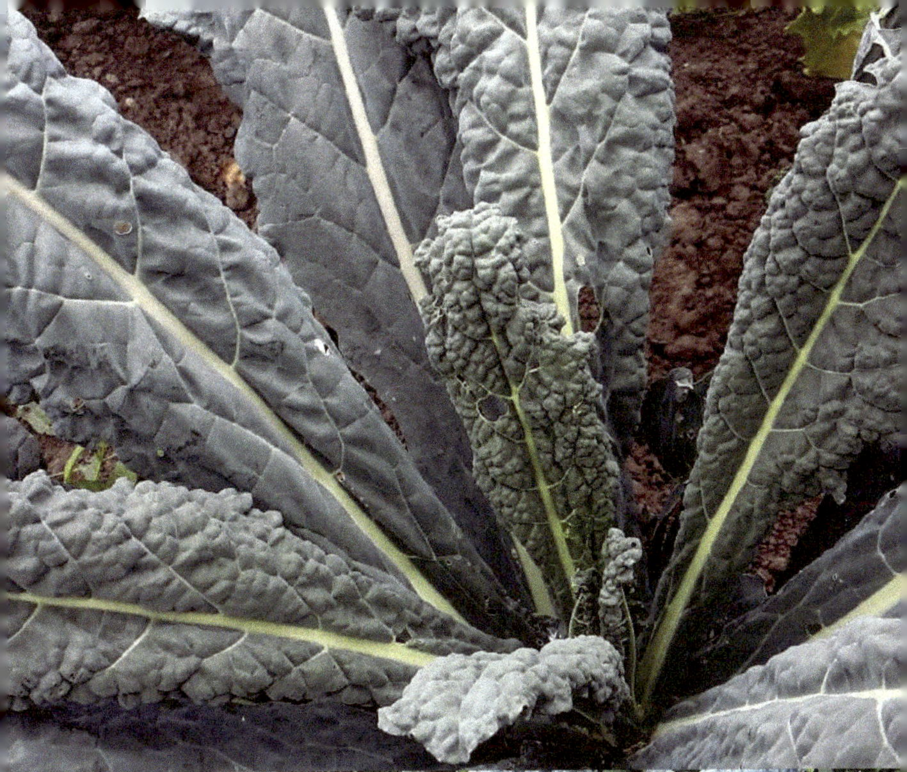
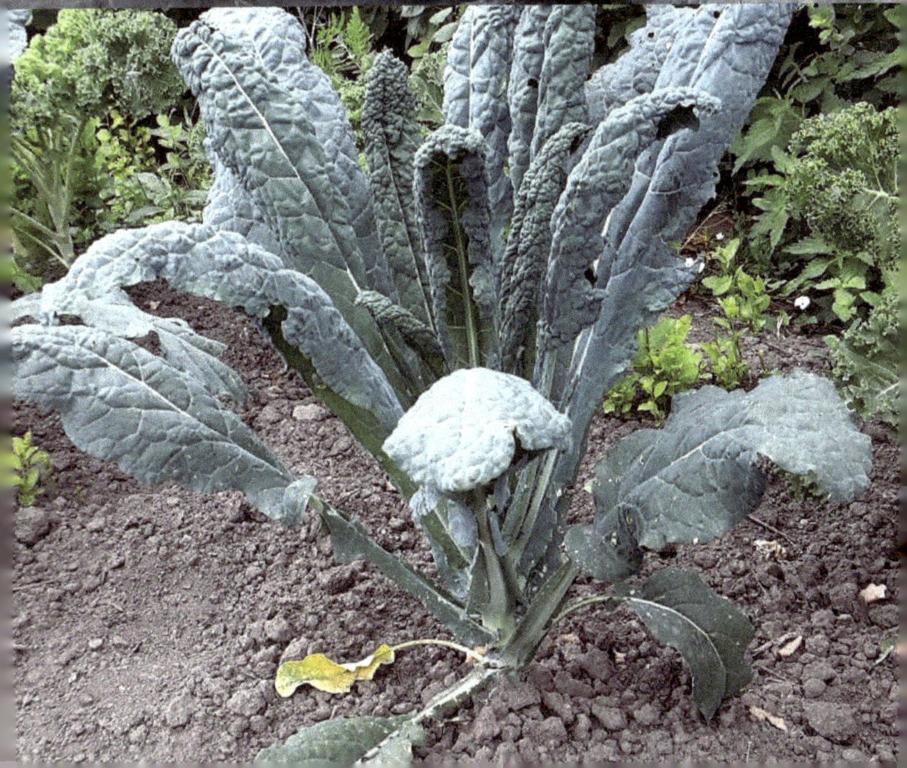

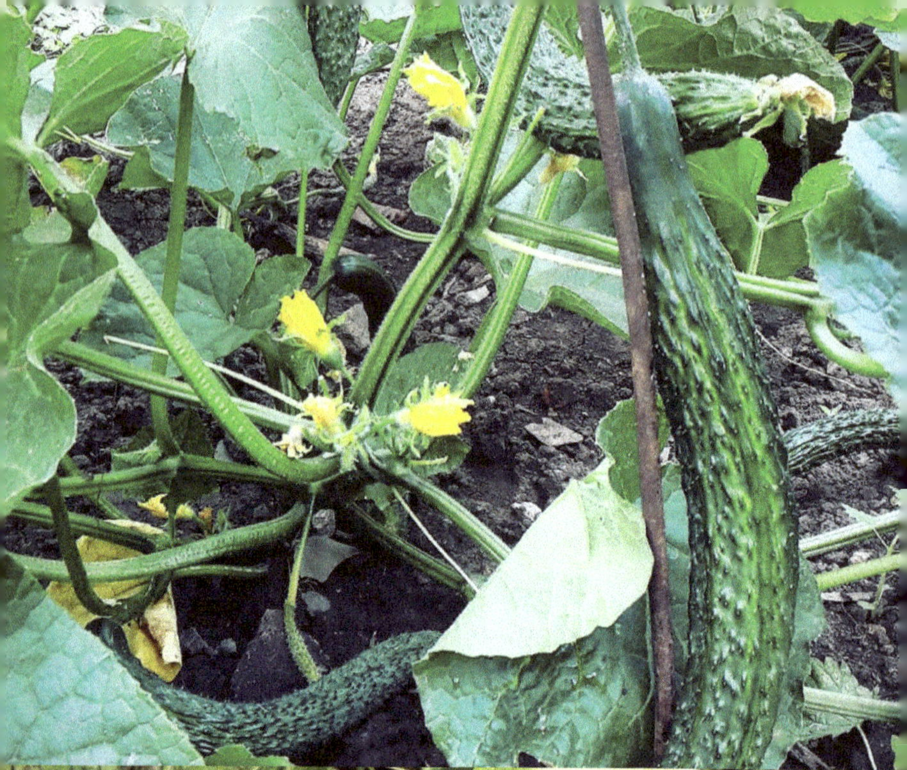

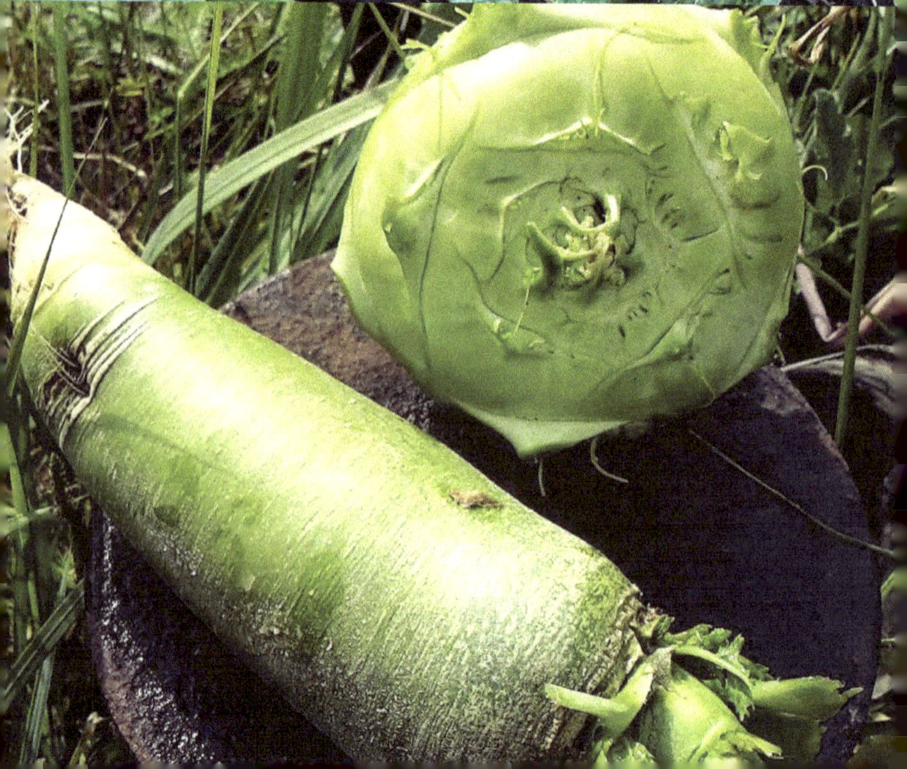

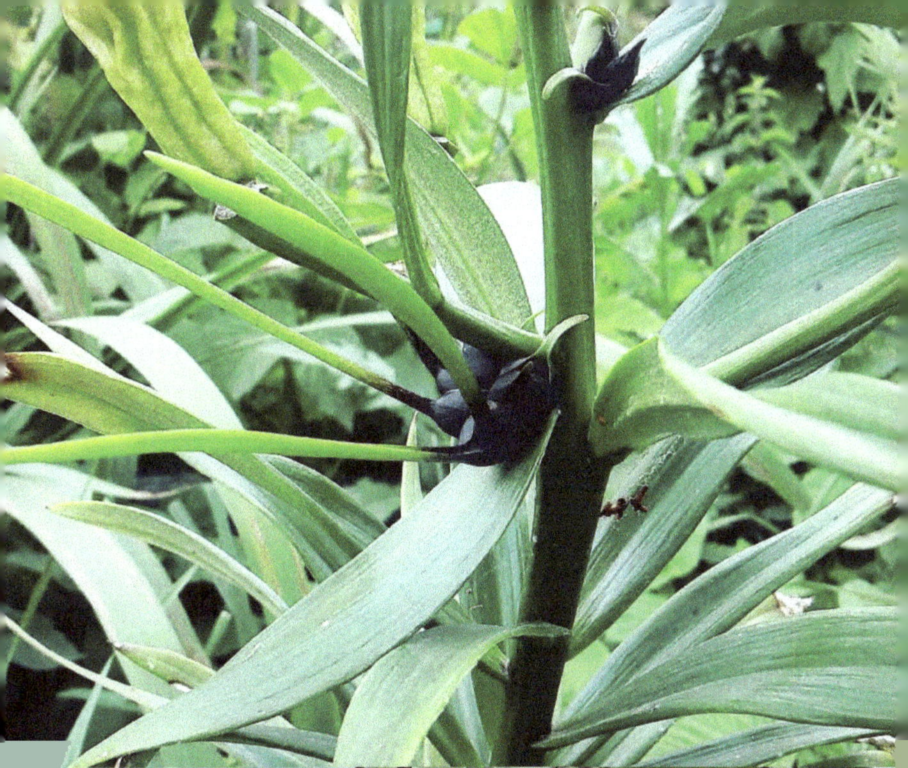

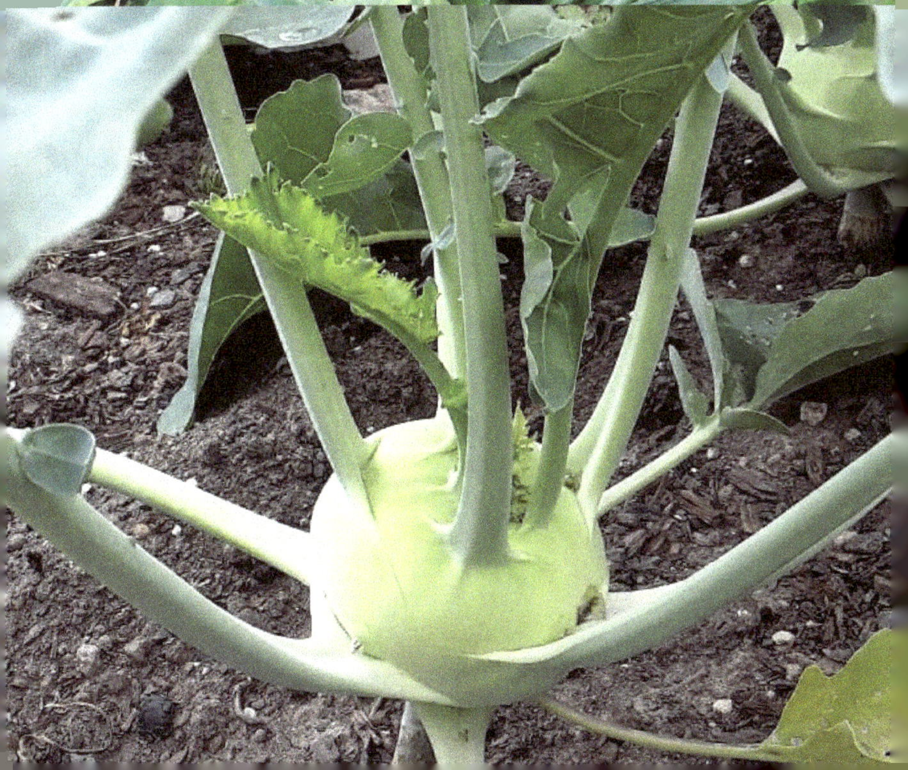

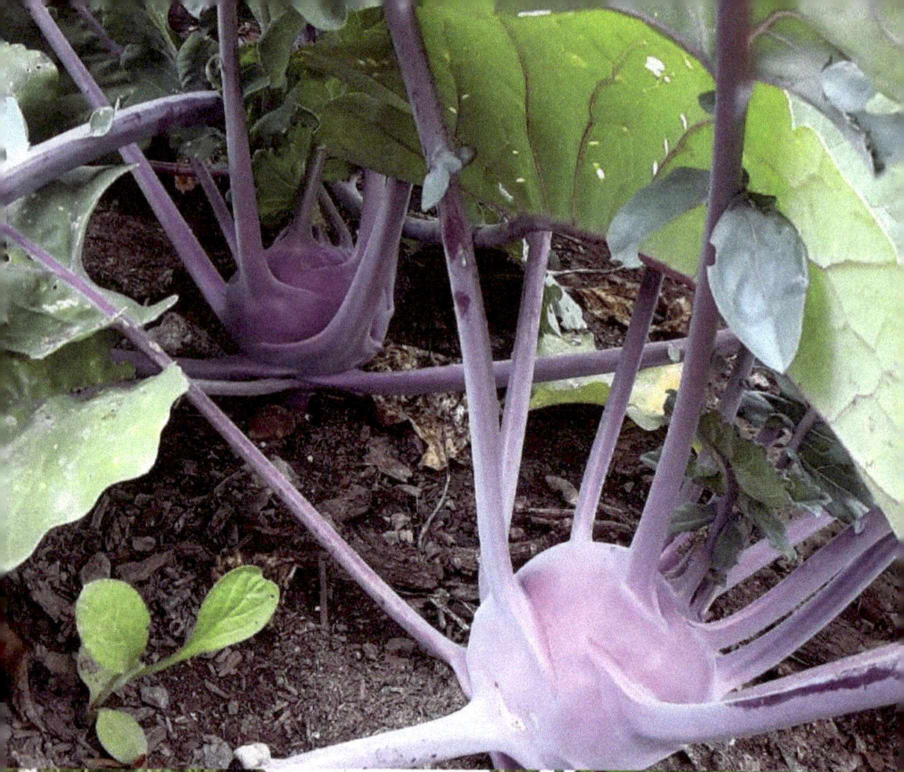

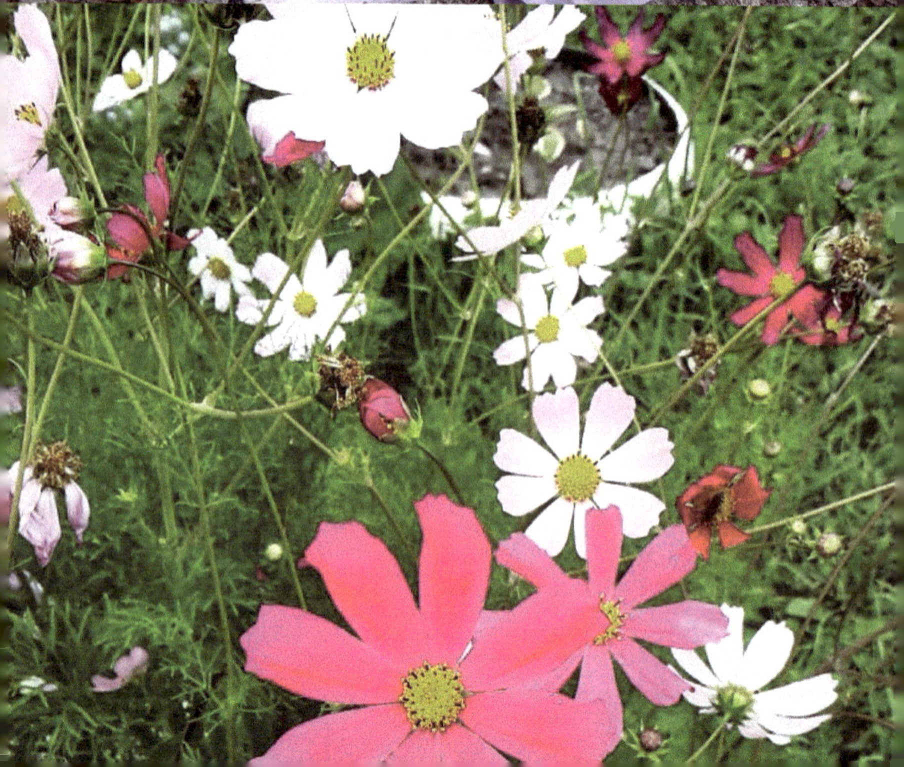

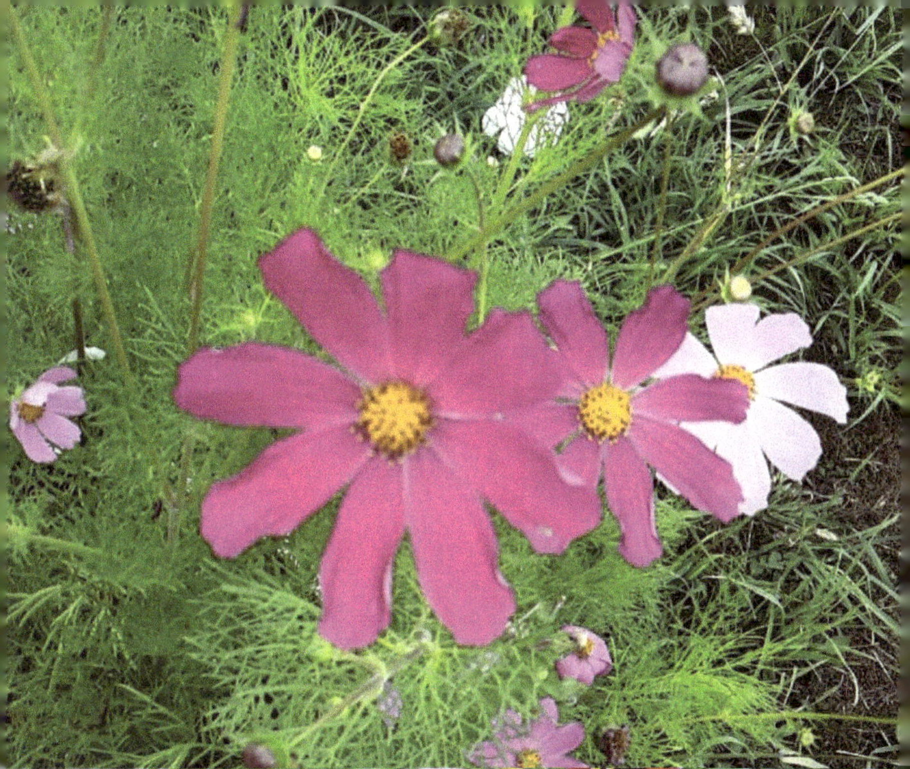
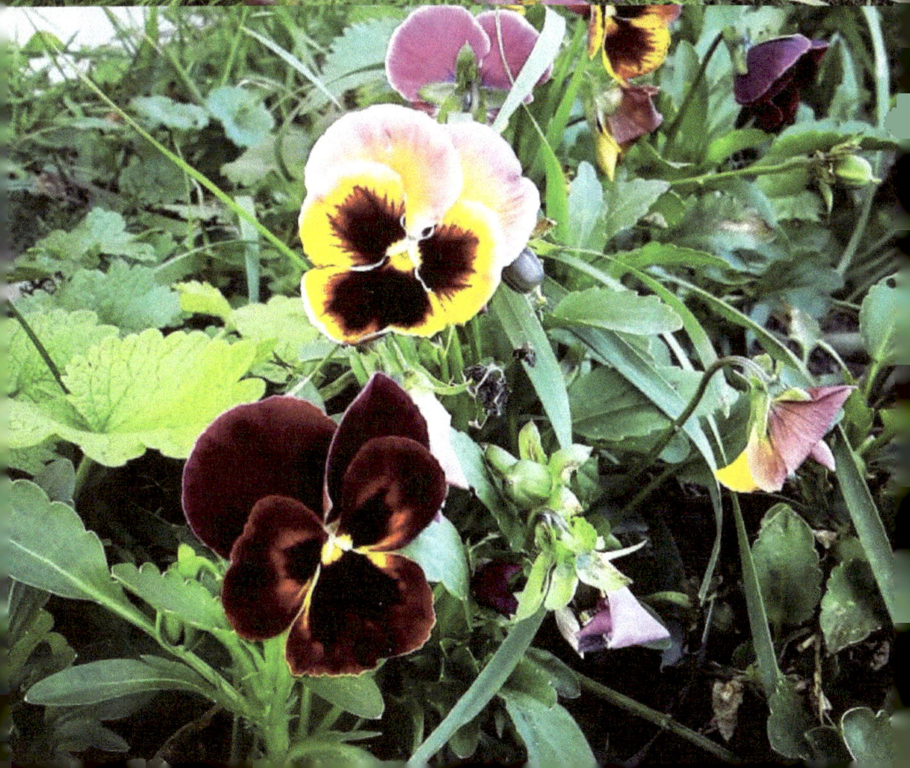

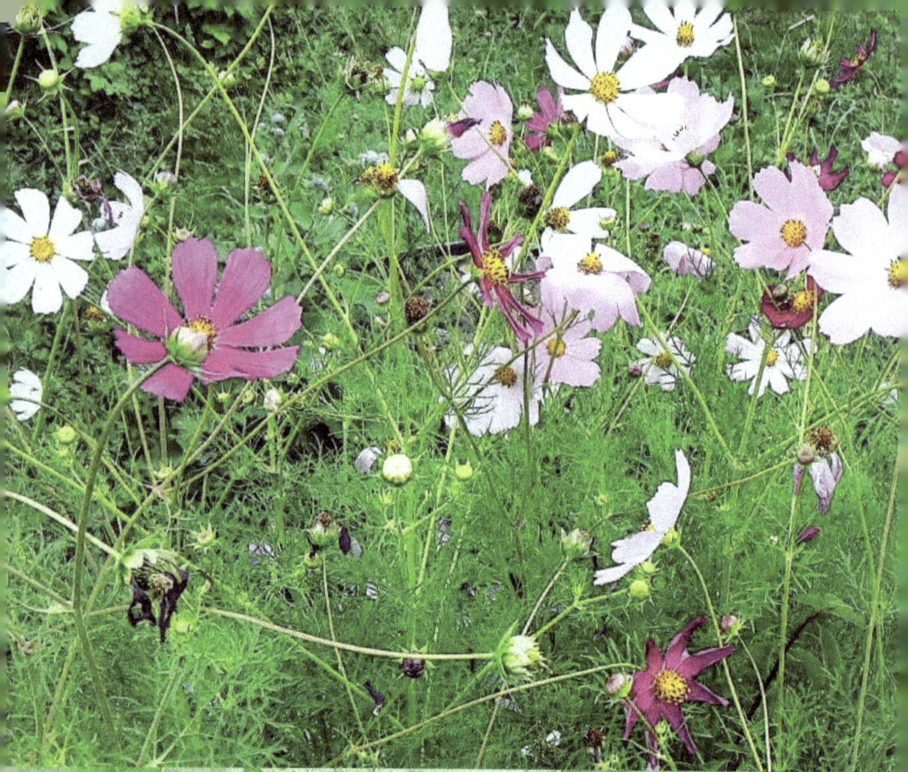
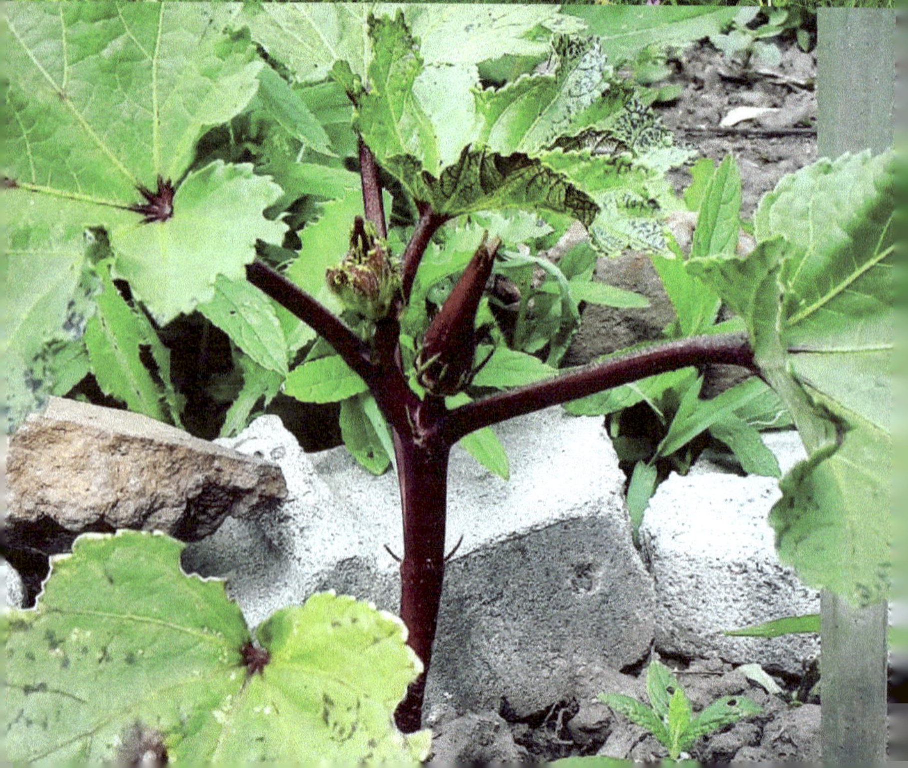

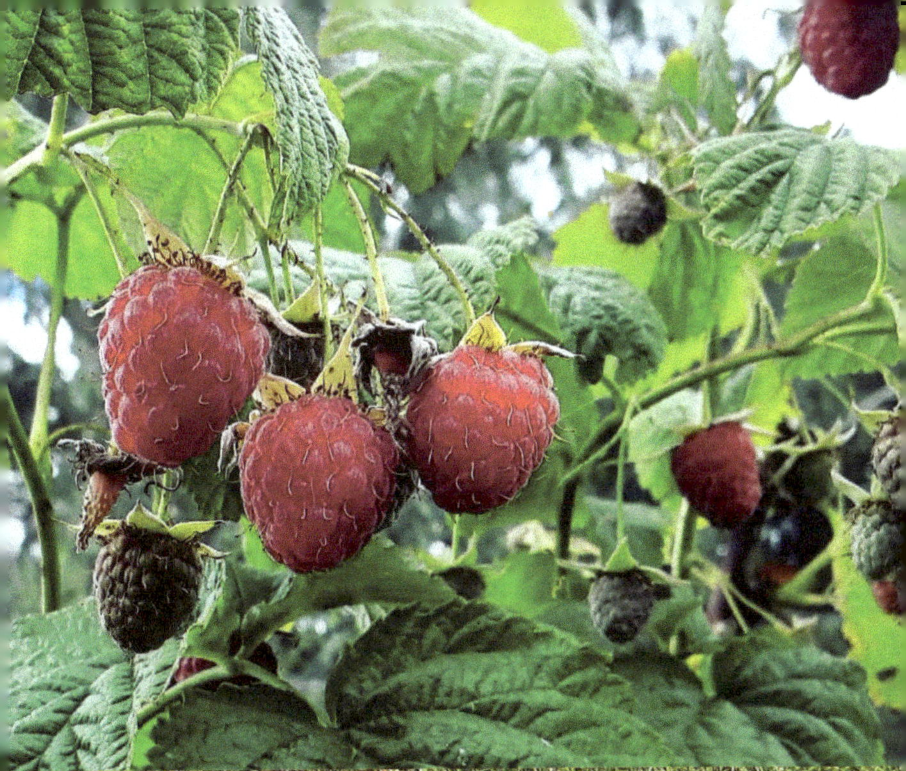

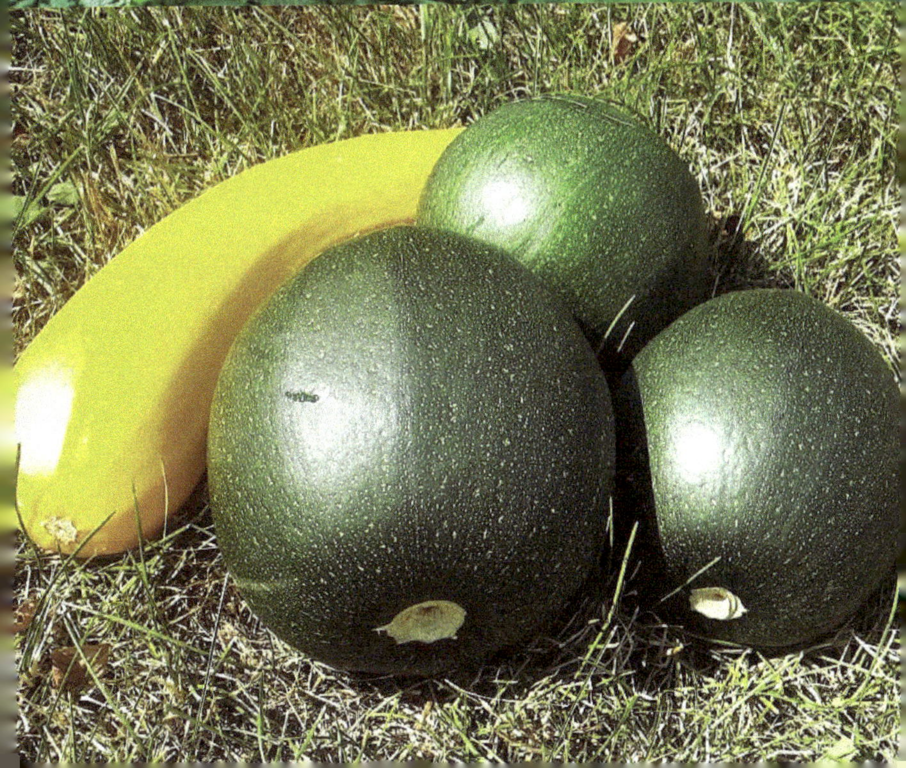

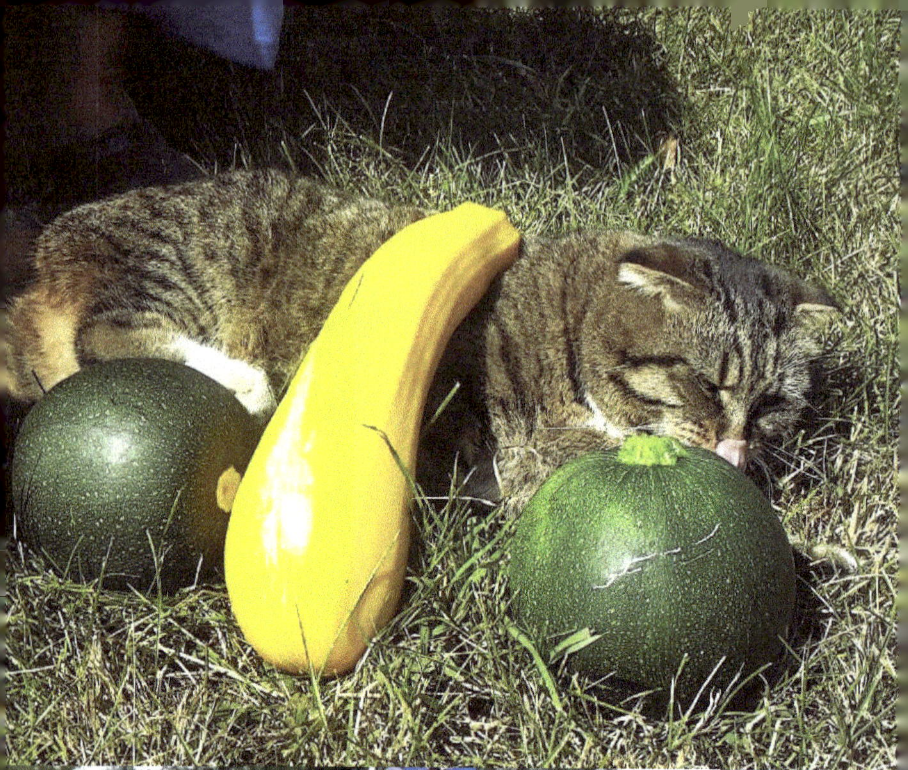

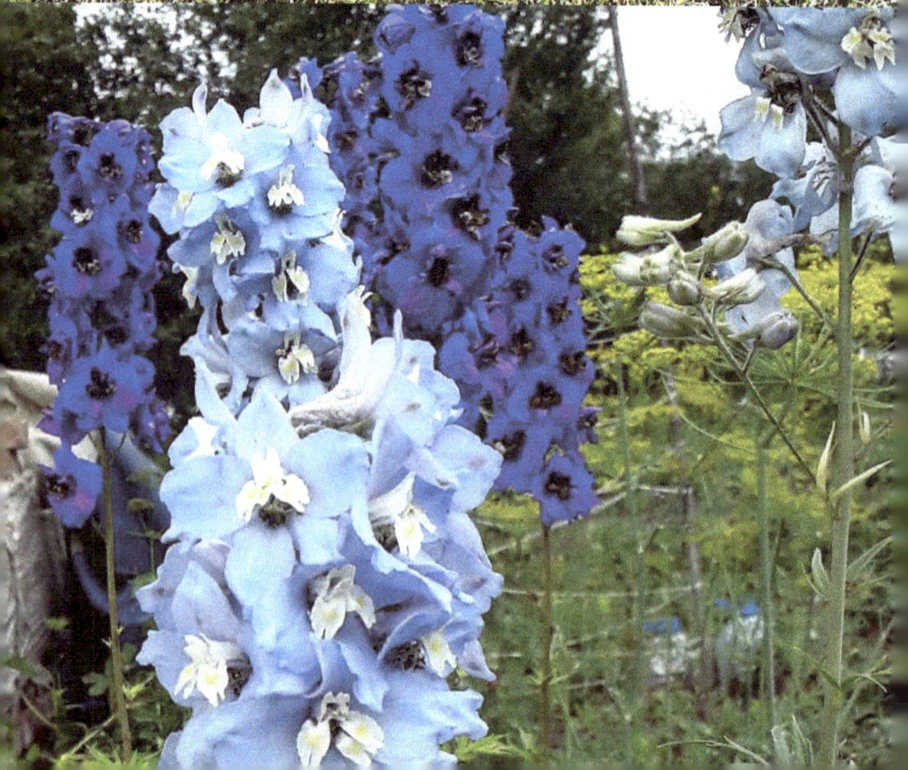

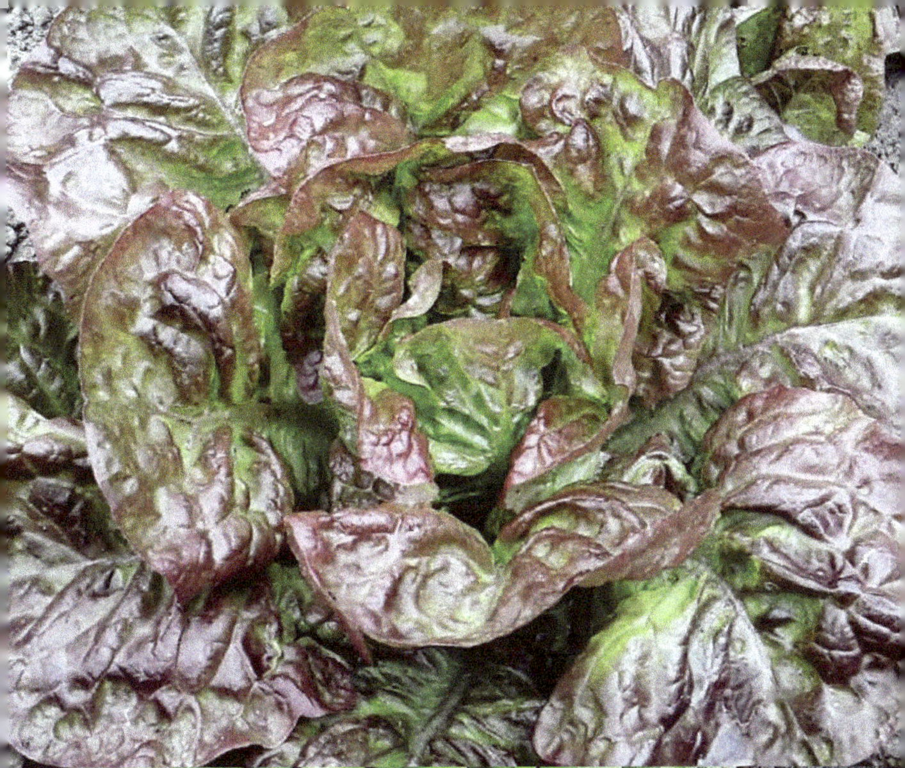

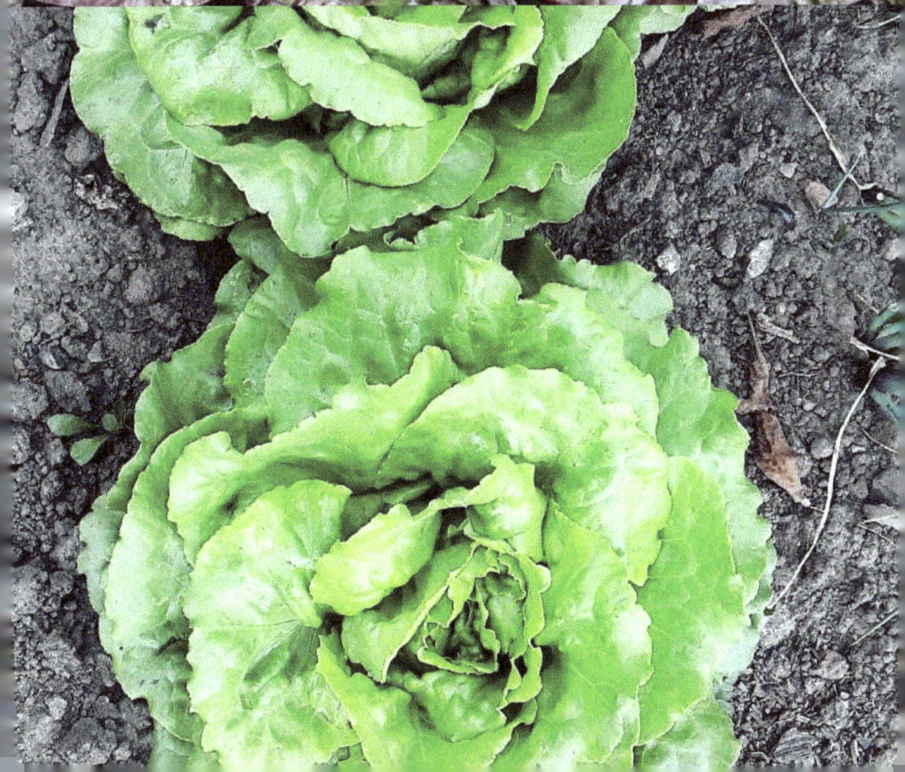

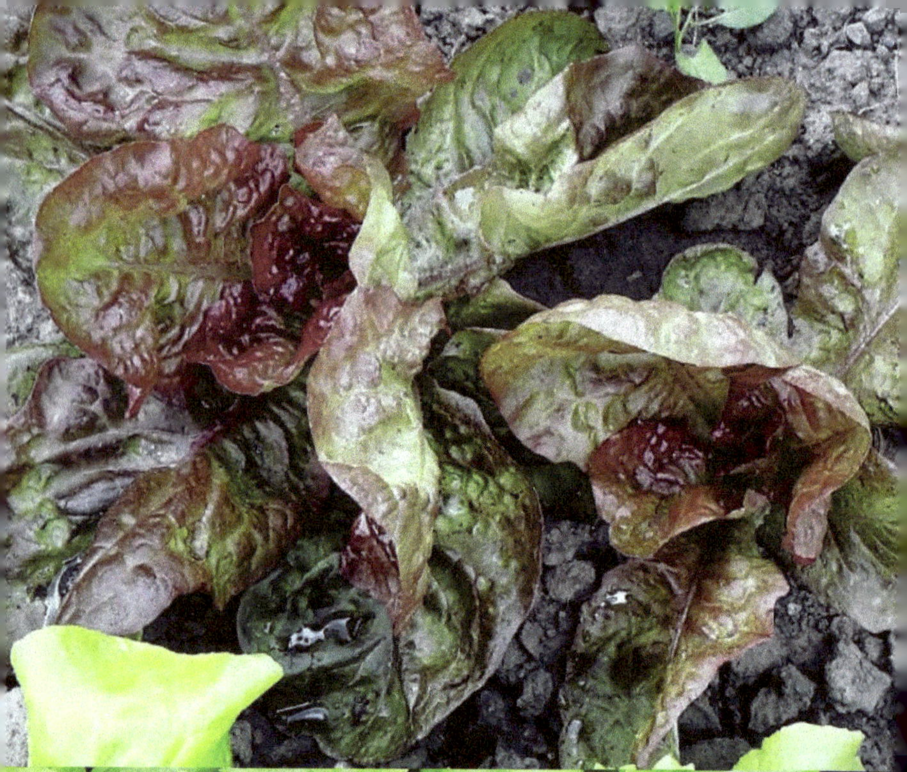

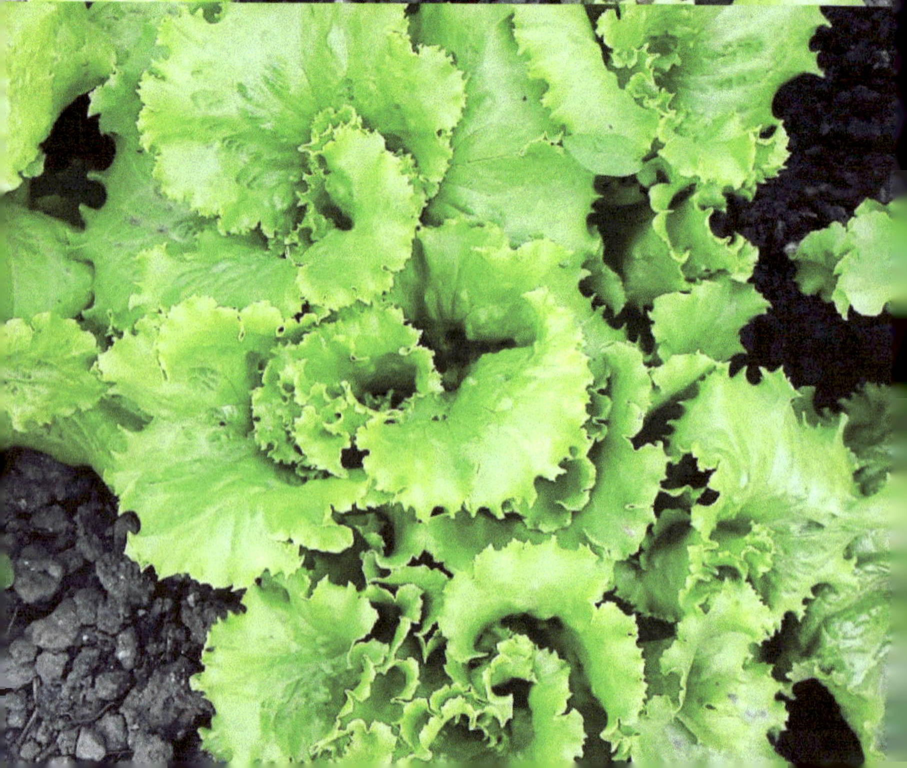

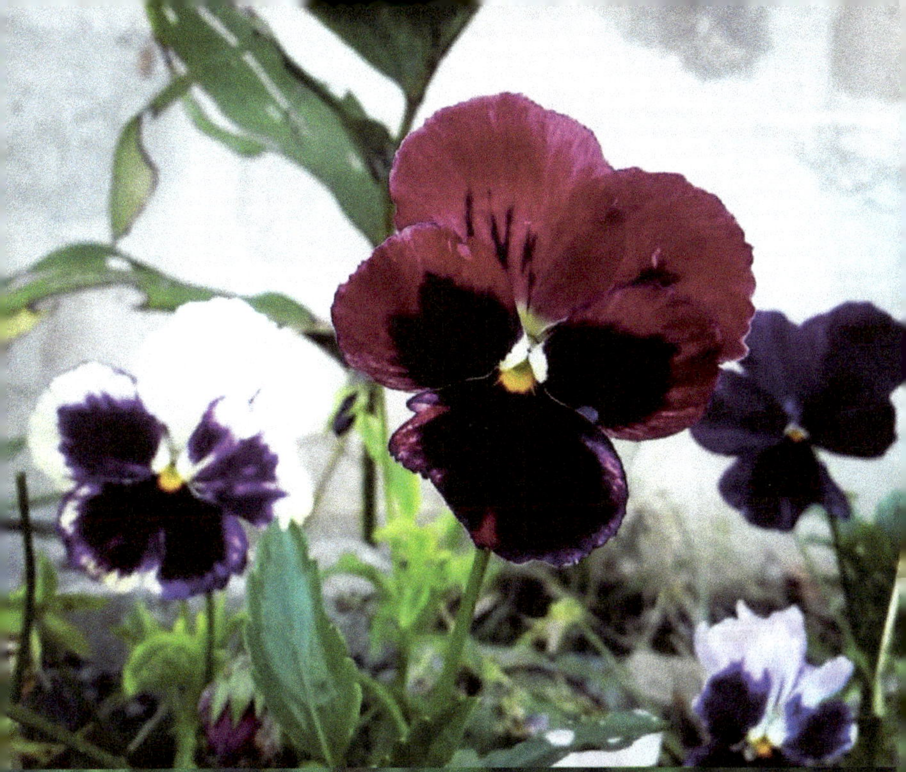

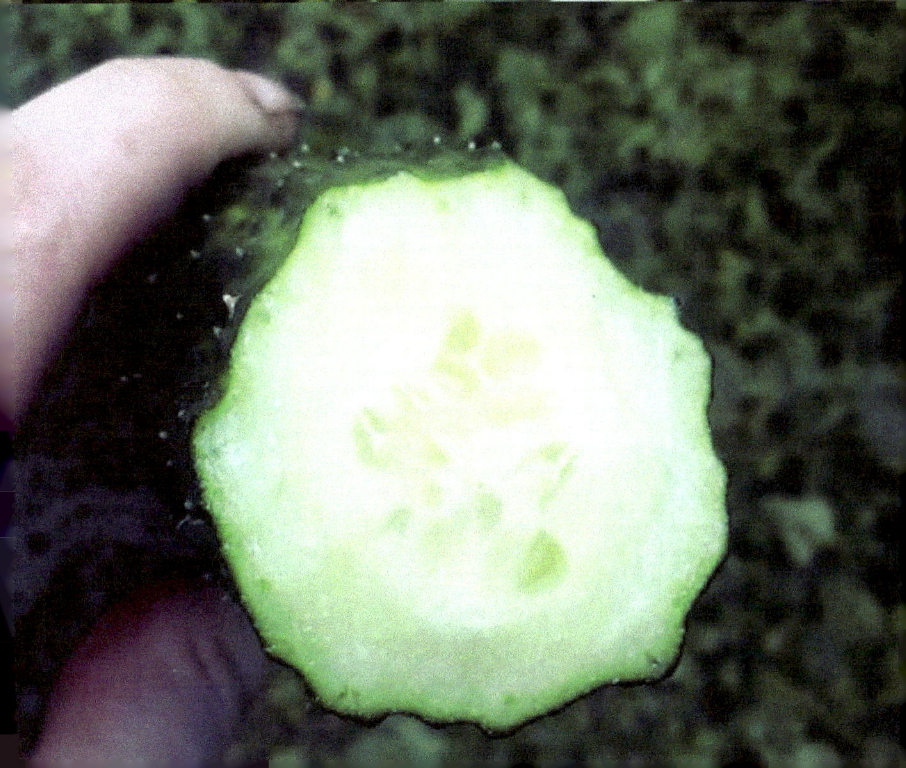

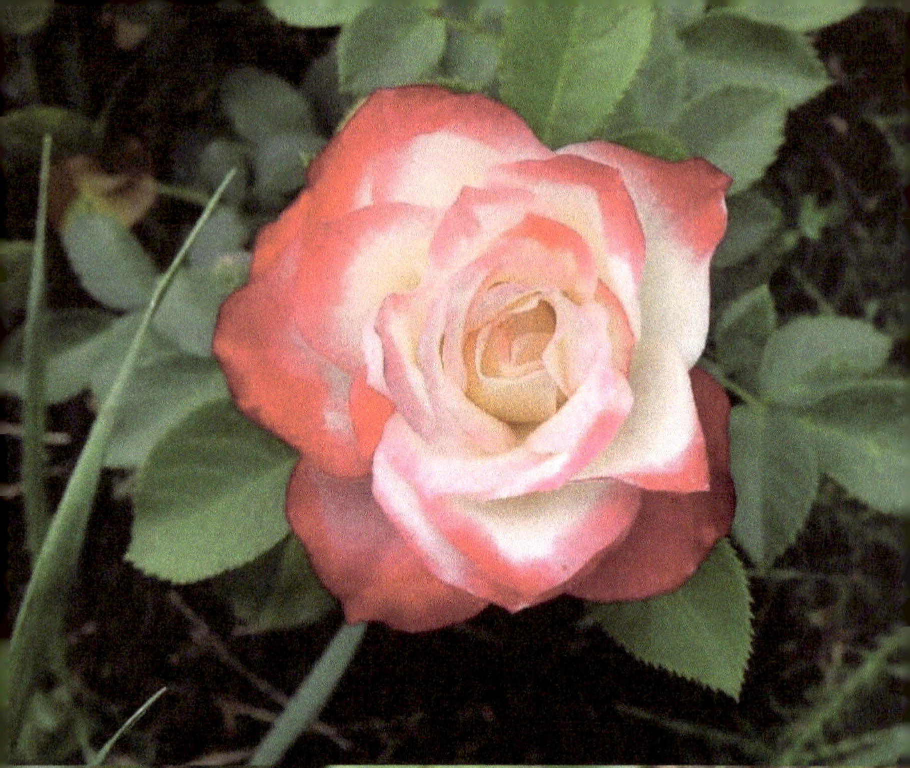

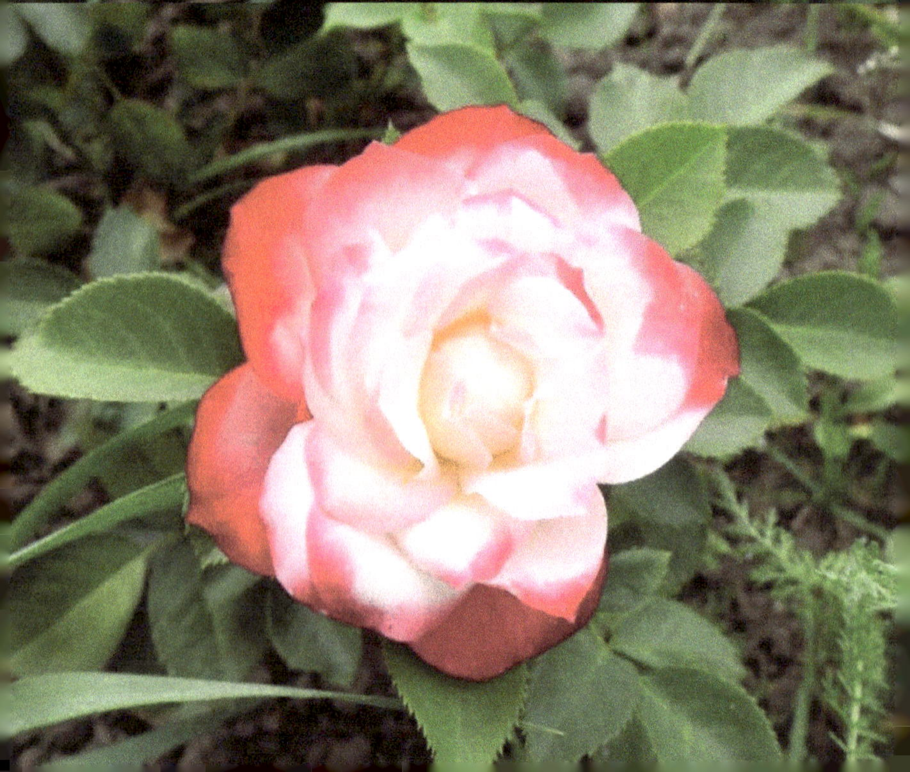

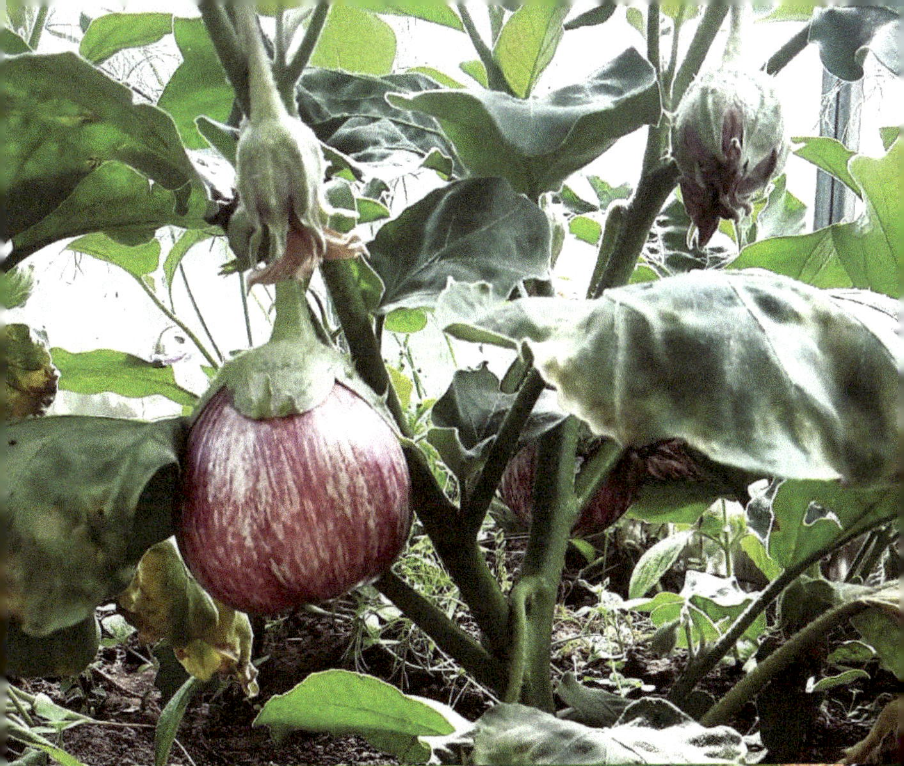

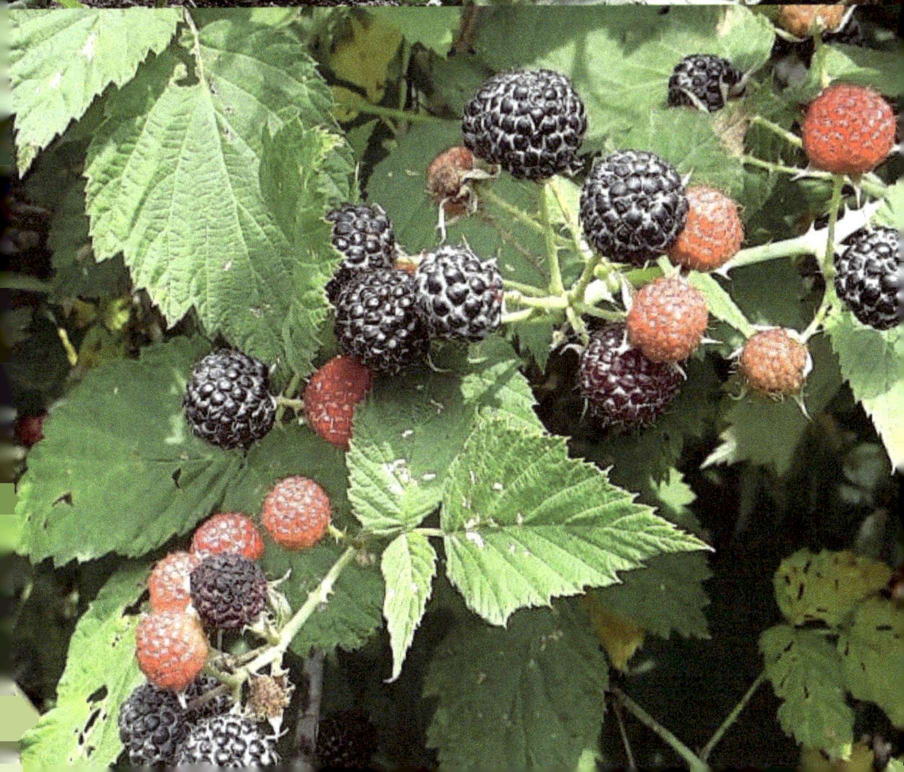

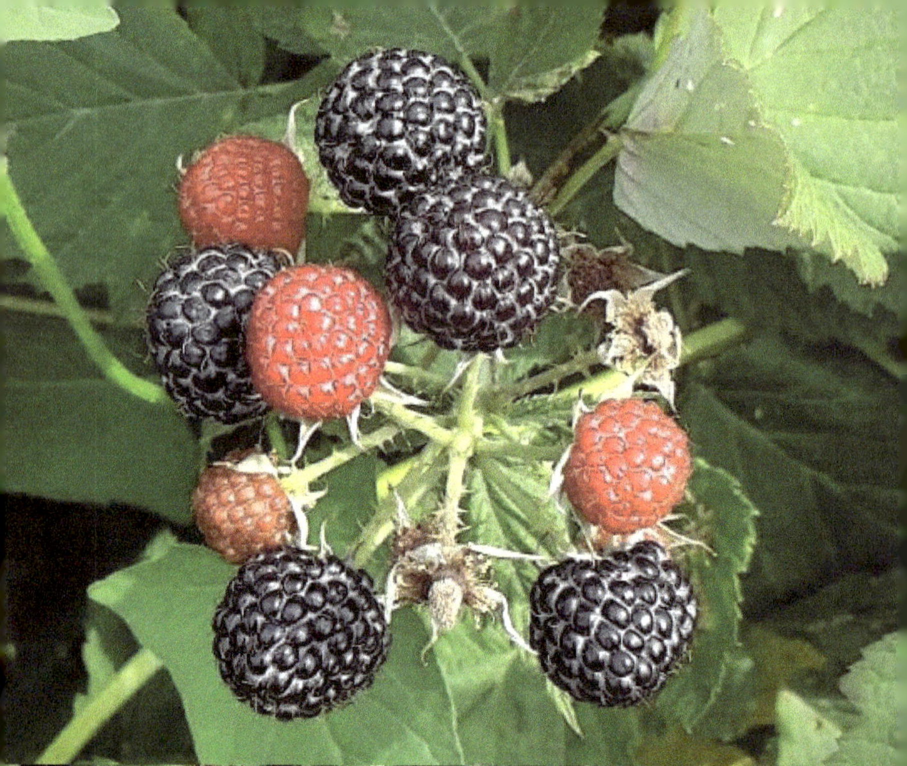

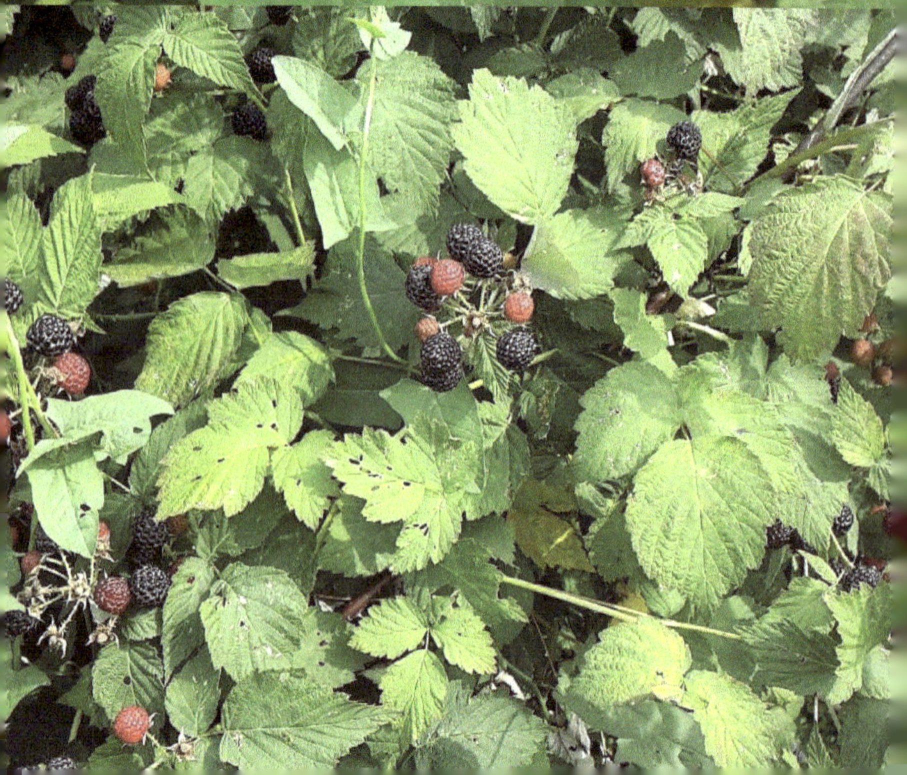

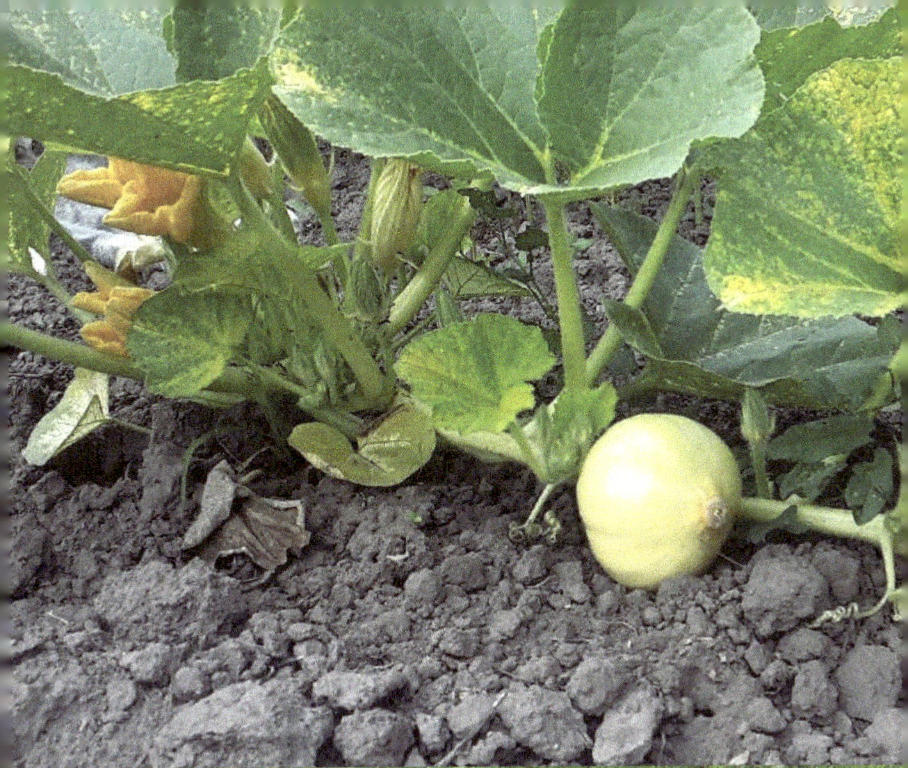

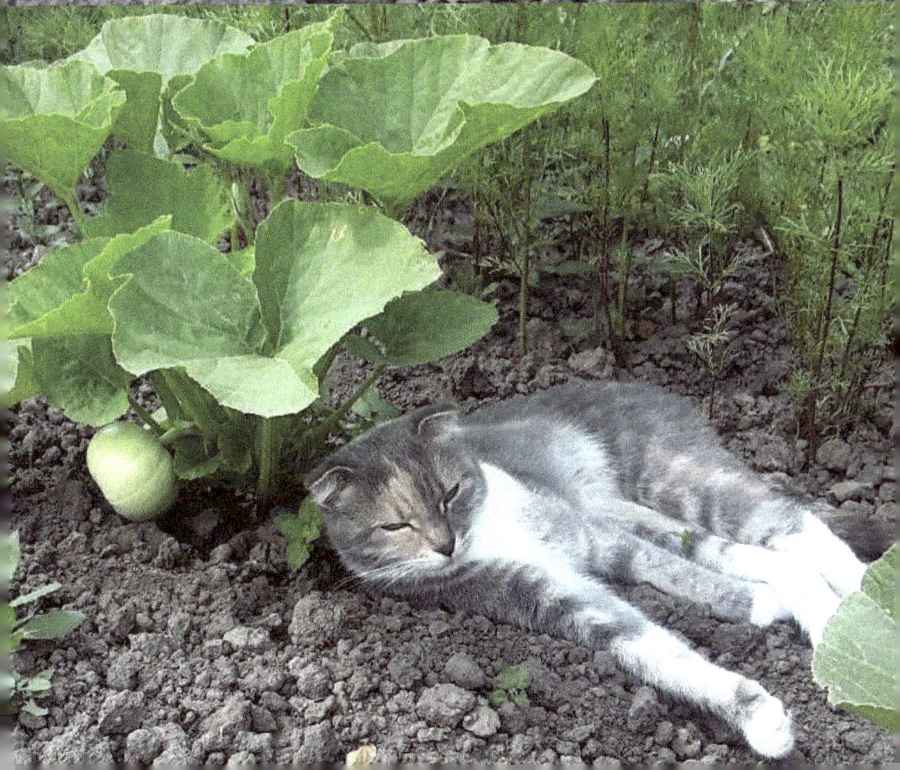

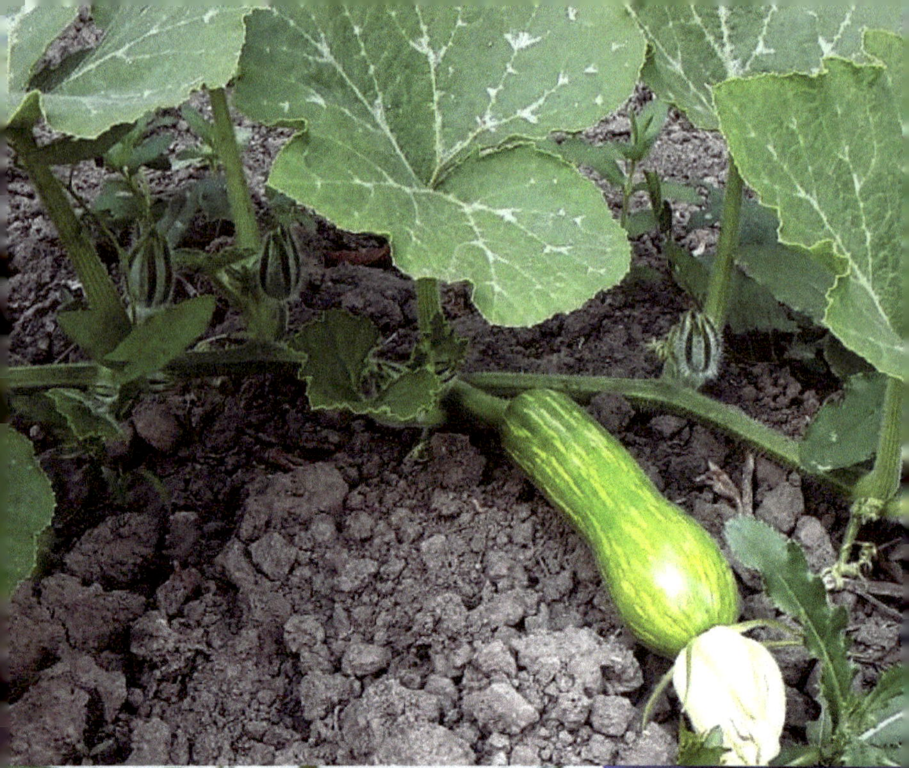
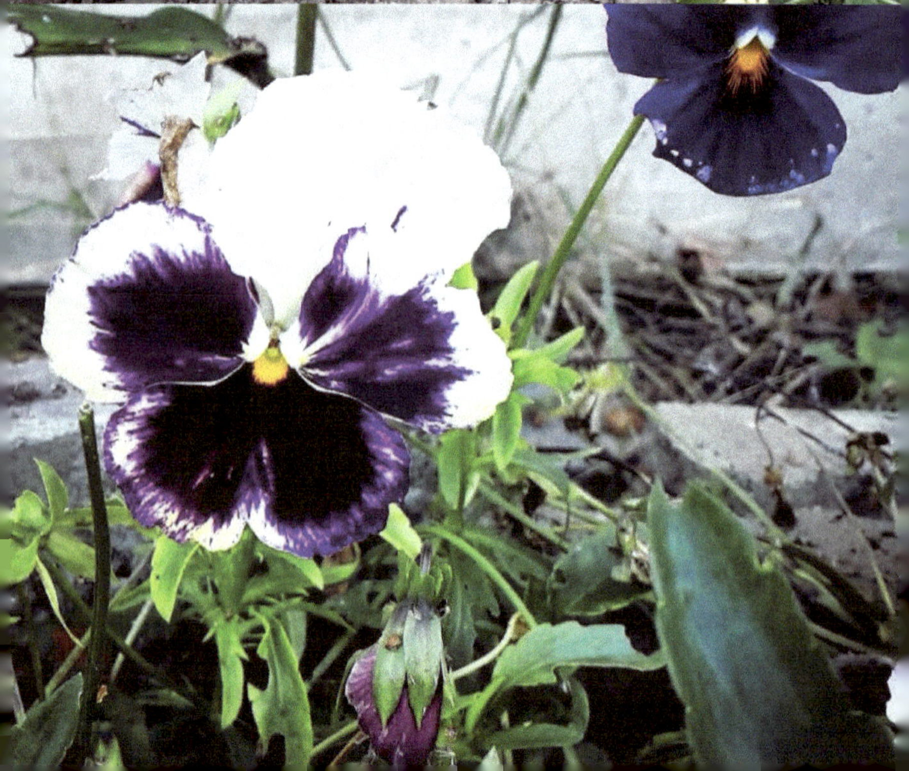

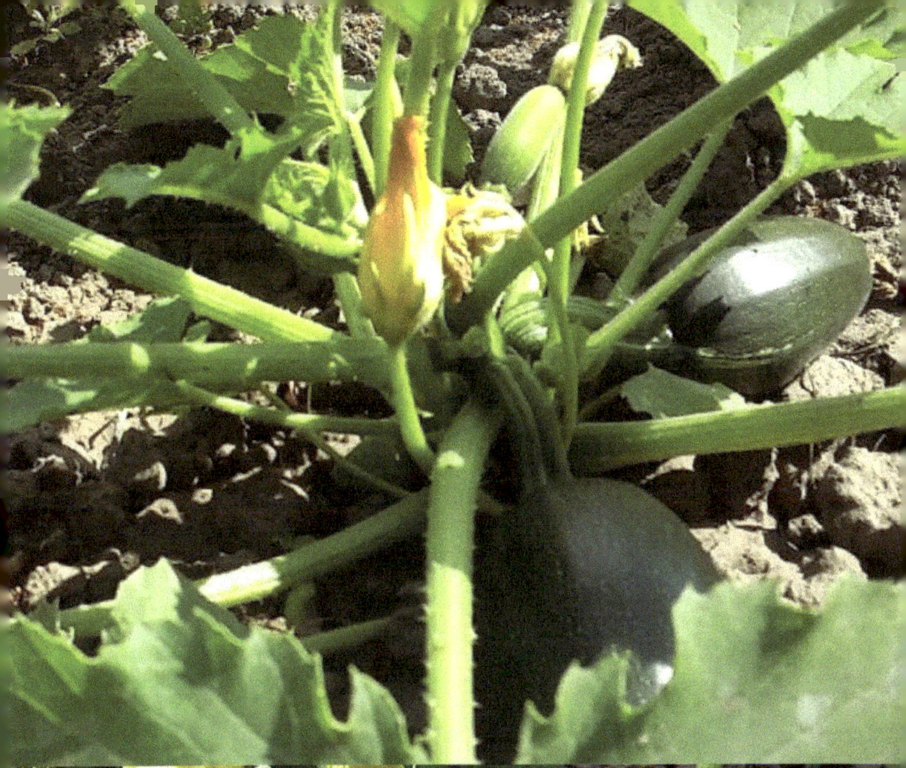

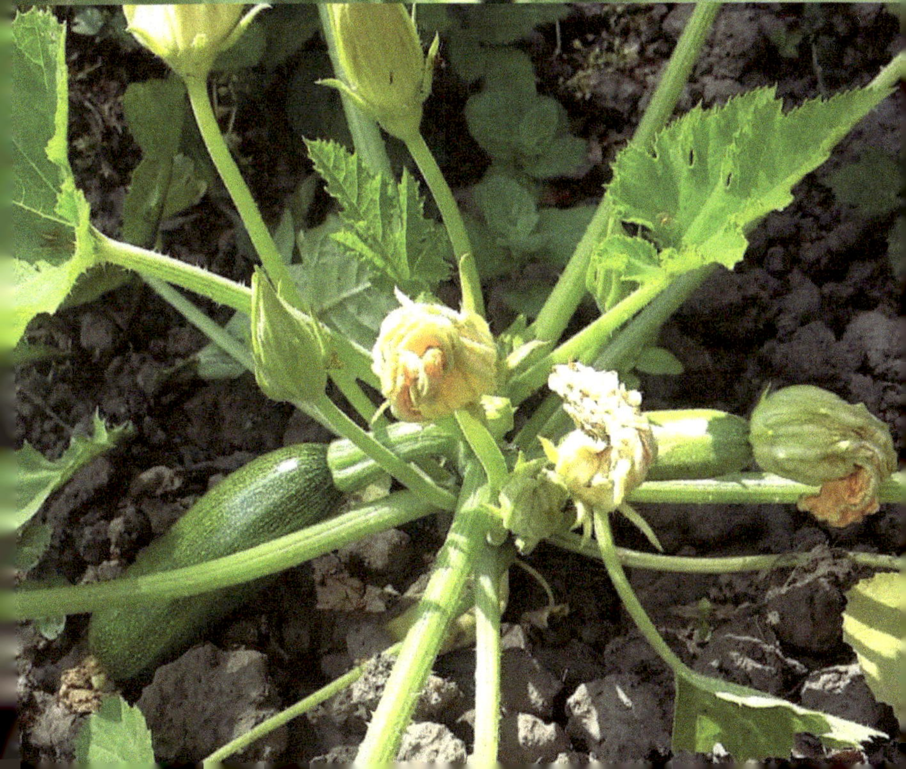

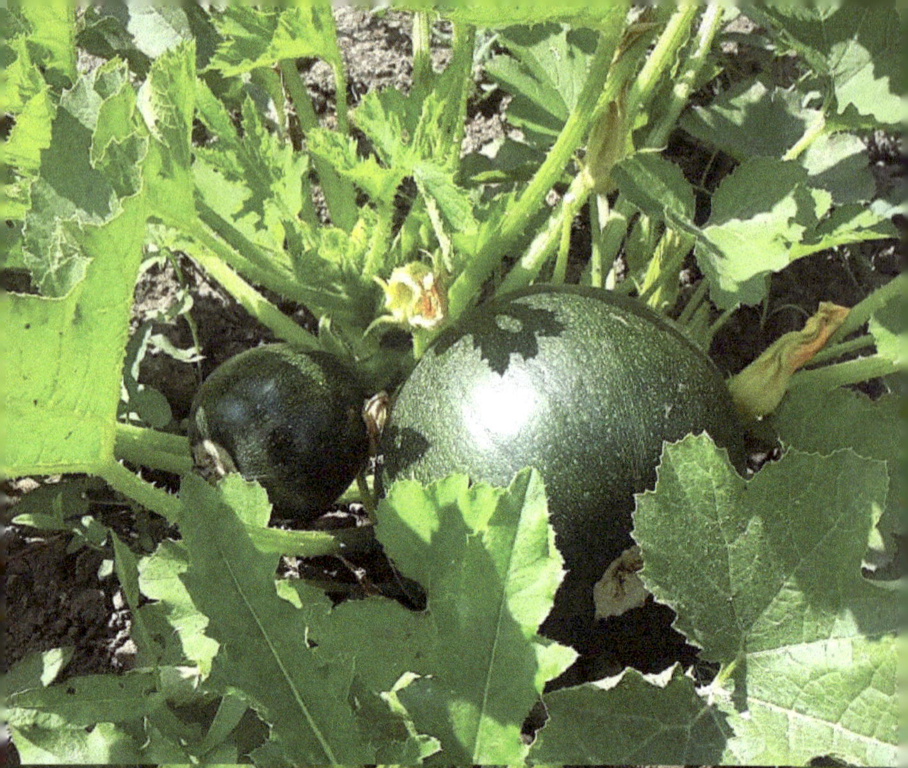

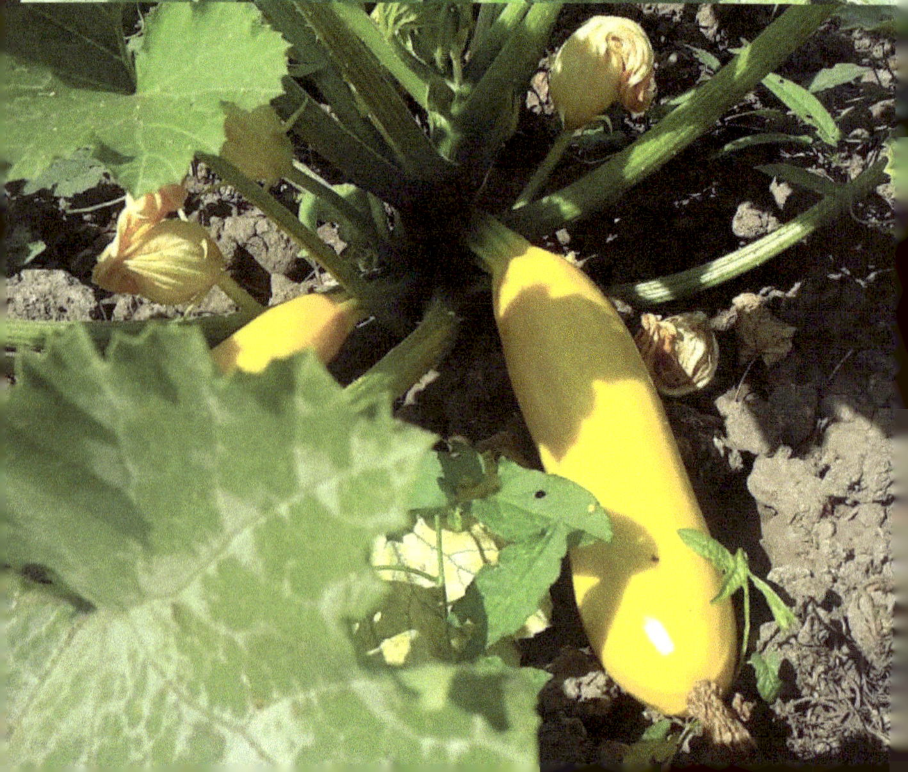

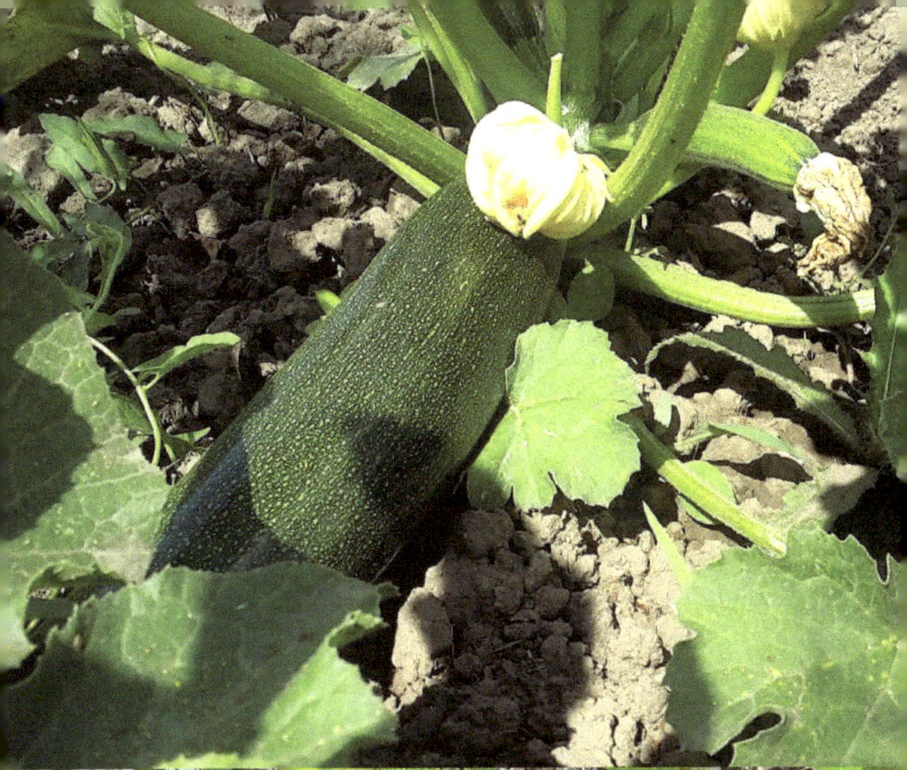

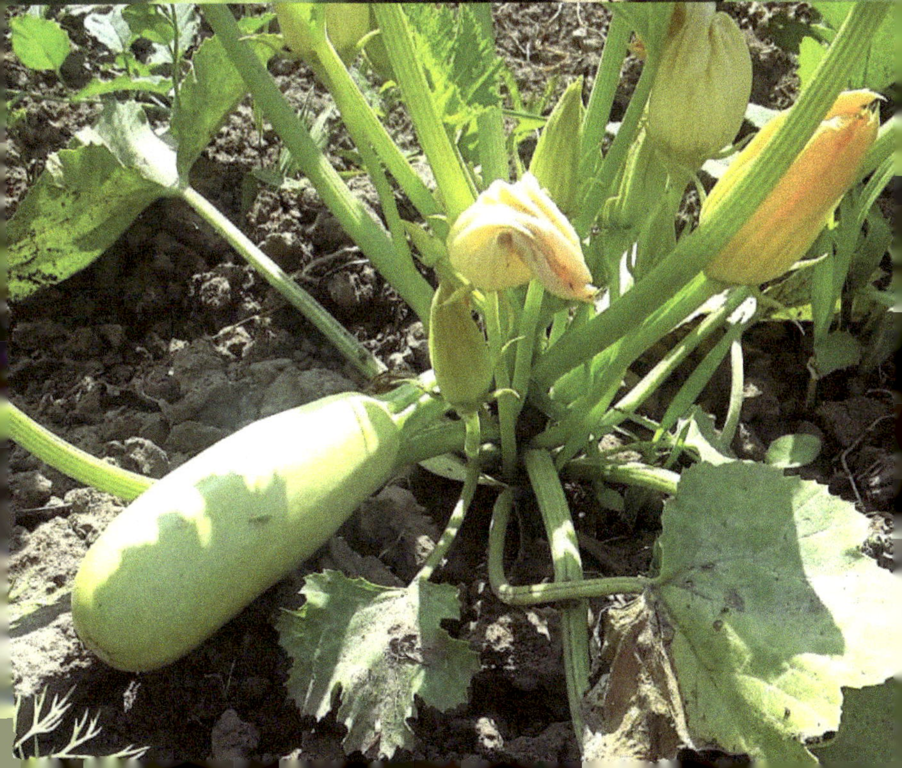

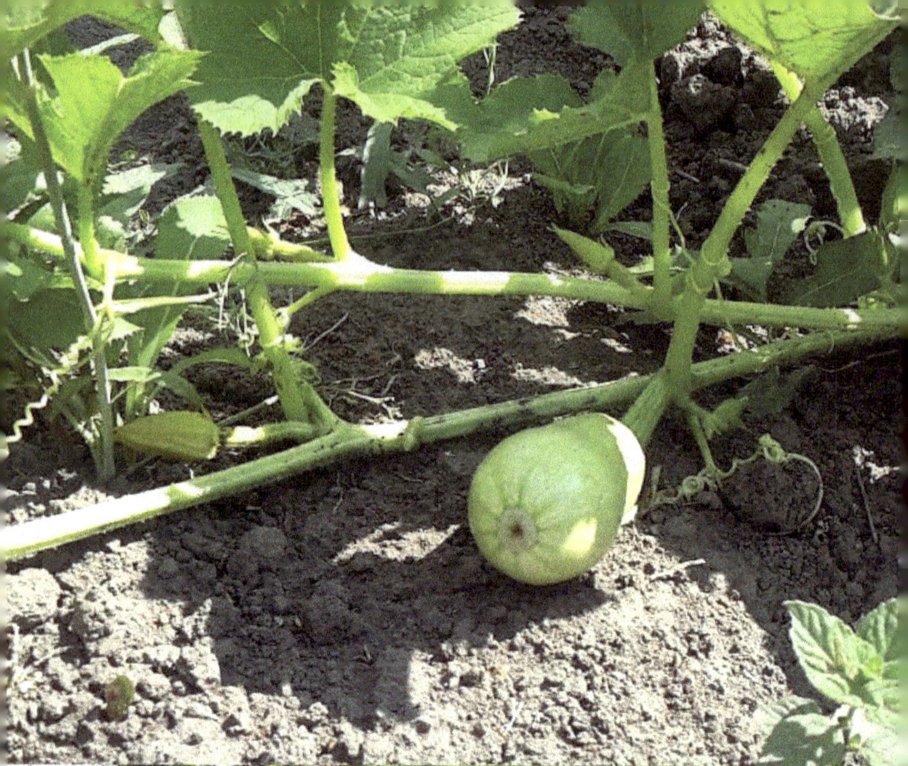

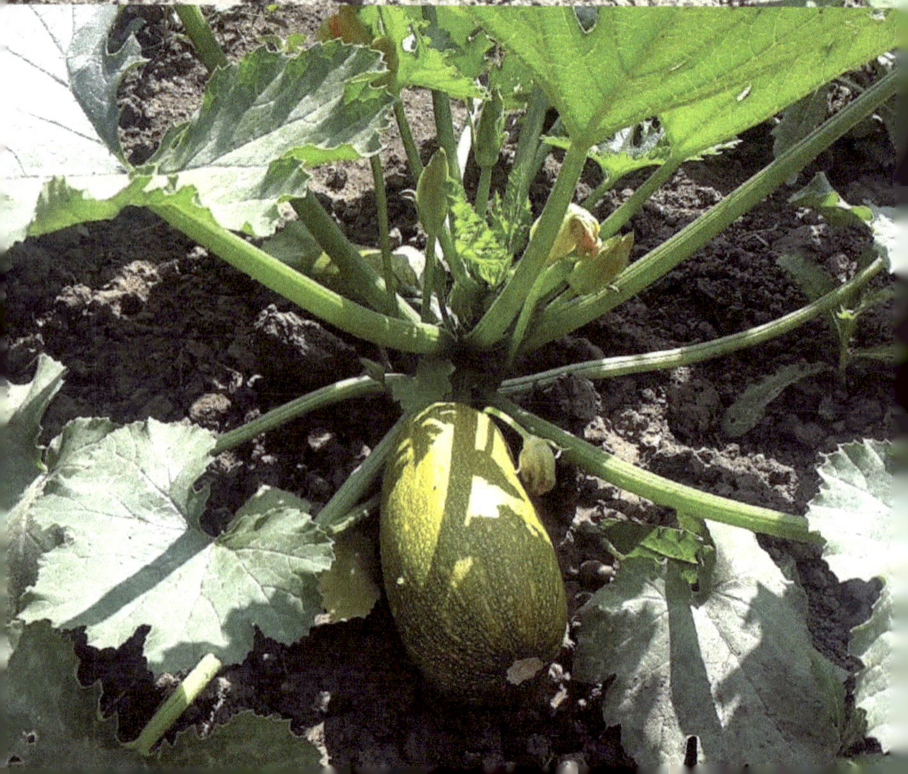

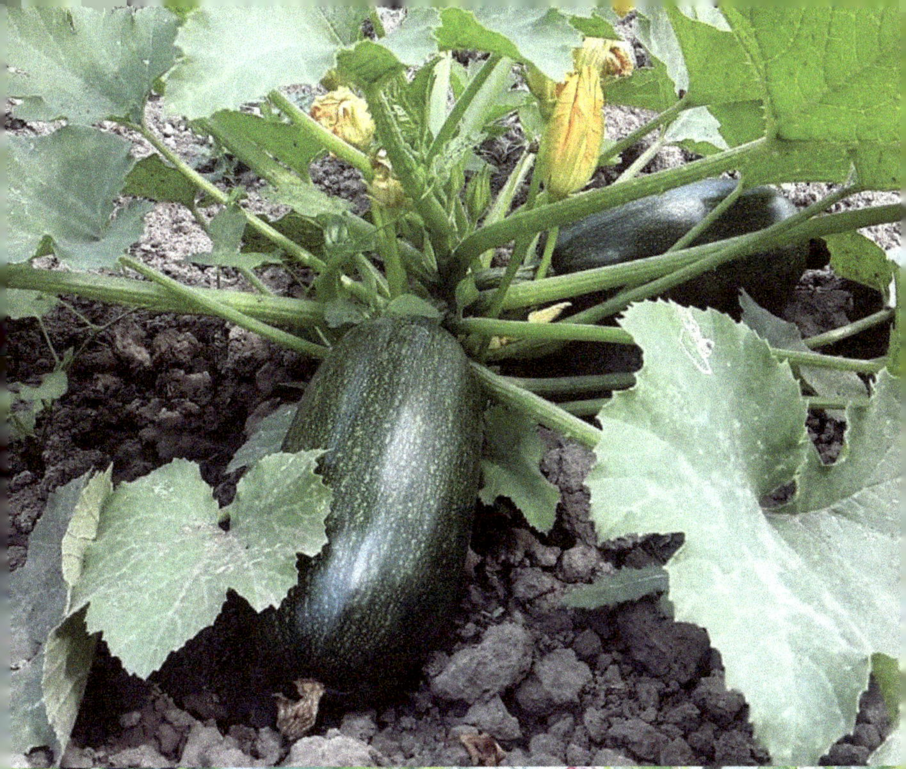

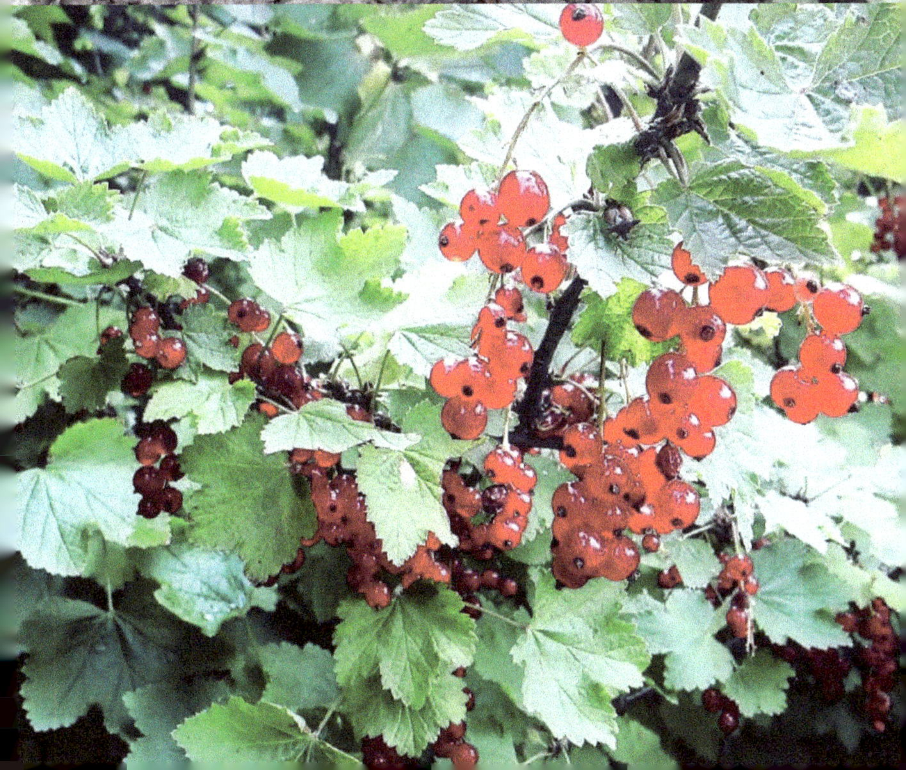

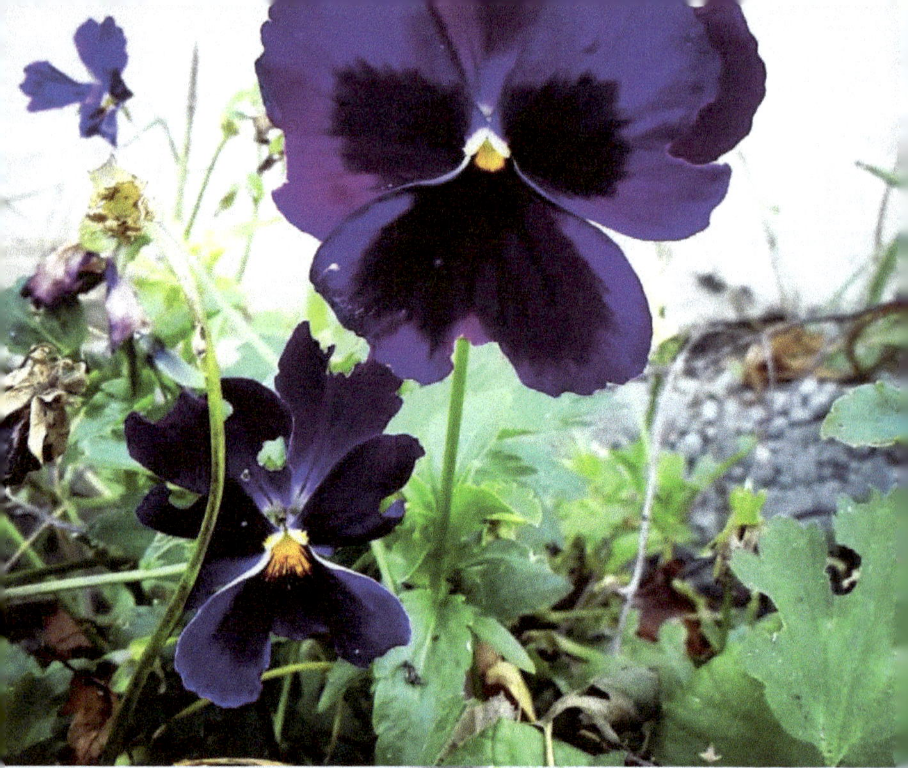

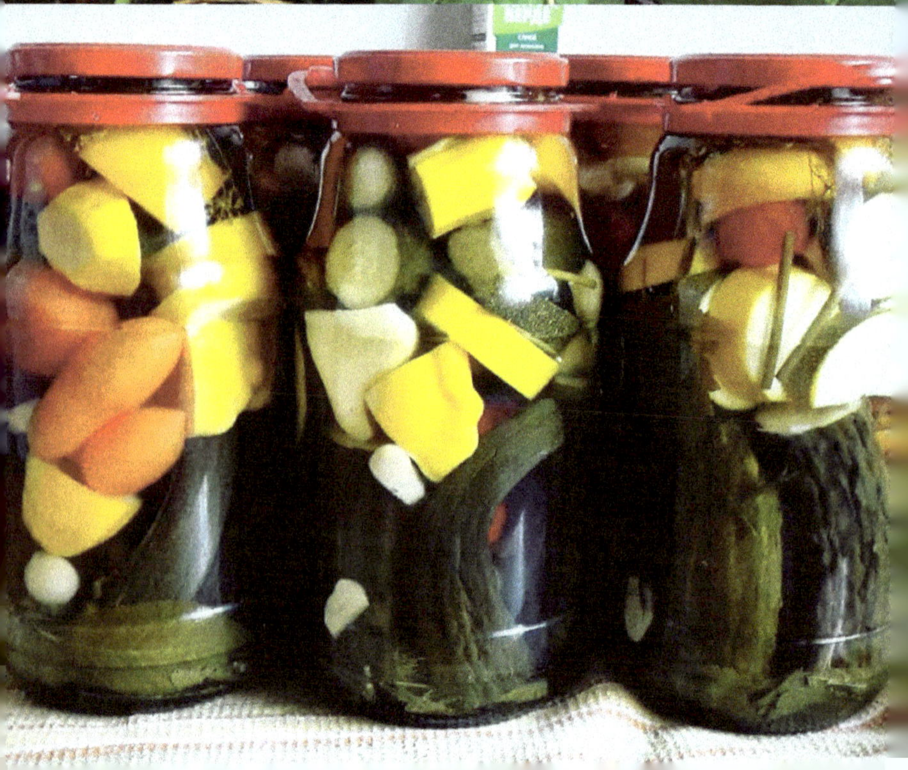

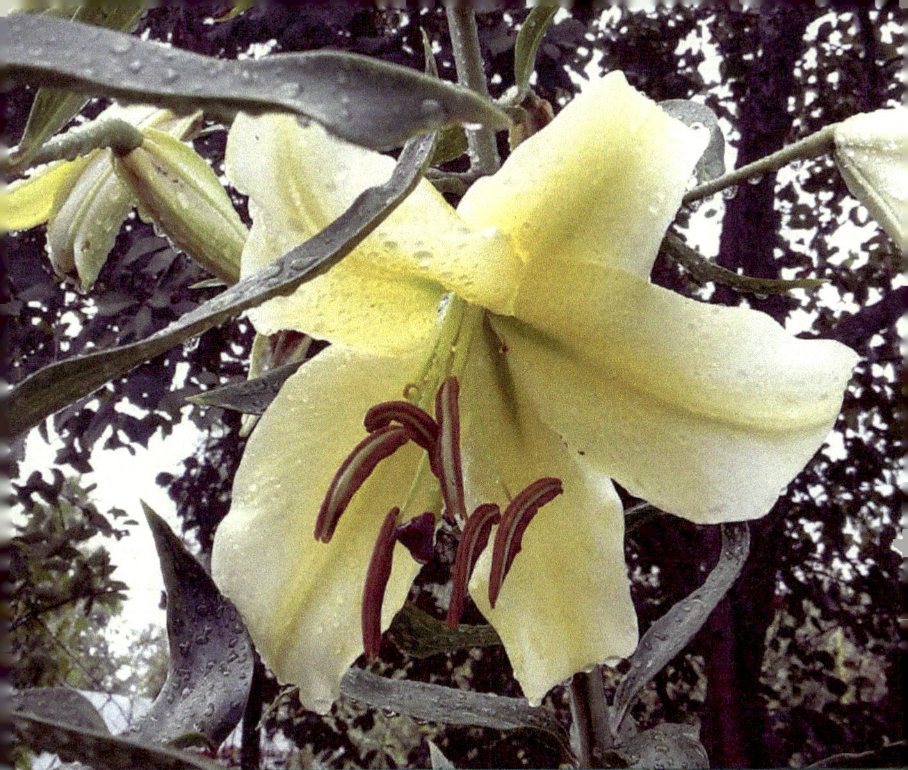

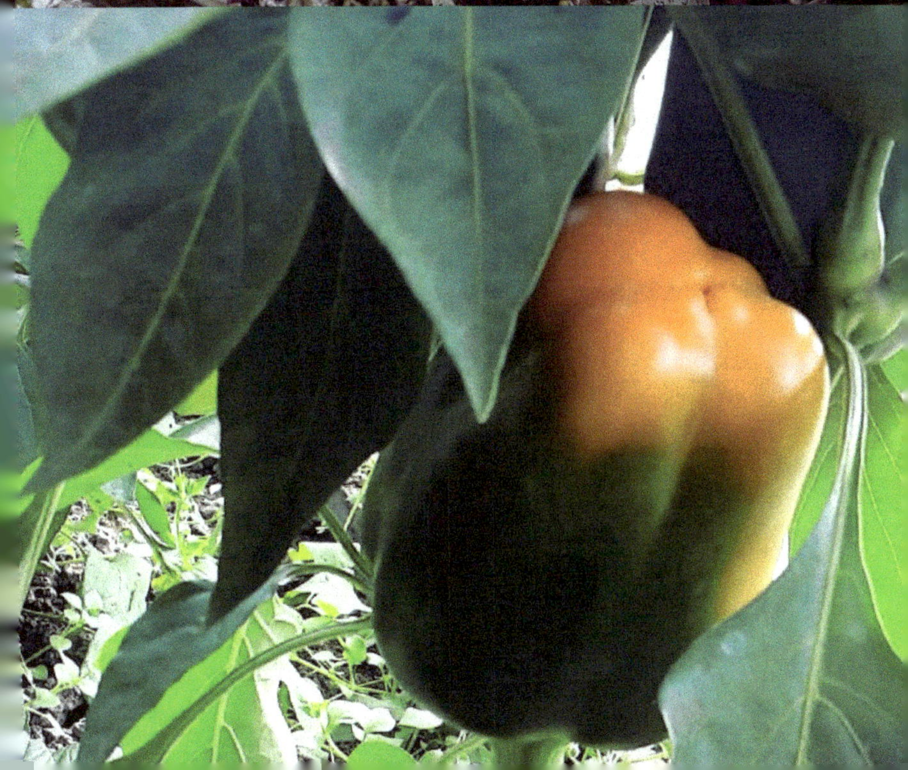

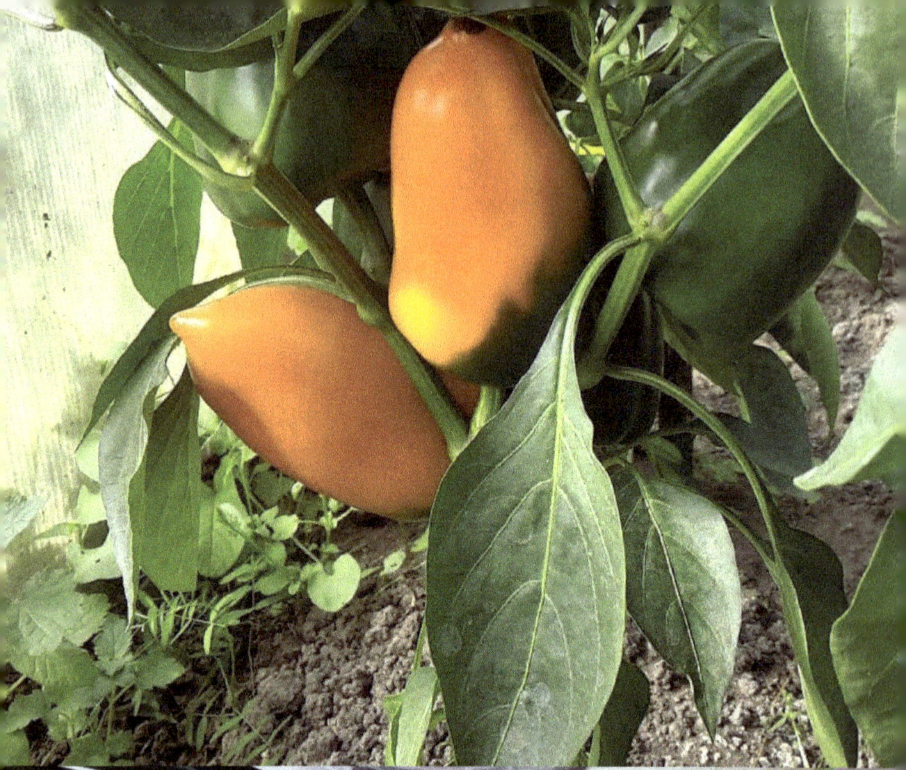

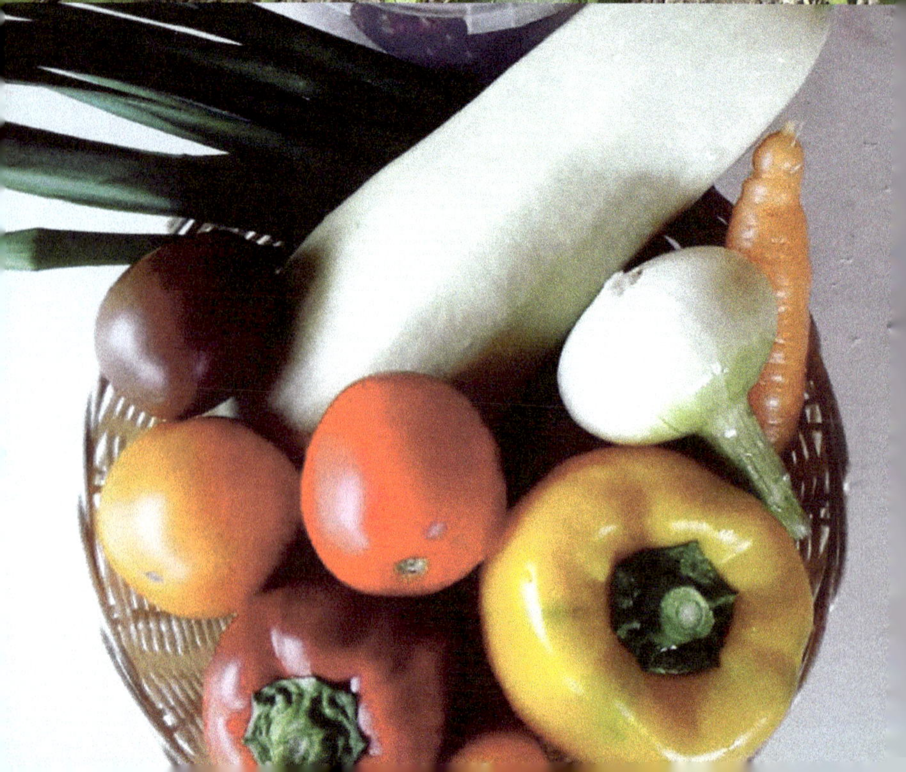

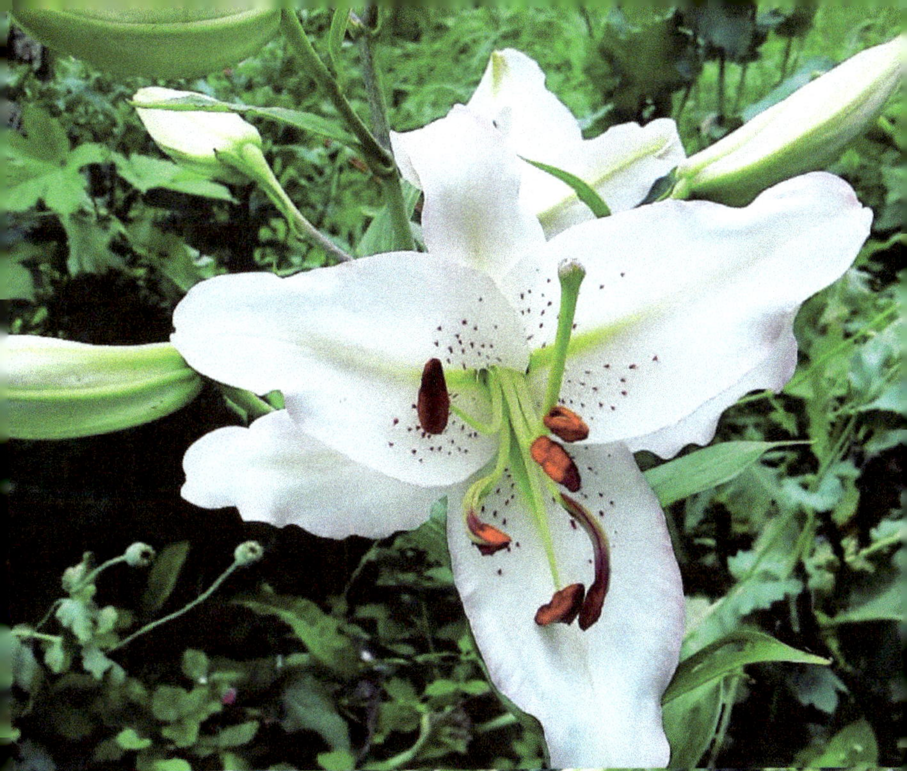

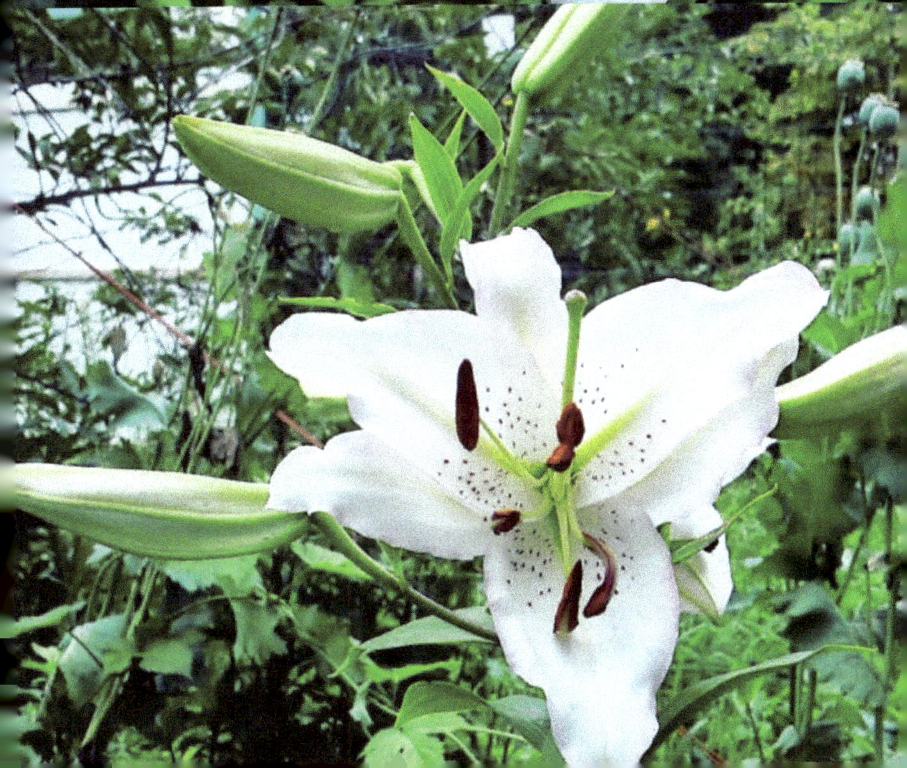

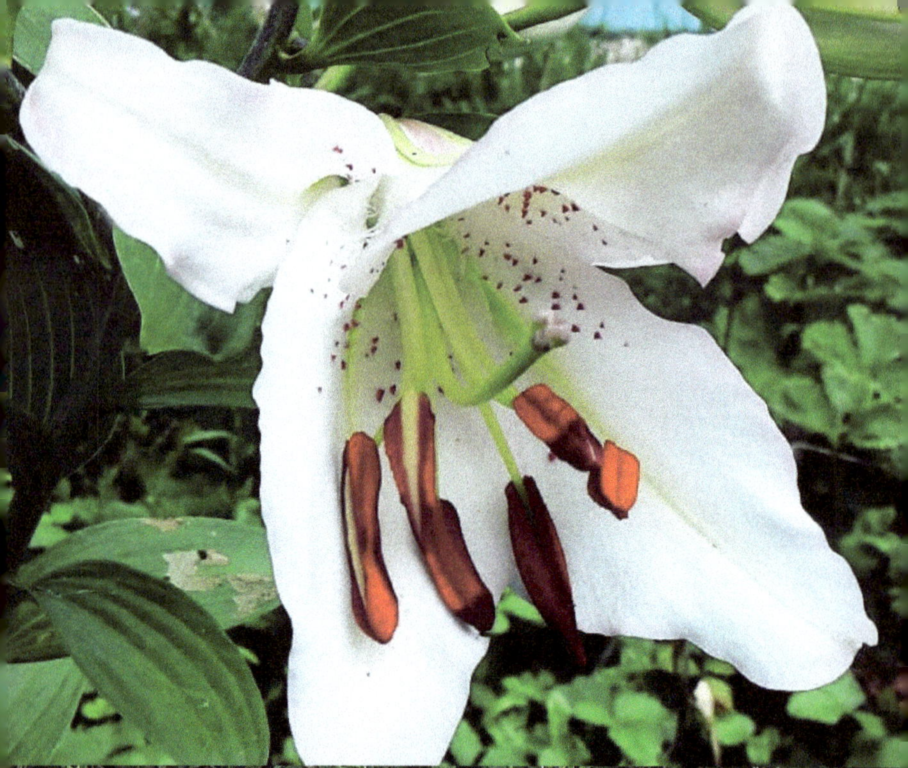

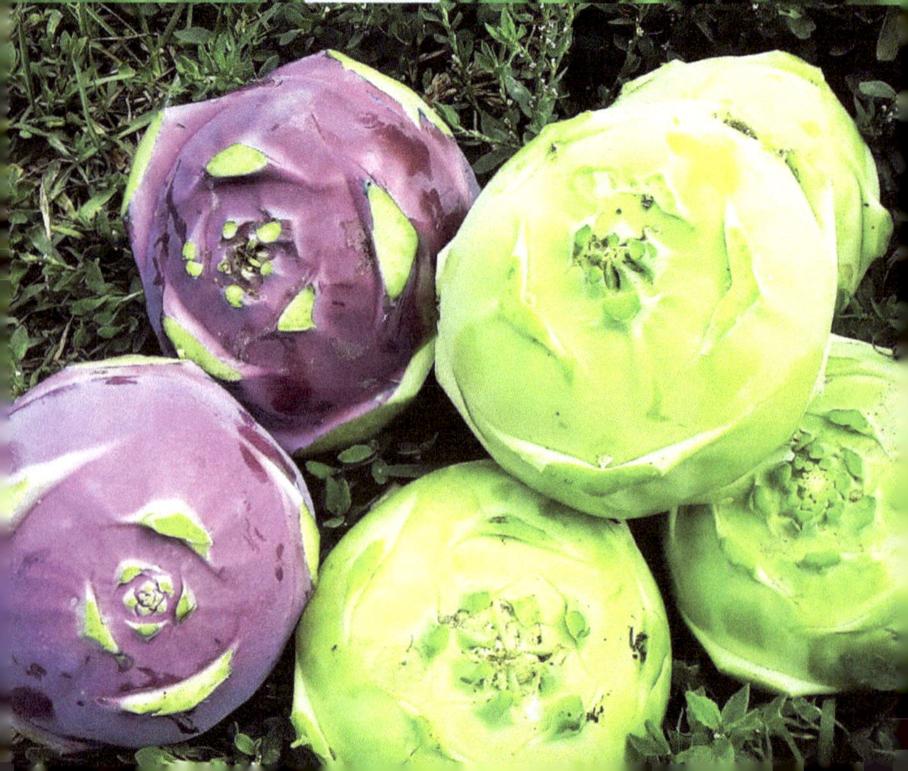

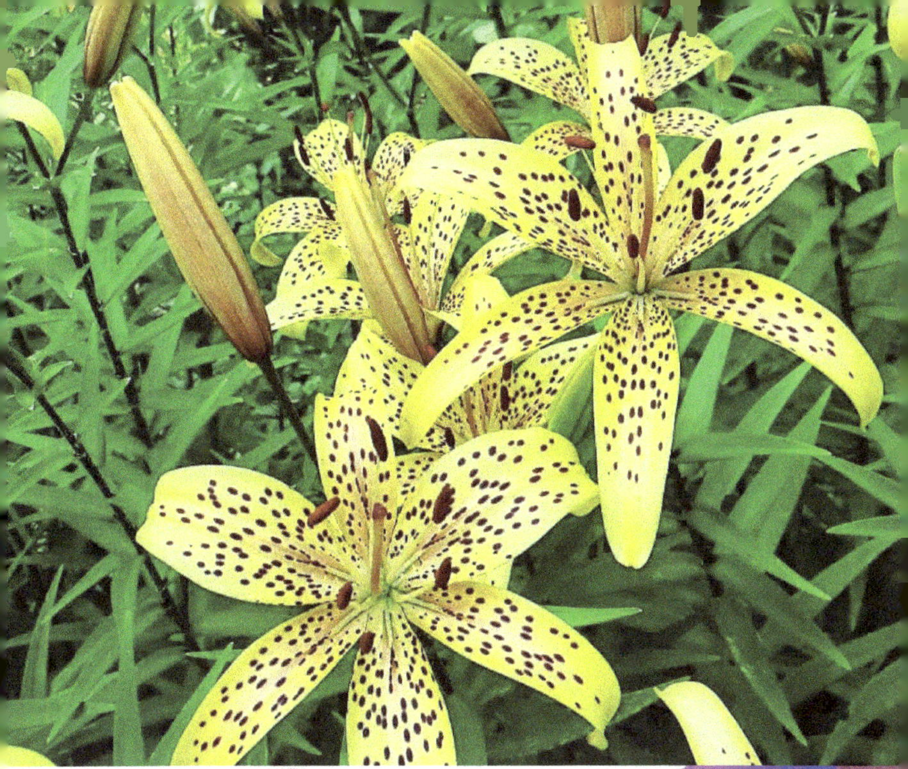
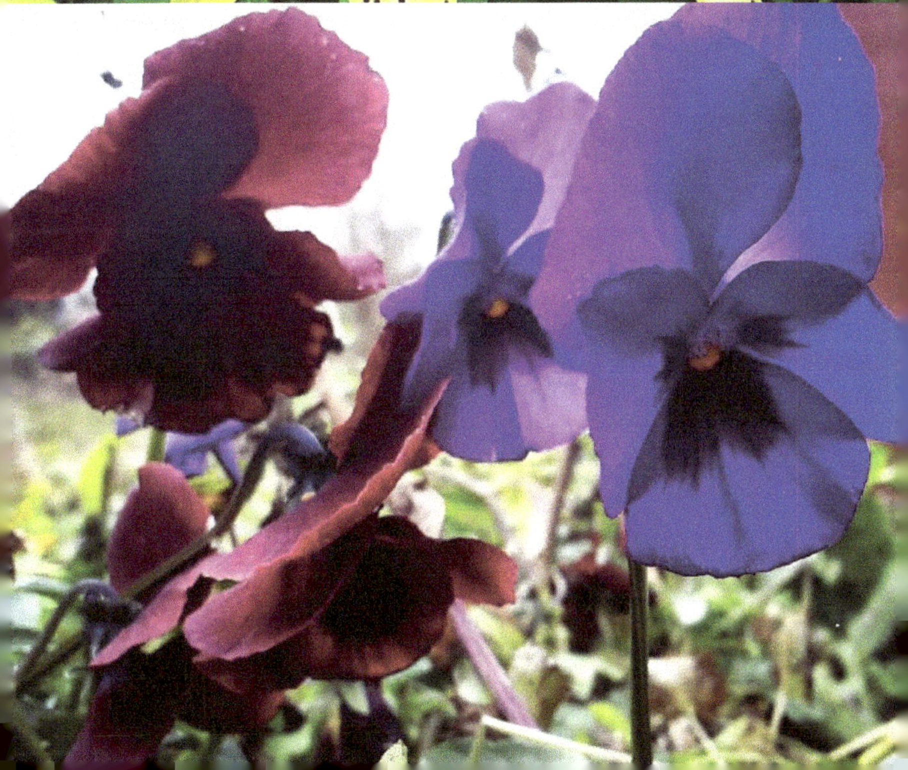

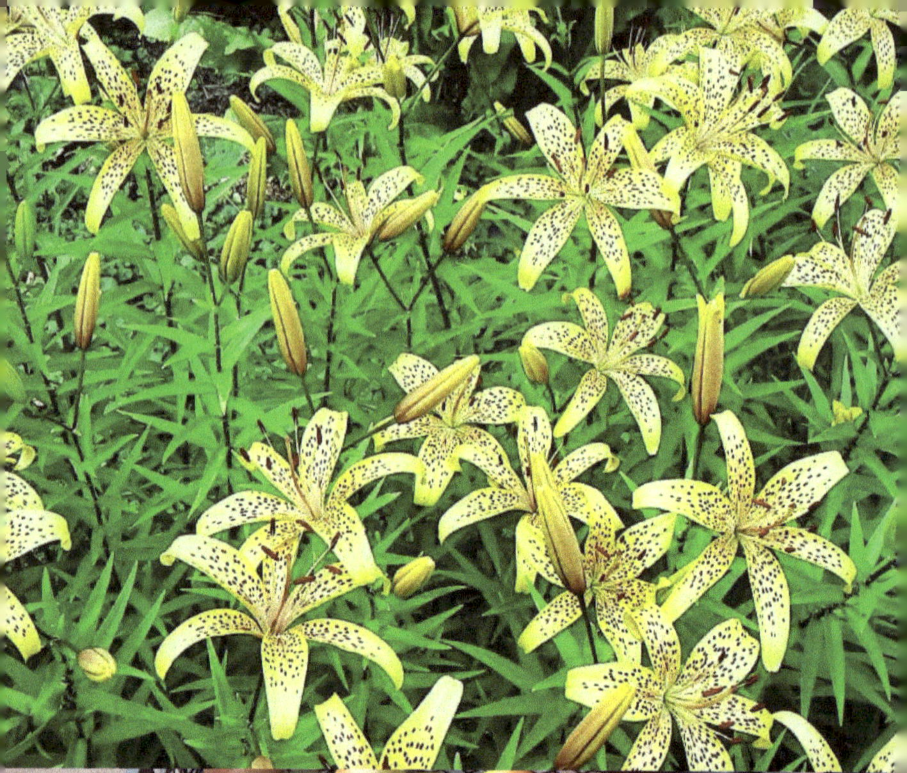
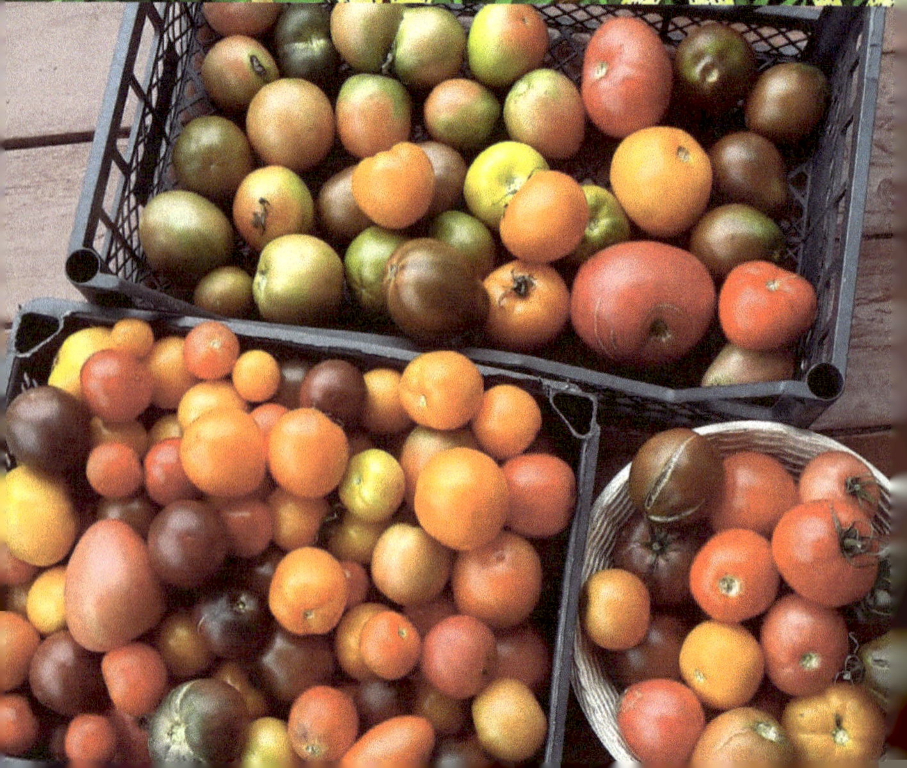

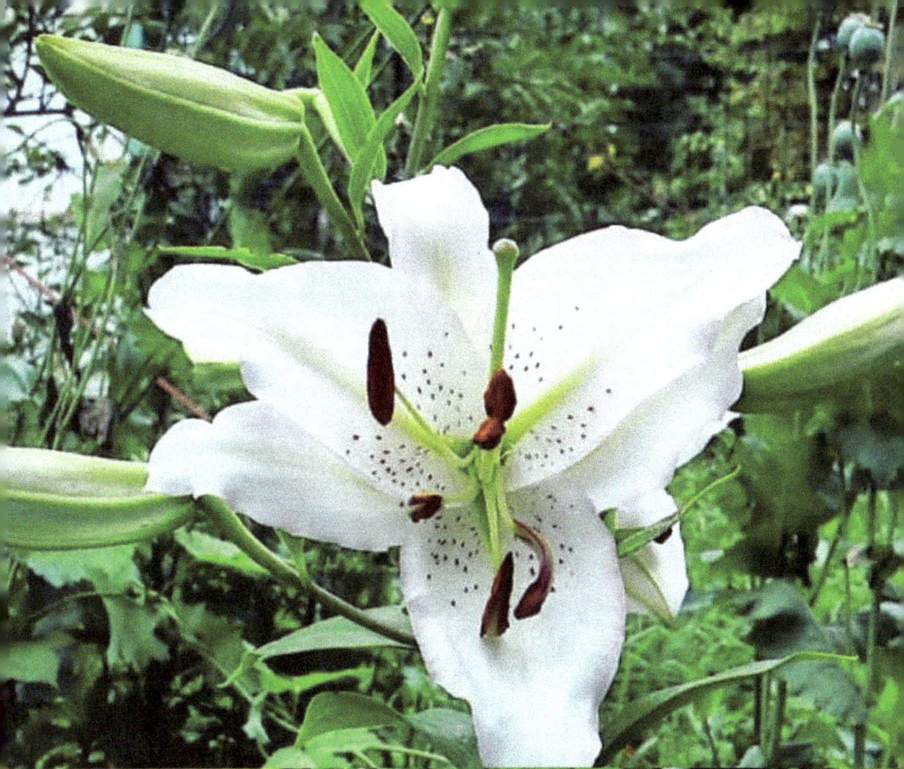

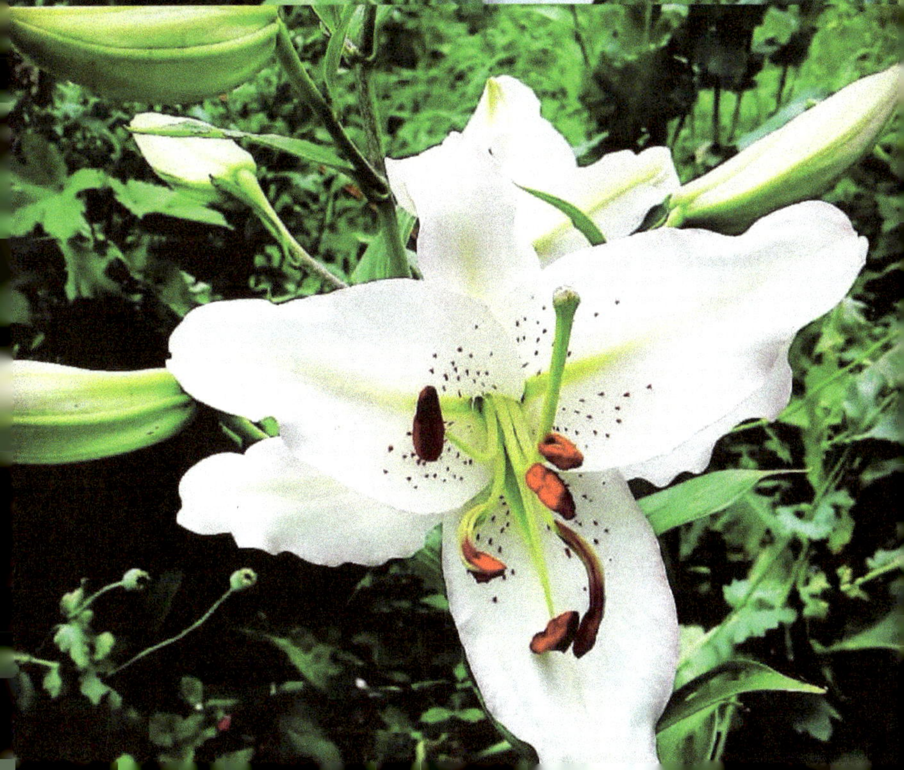

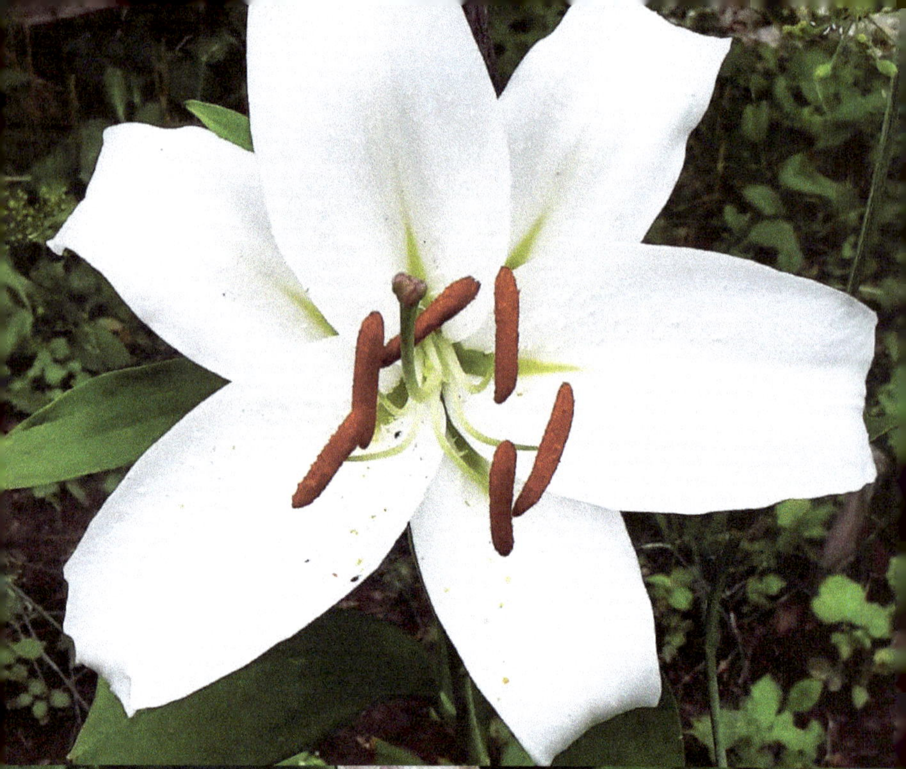

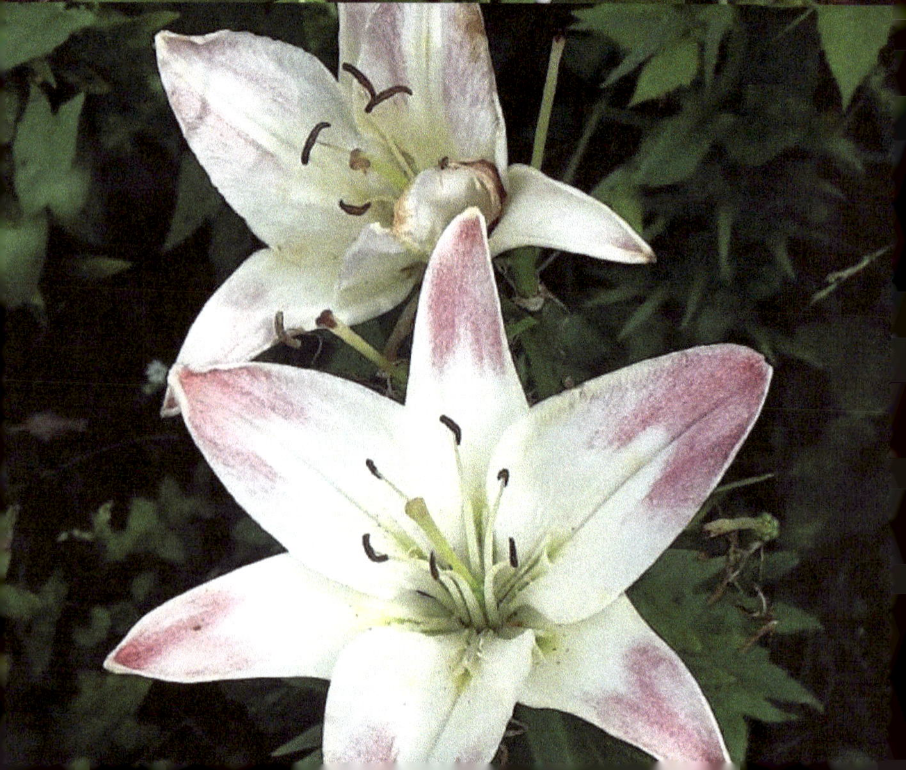

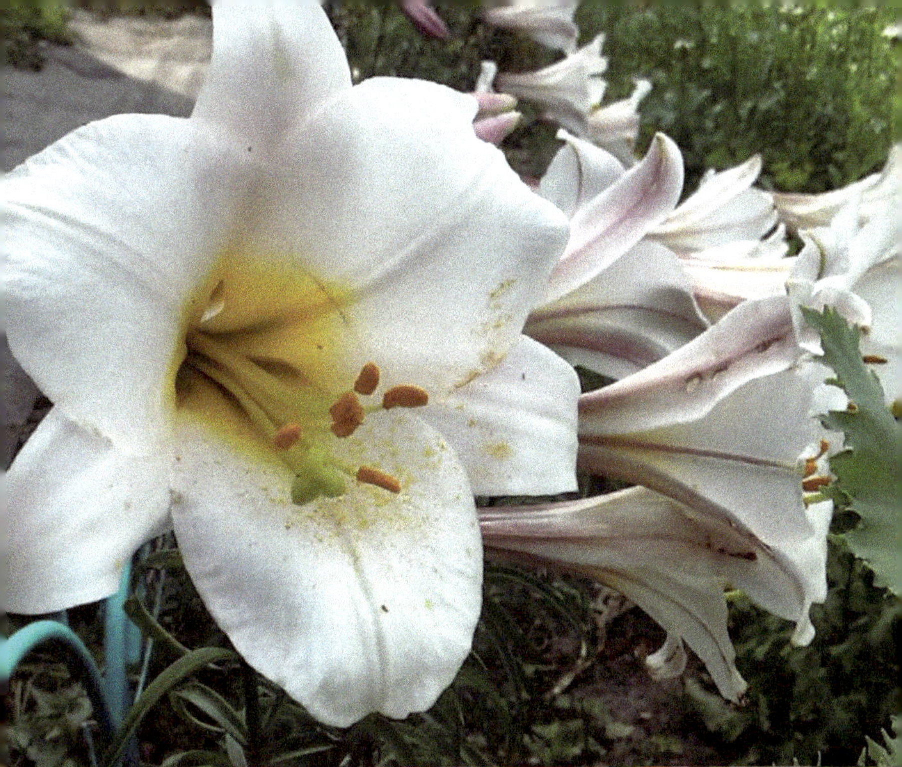

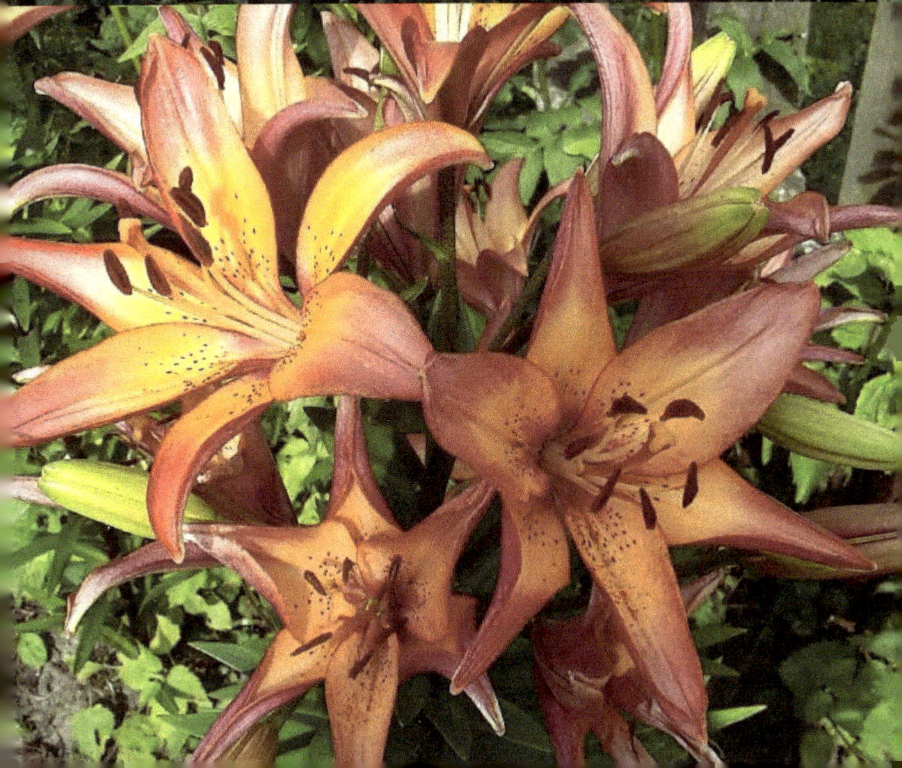

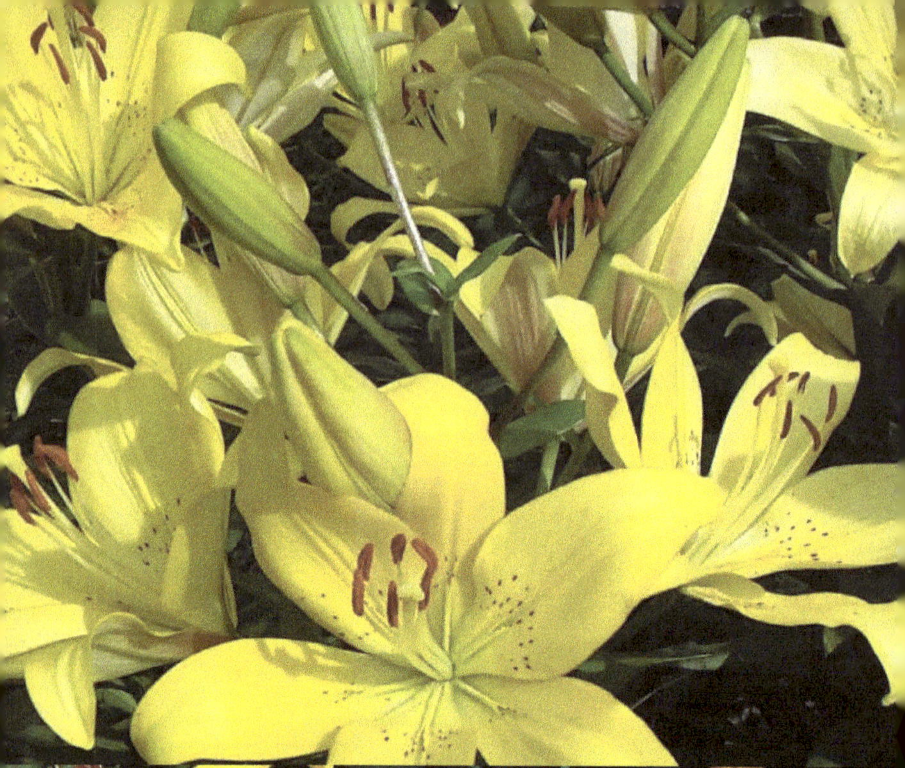
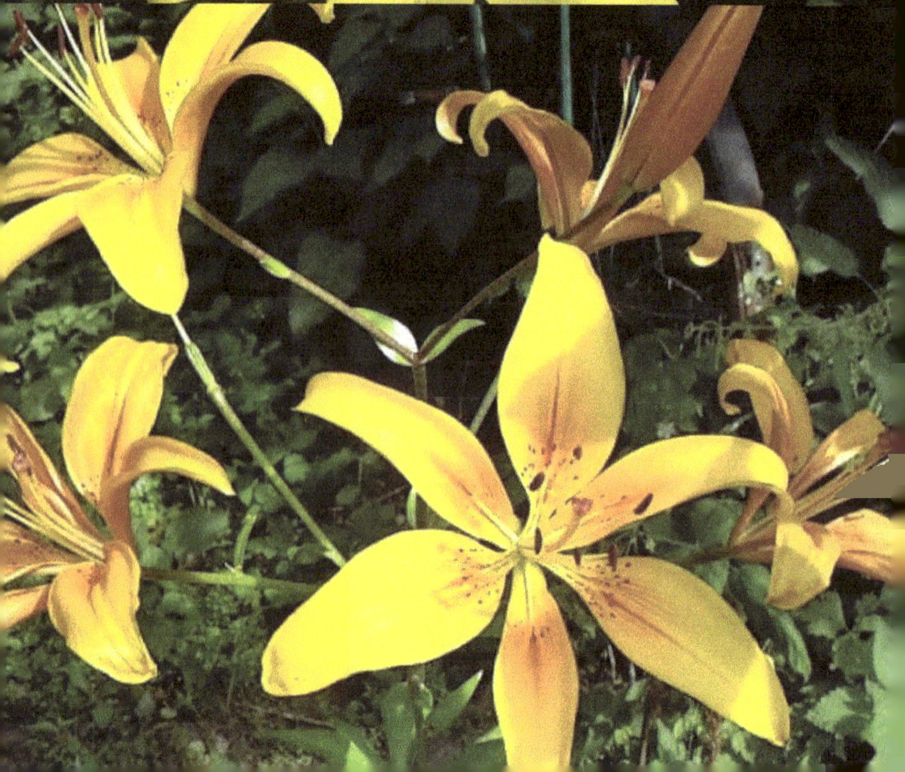

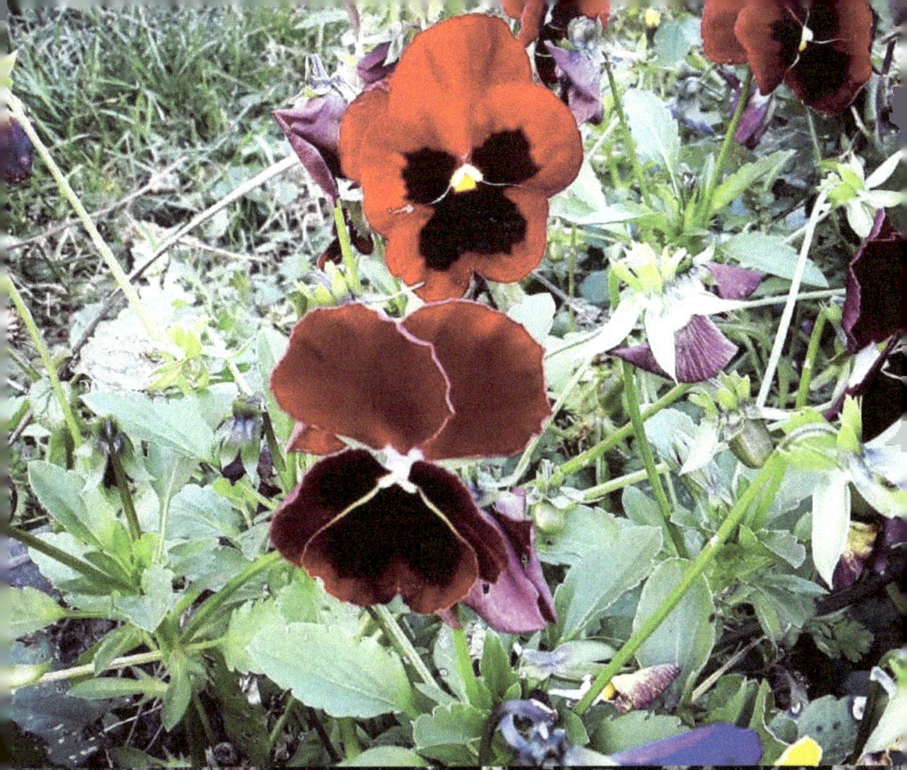
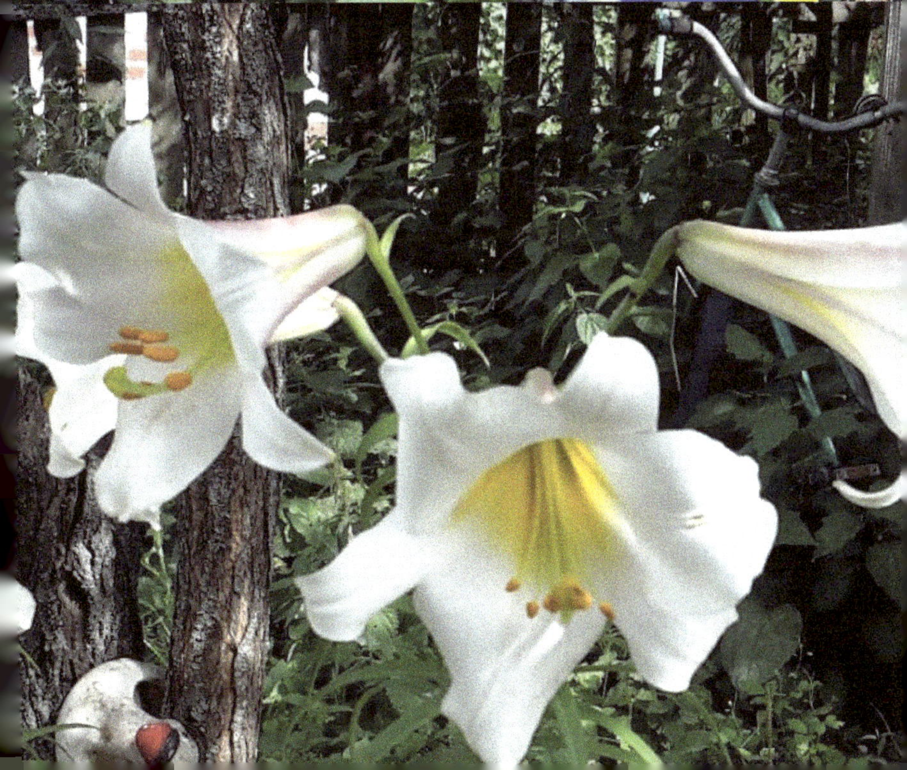

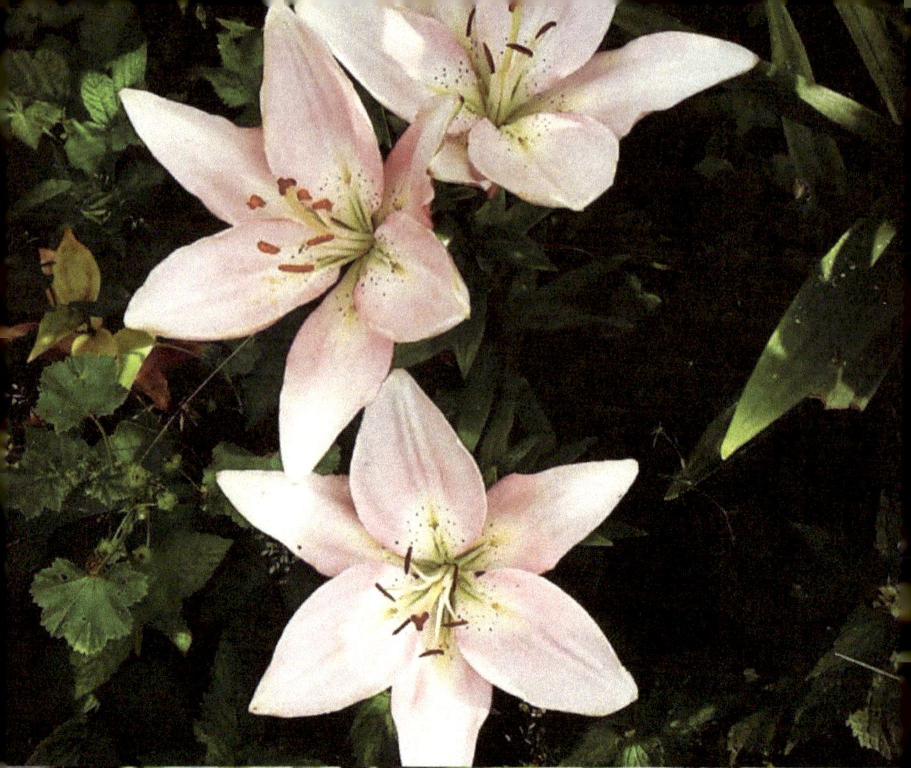

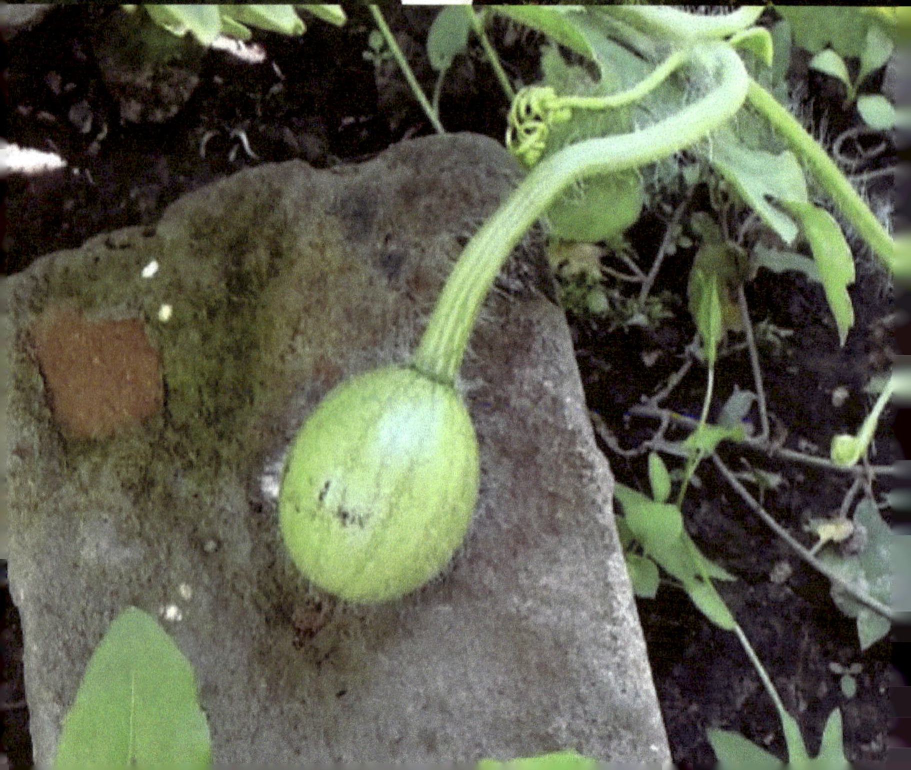

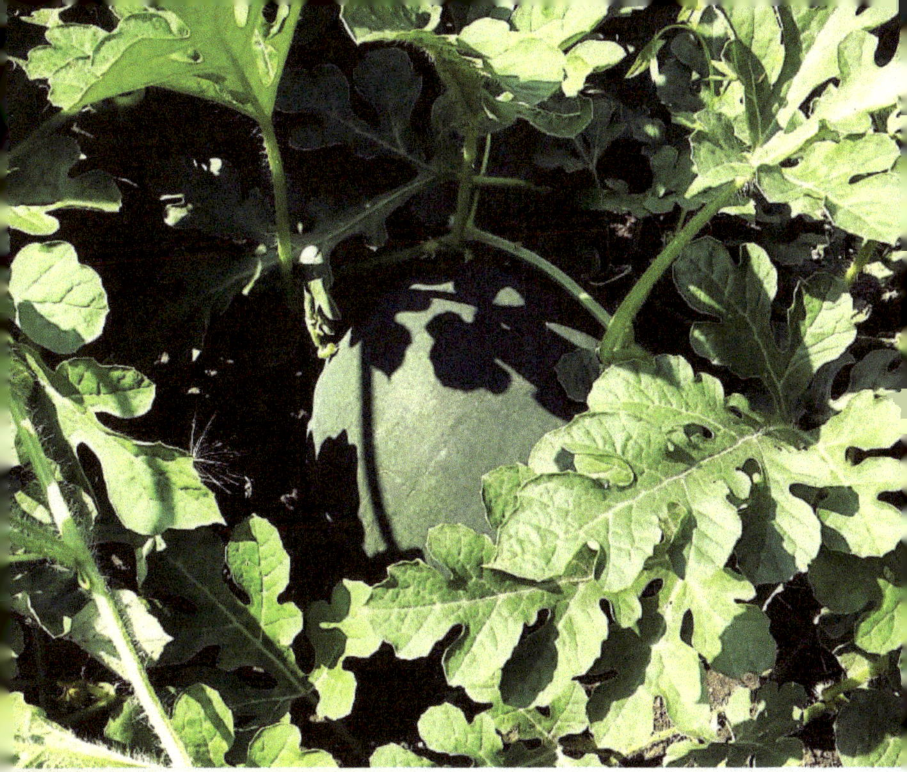
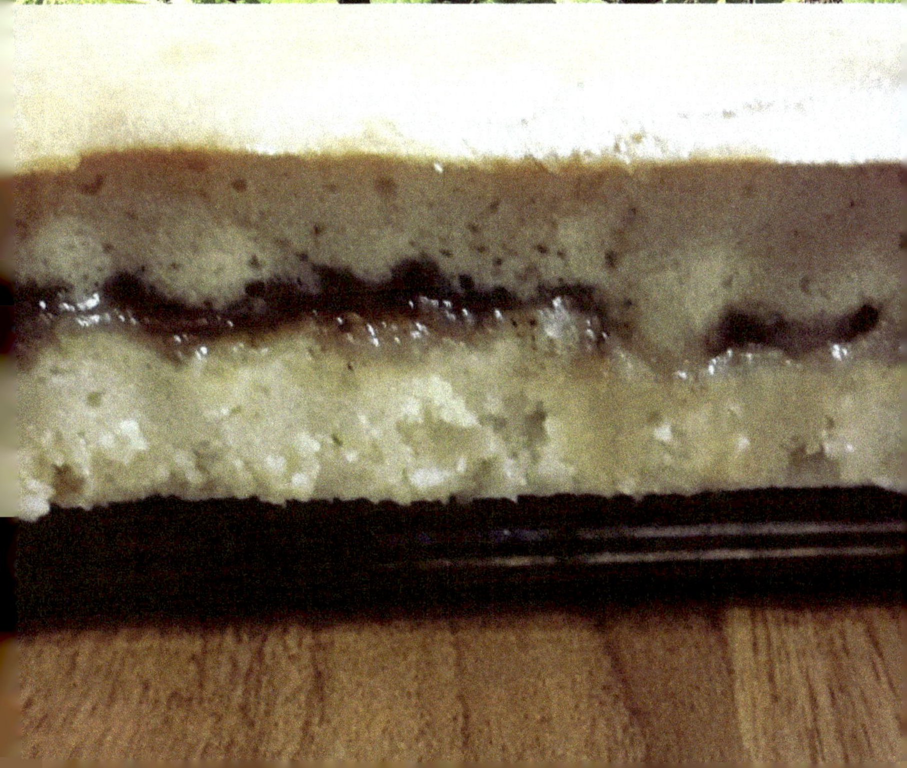

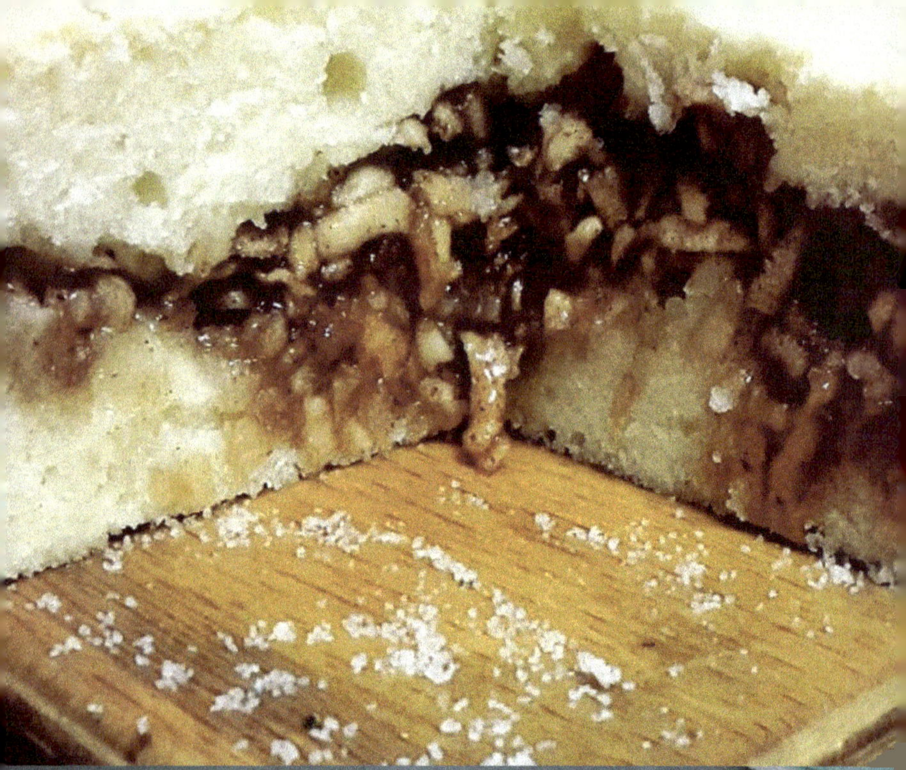

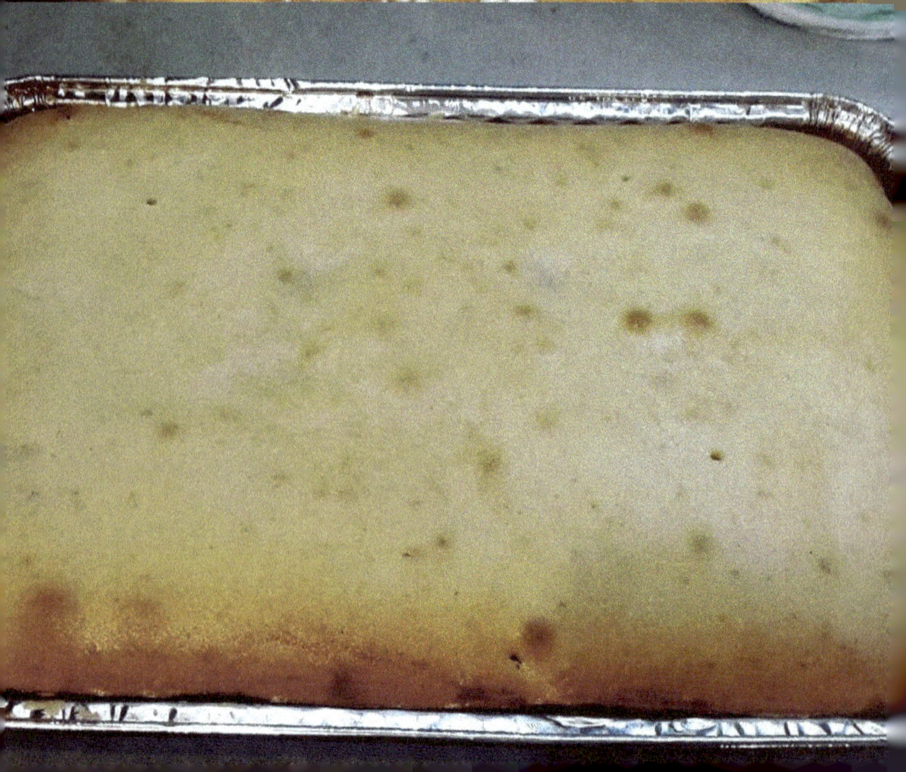

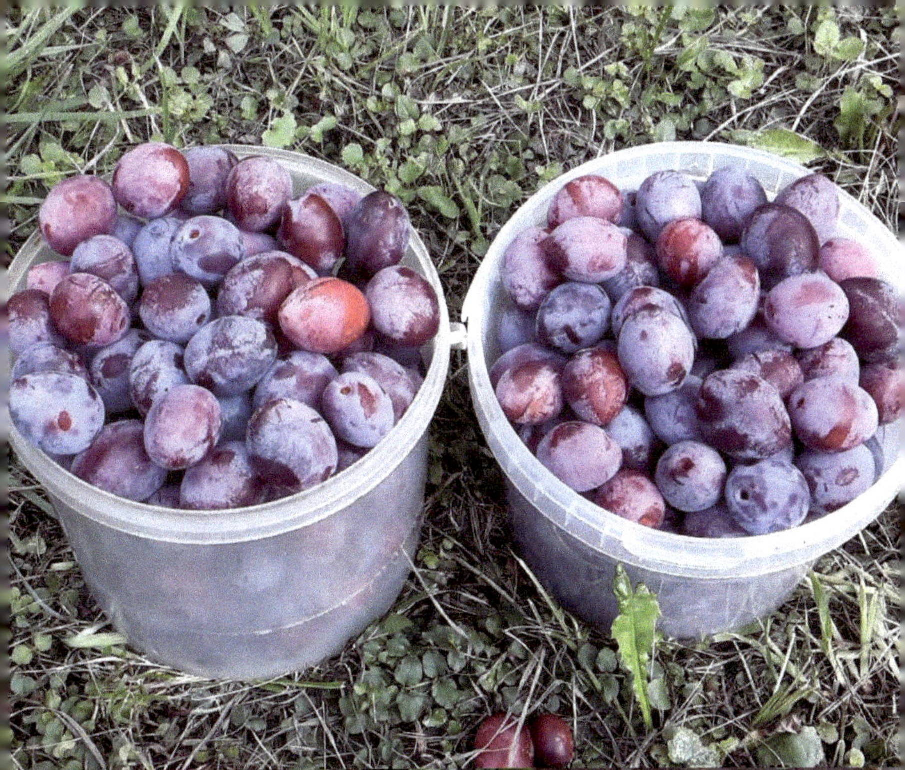

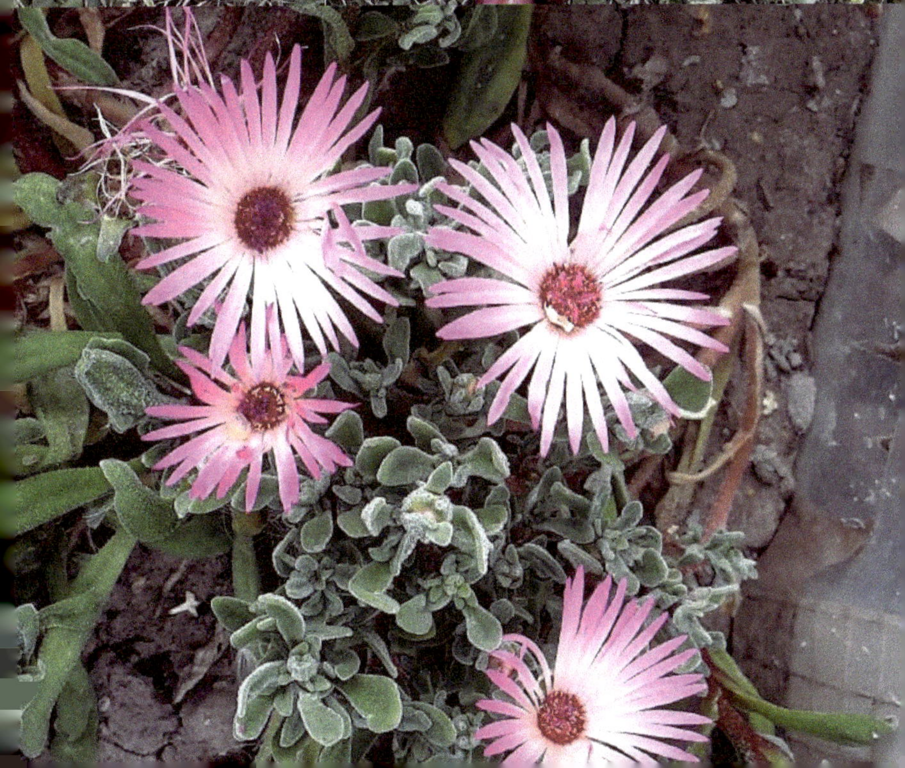

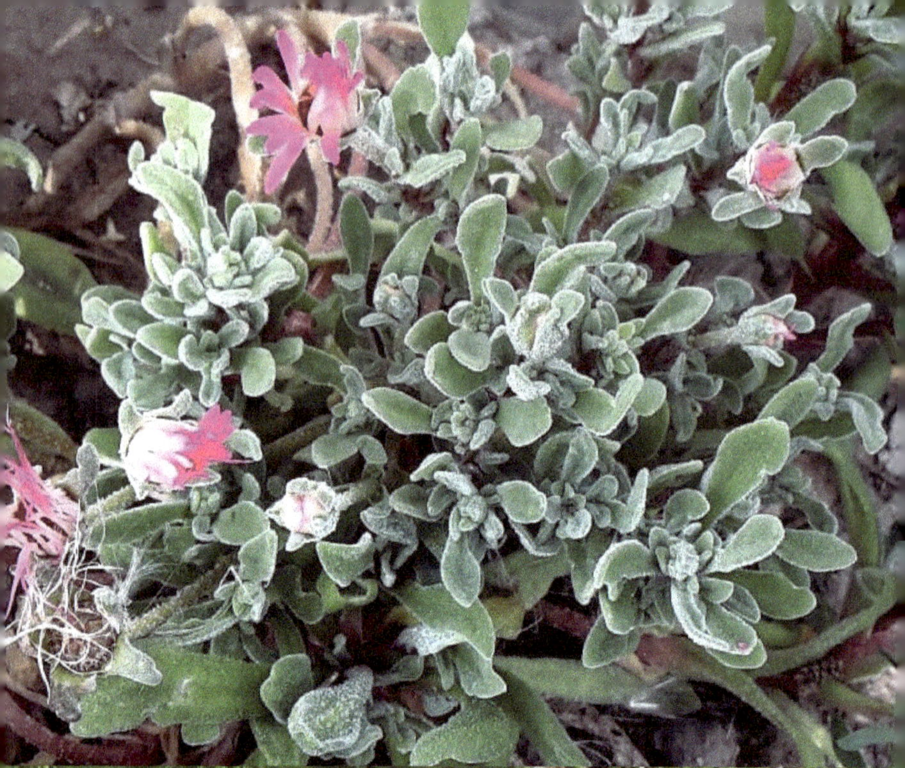

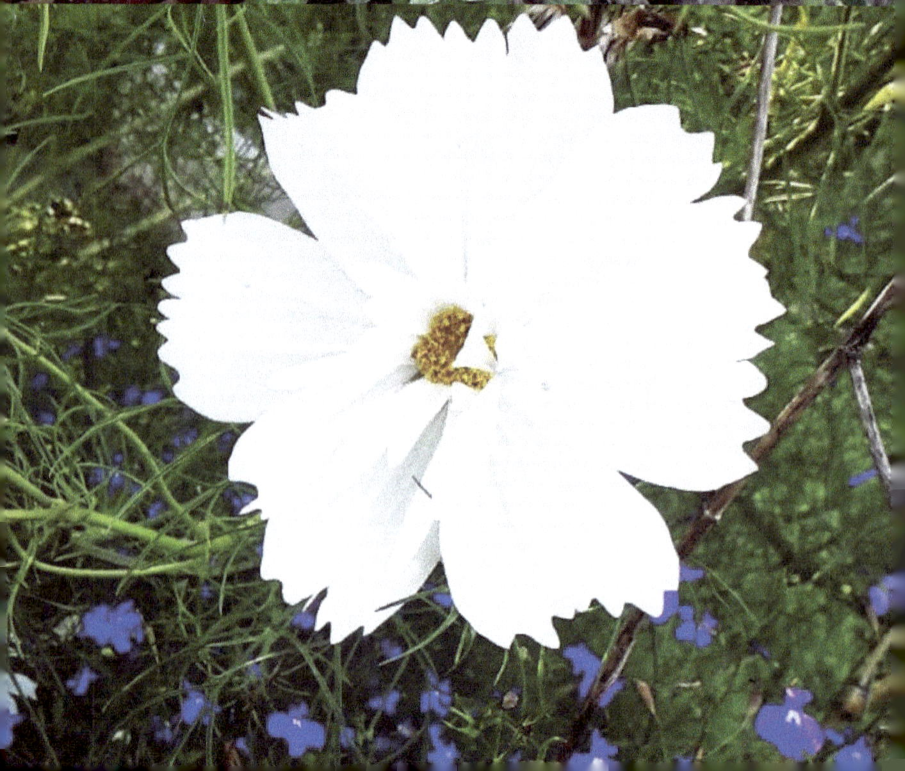

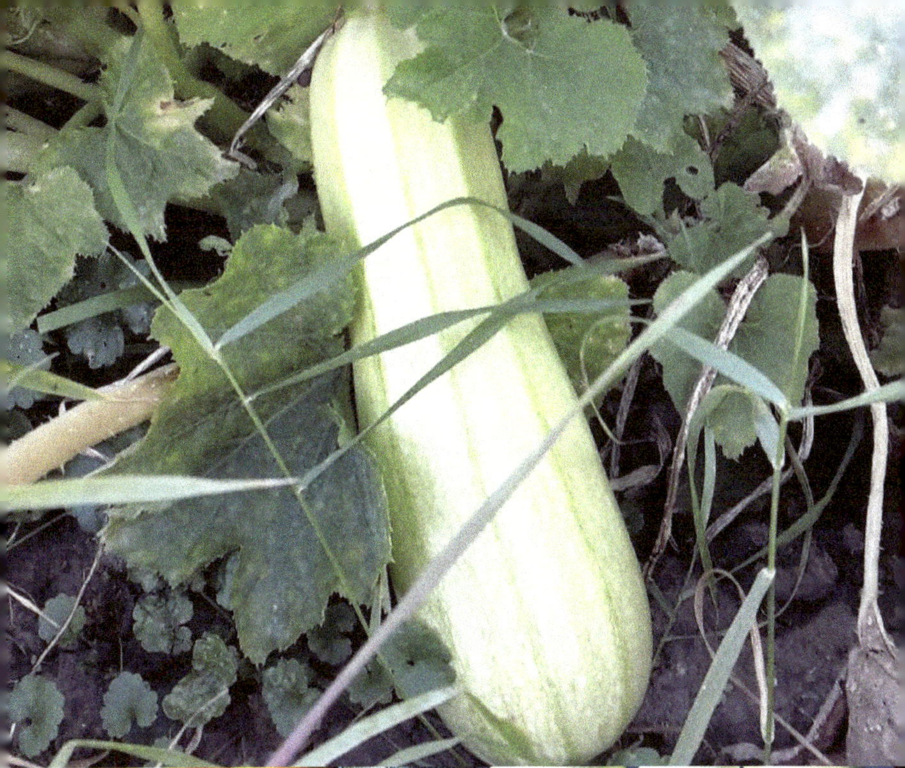
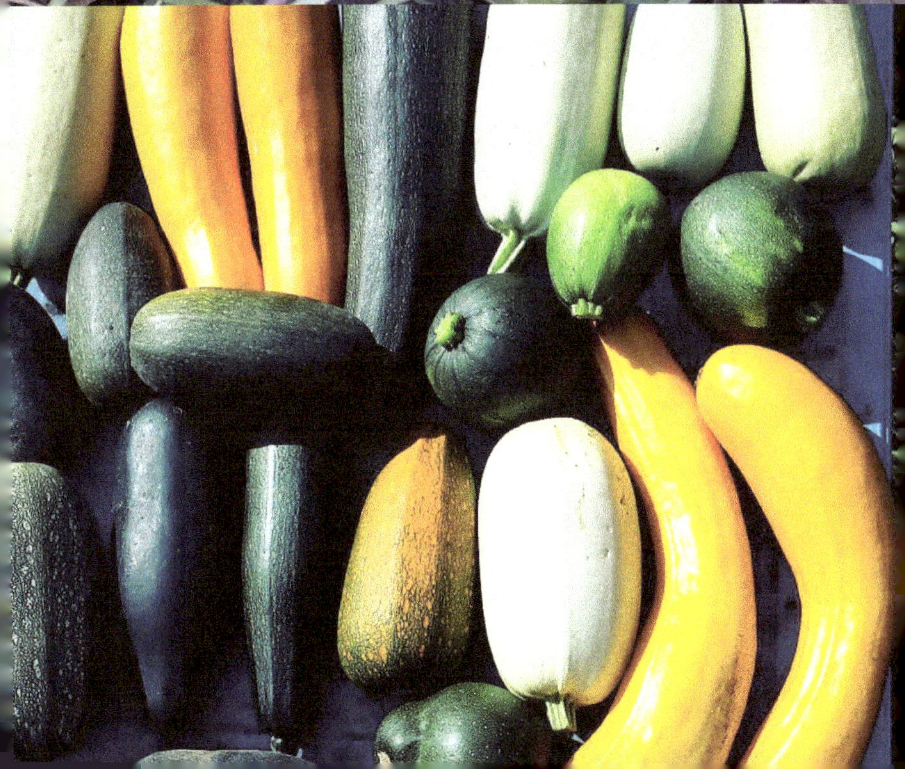

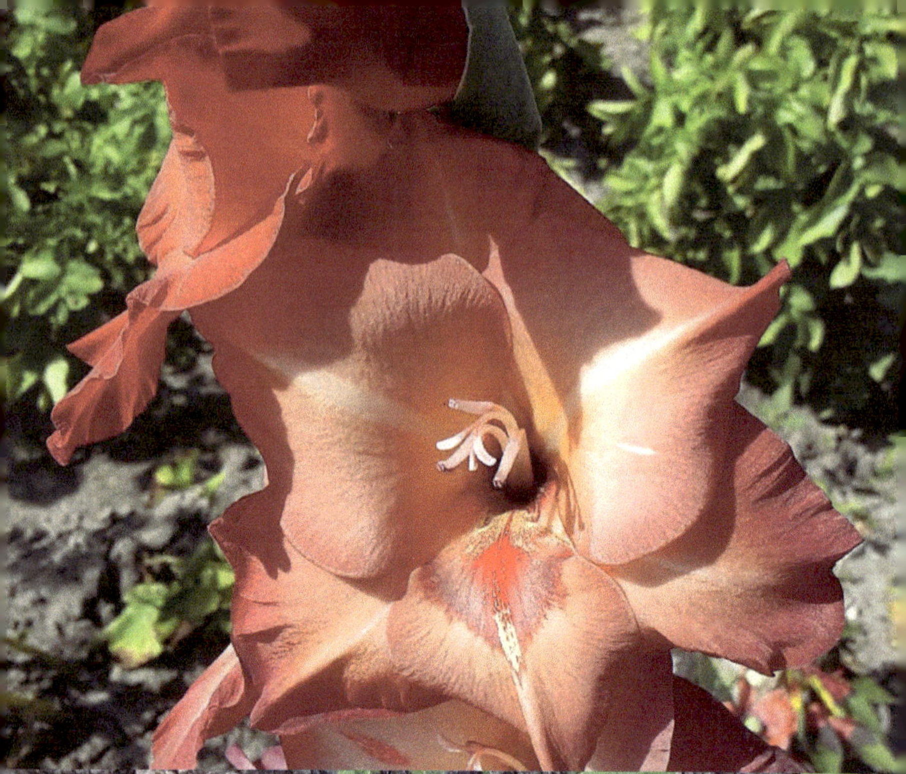

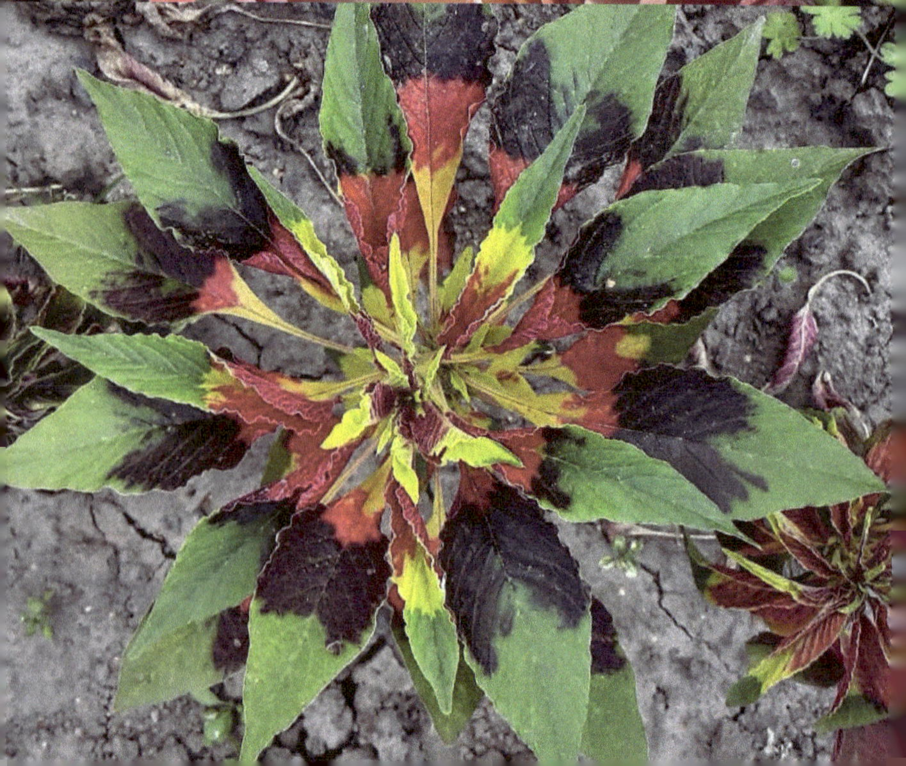

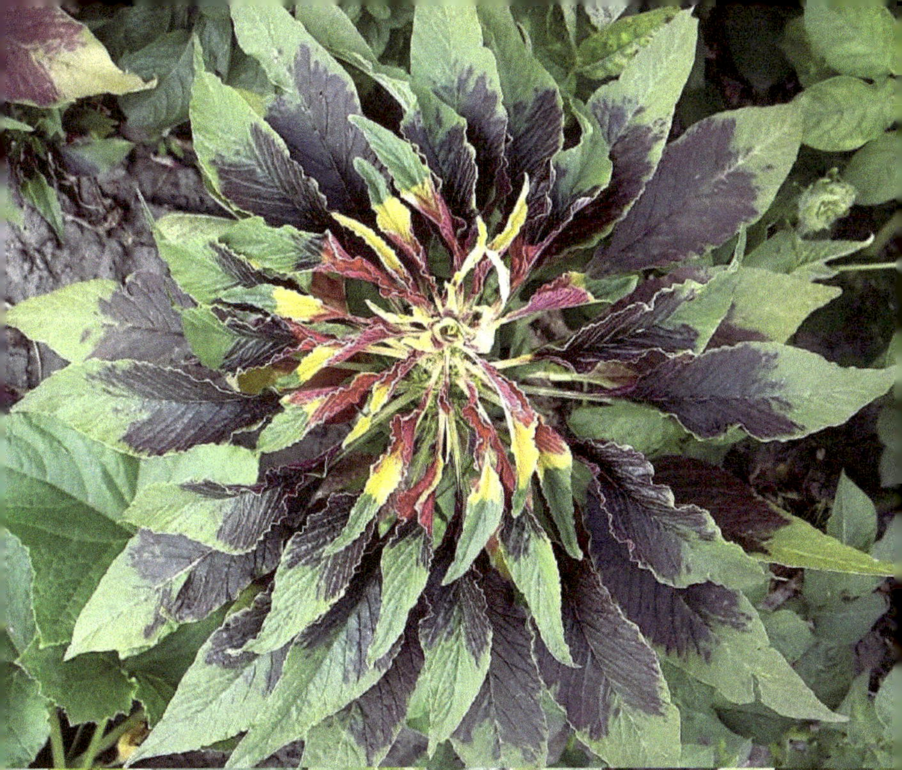

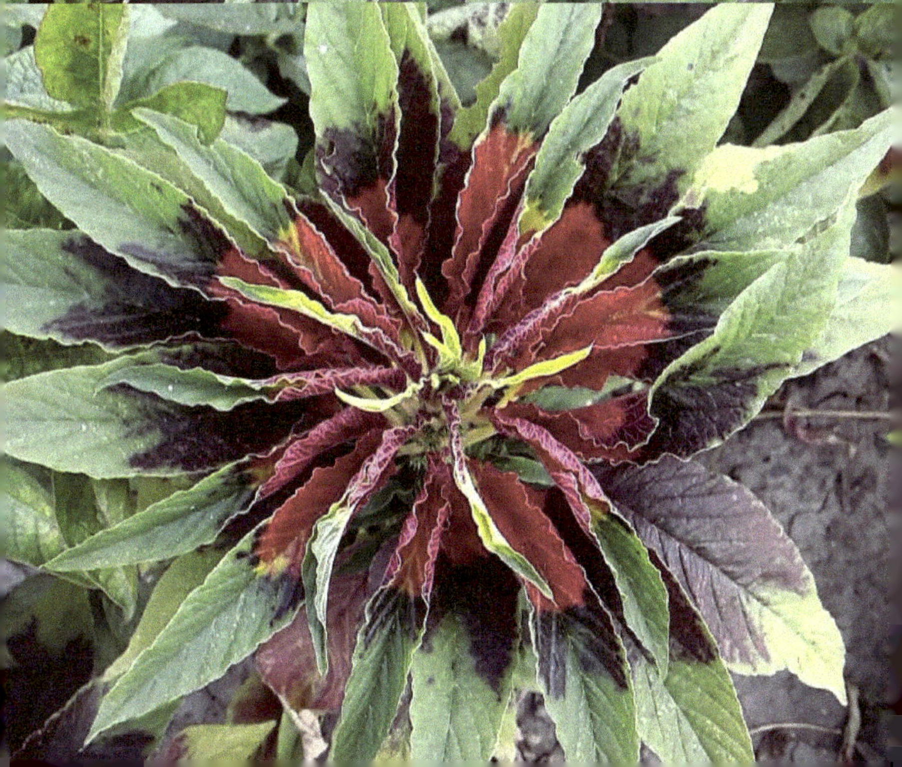

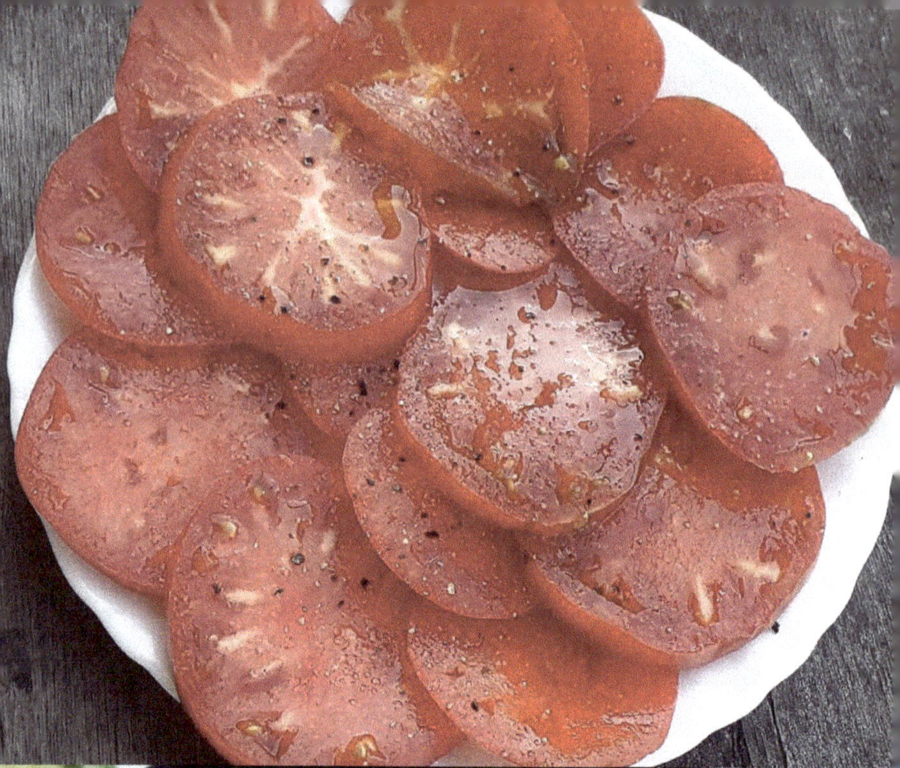

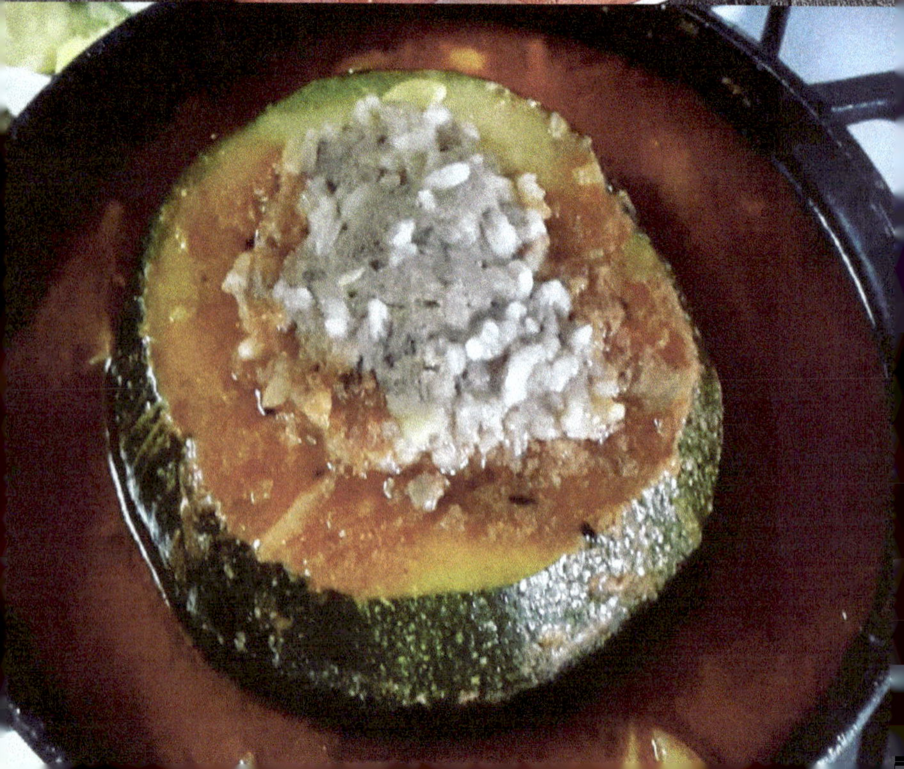

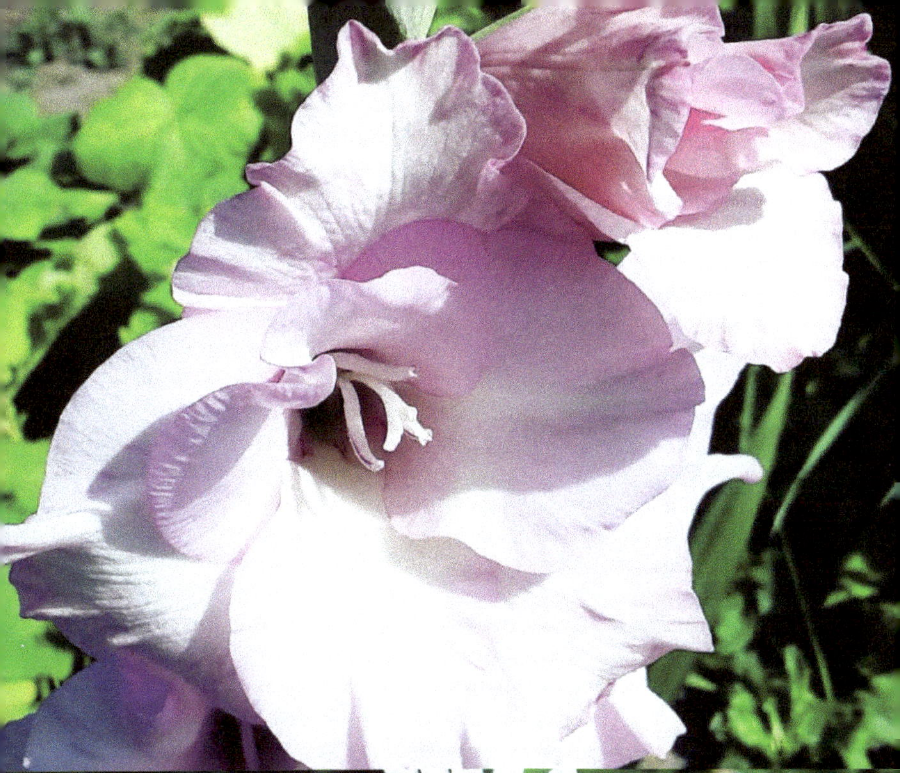

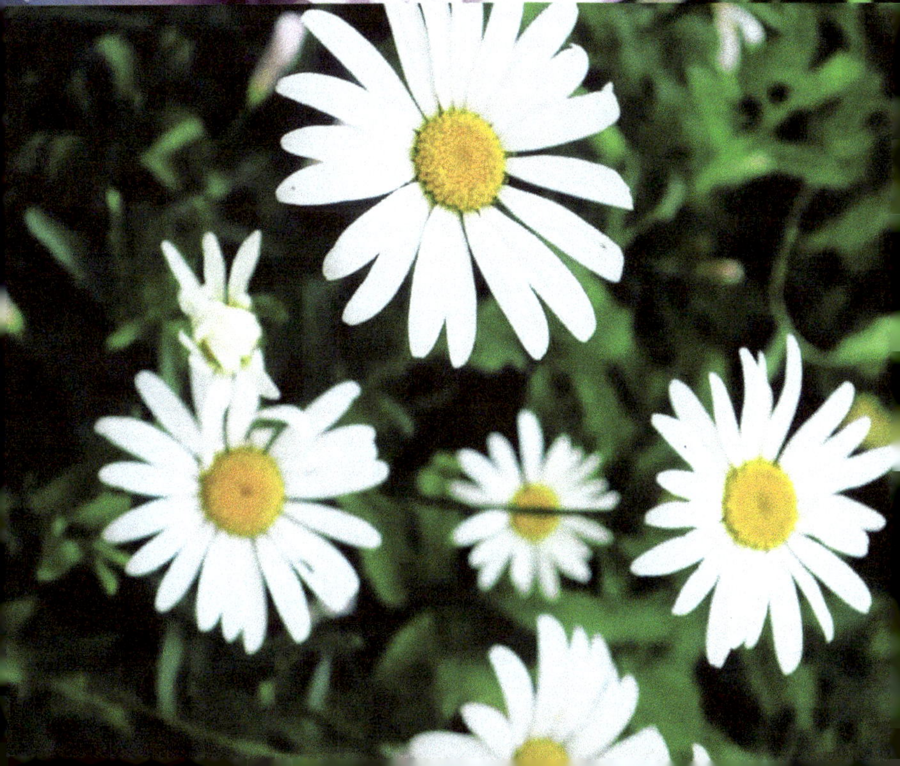

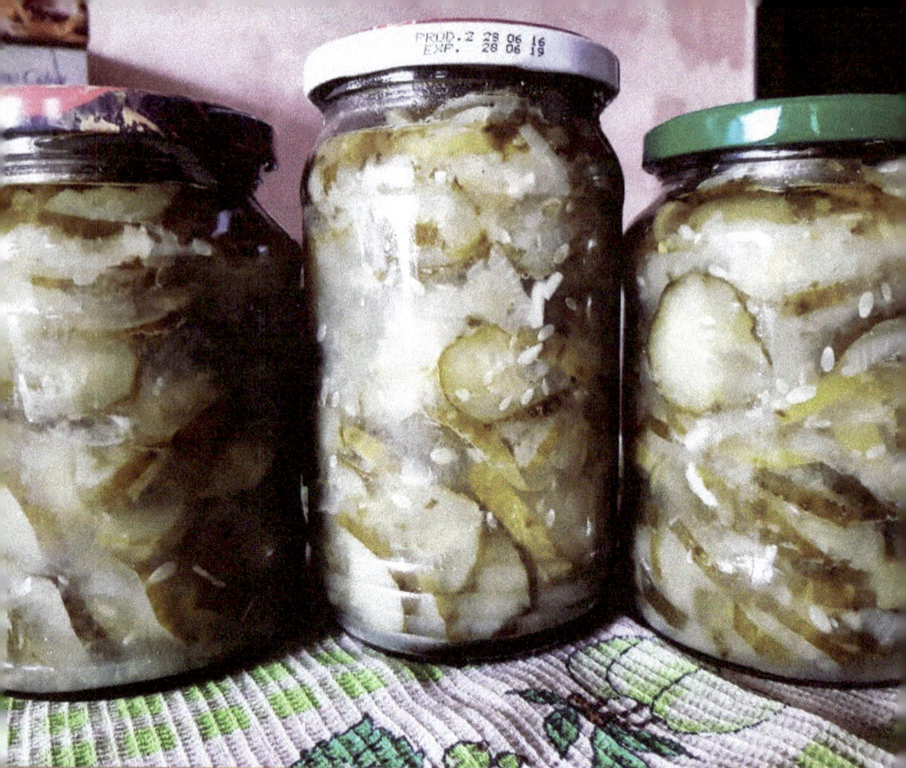
PROD.2 28 06 16
EXP. 28 06 19
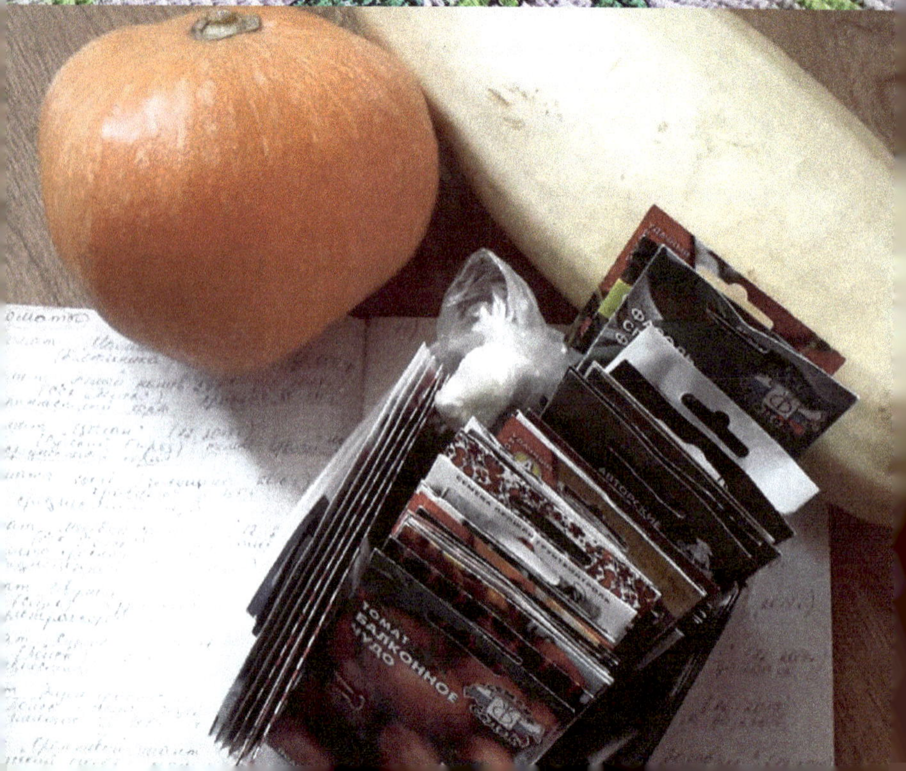
ТОМАТ
БАЛКОННОЕ
ЧУДО

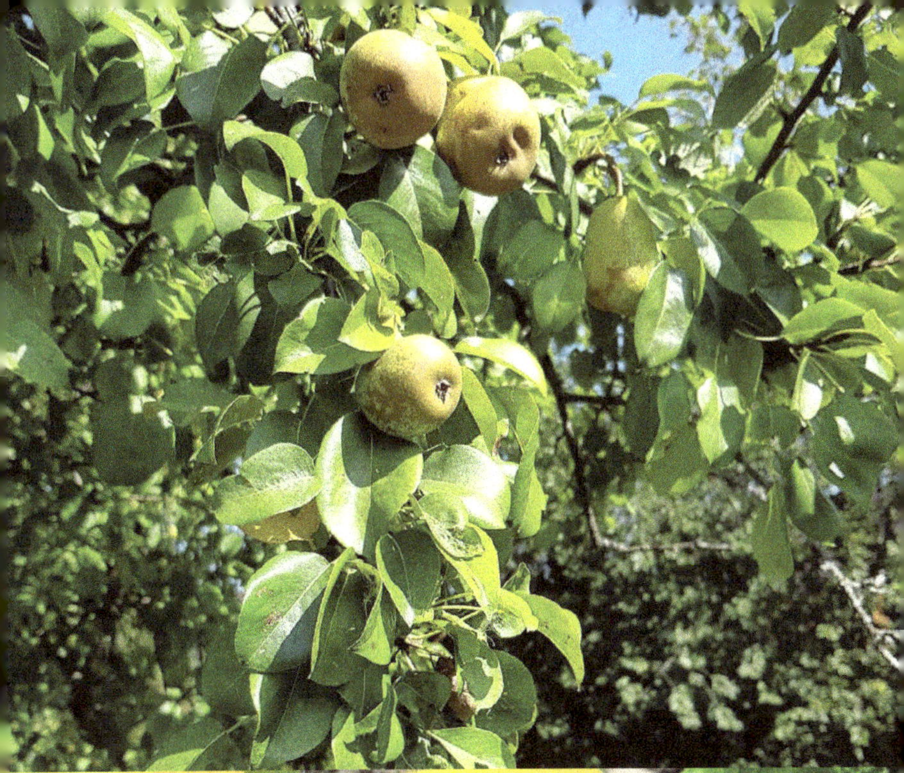

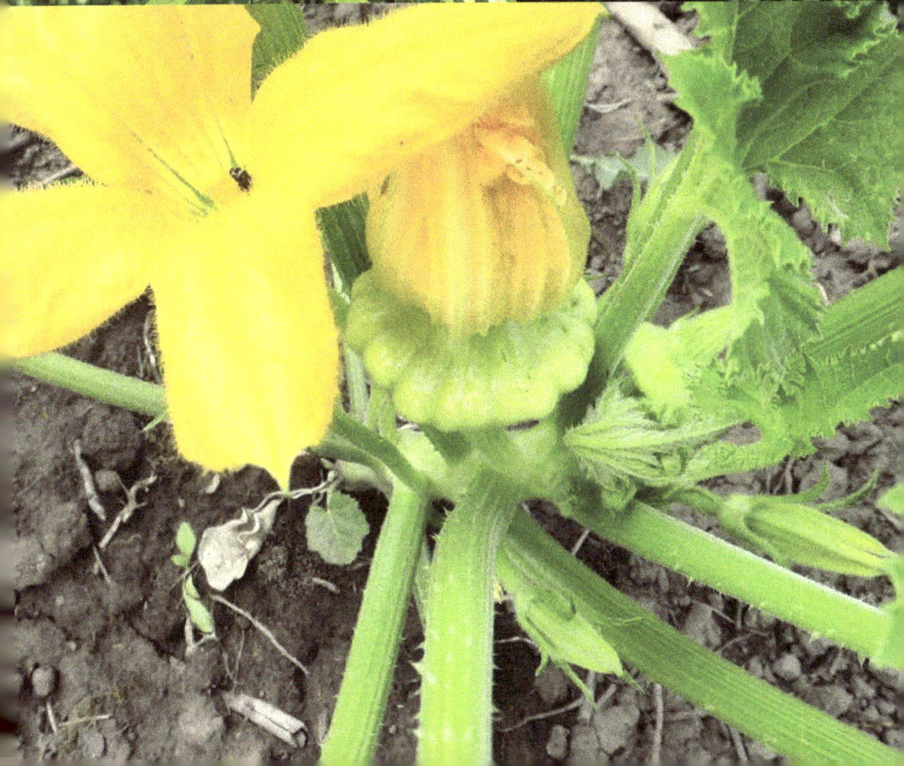

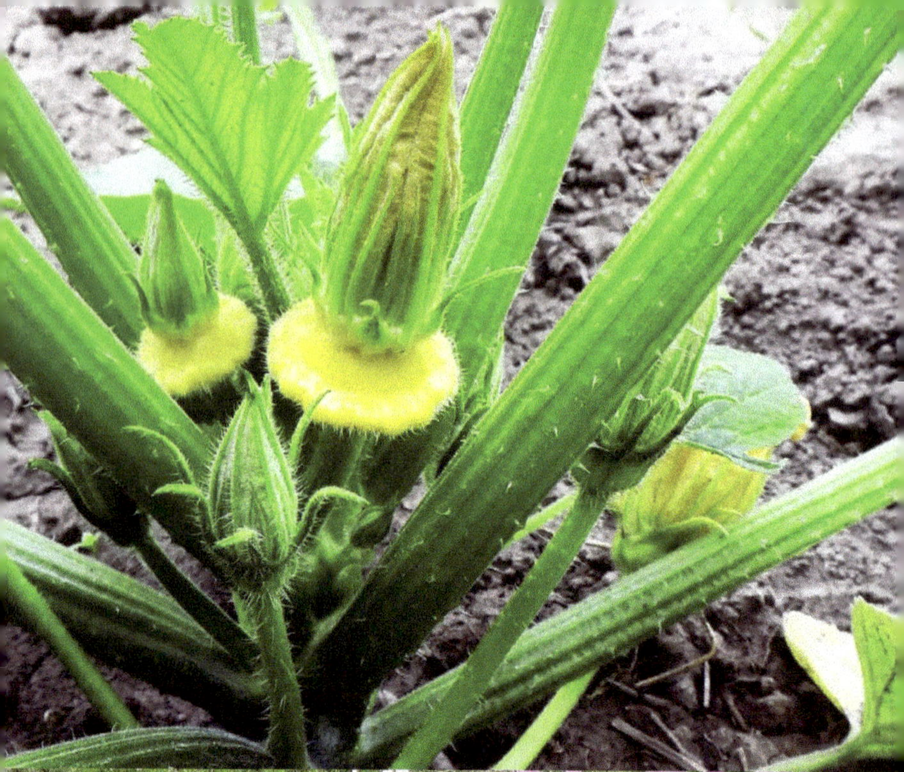
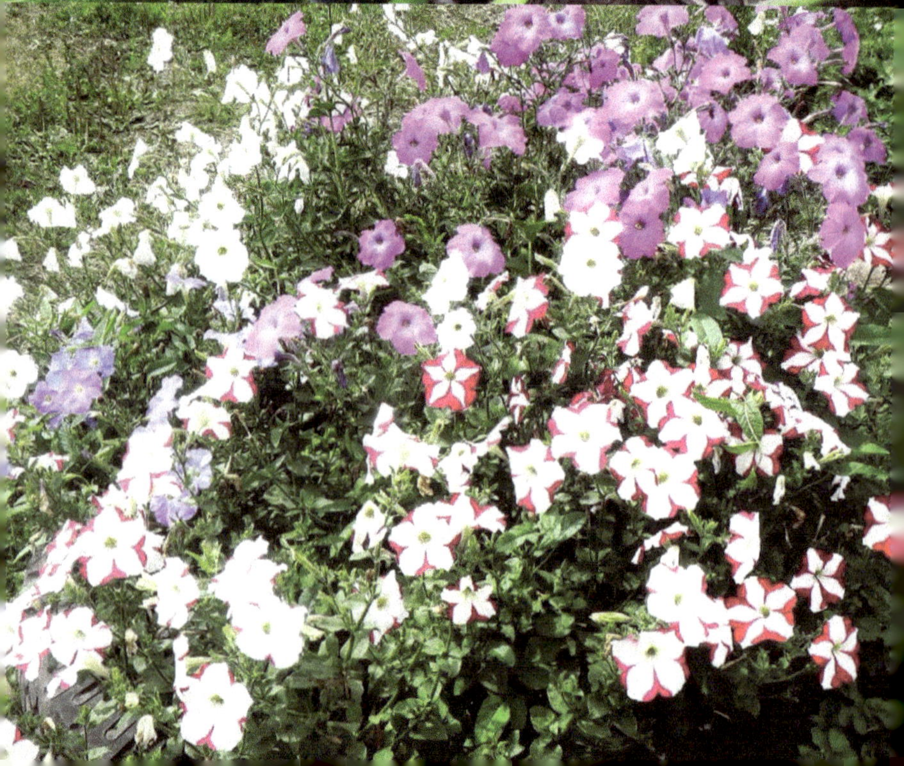

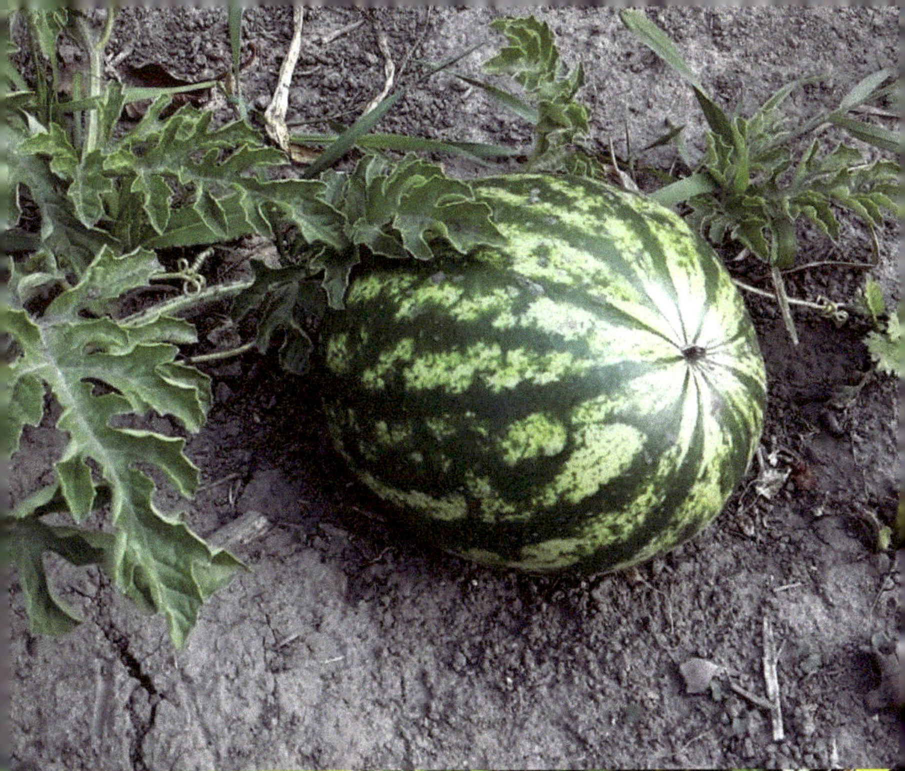

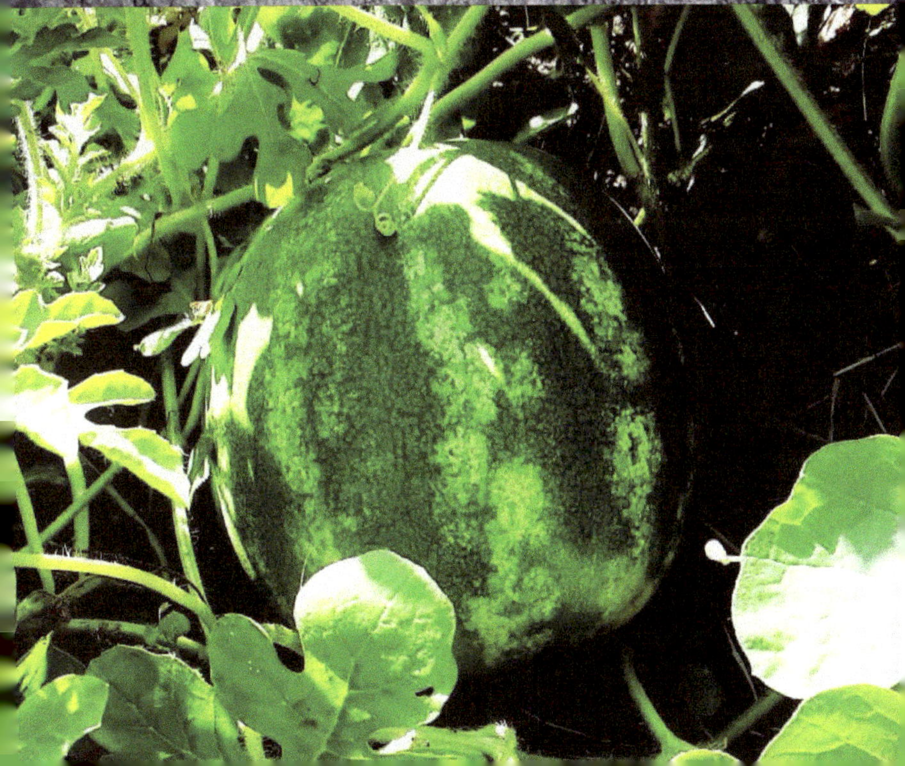

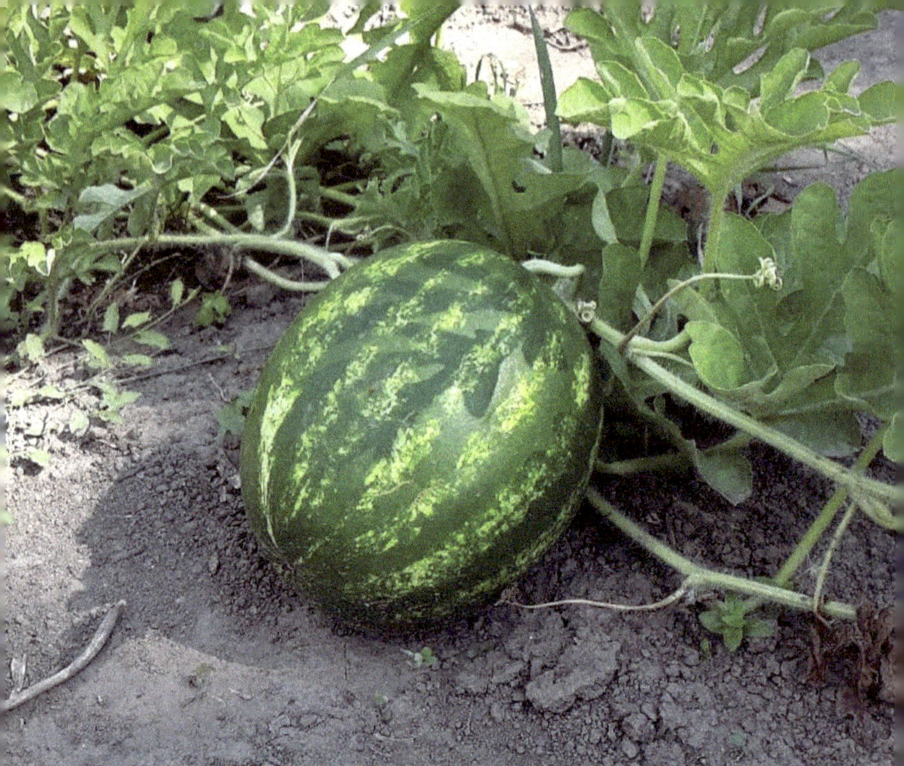

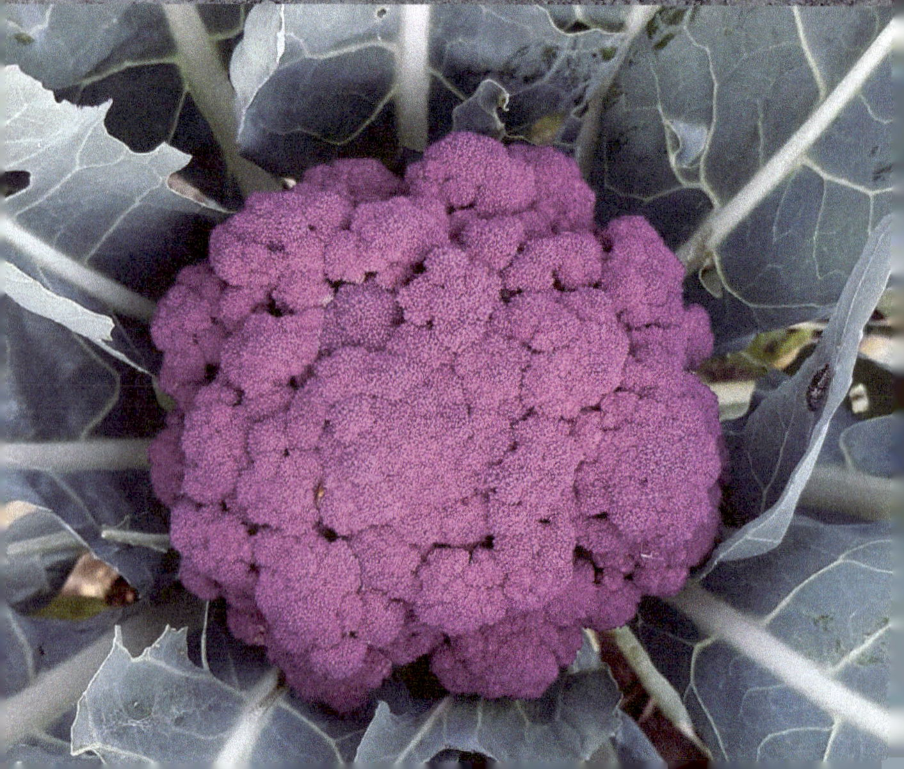

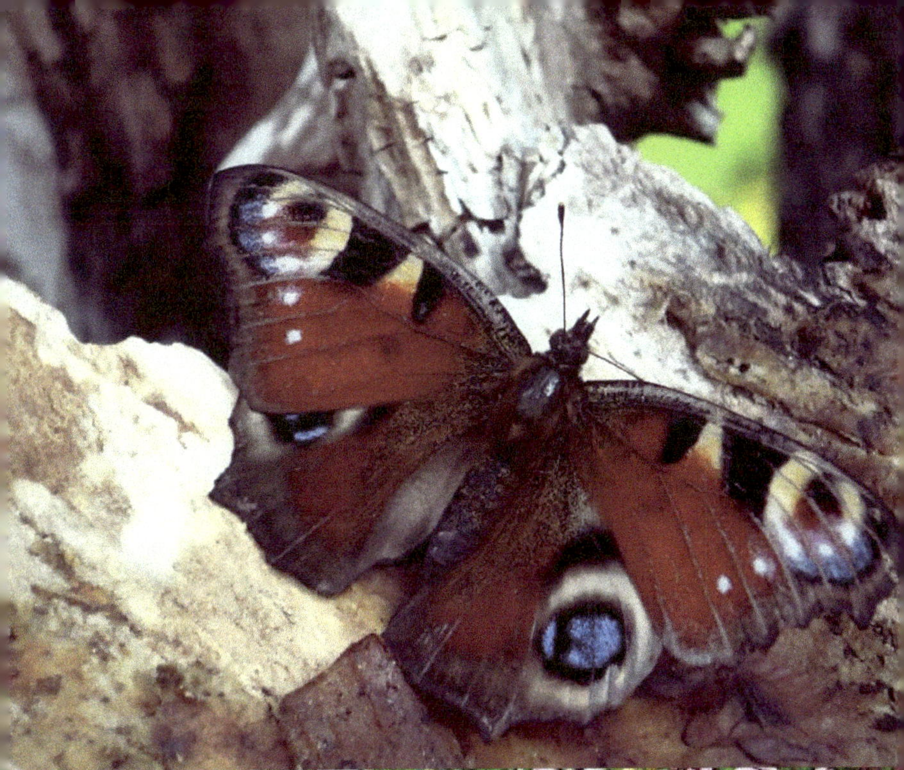

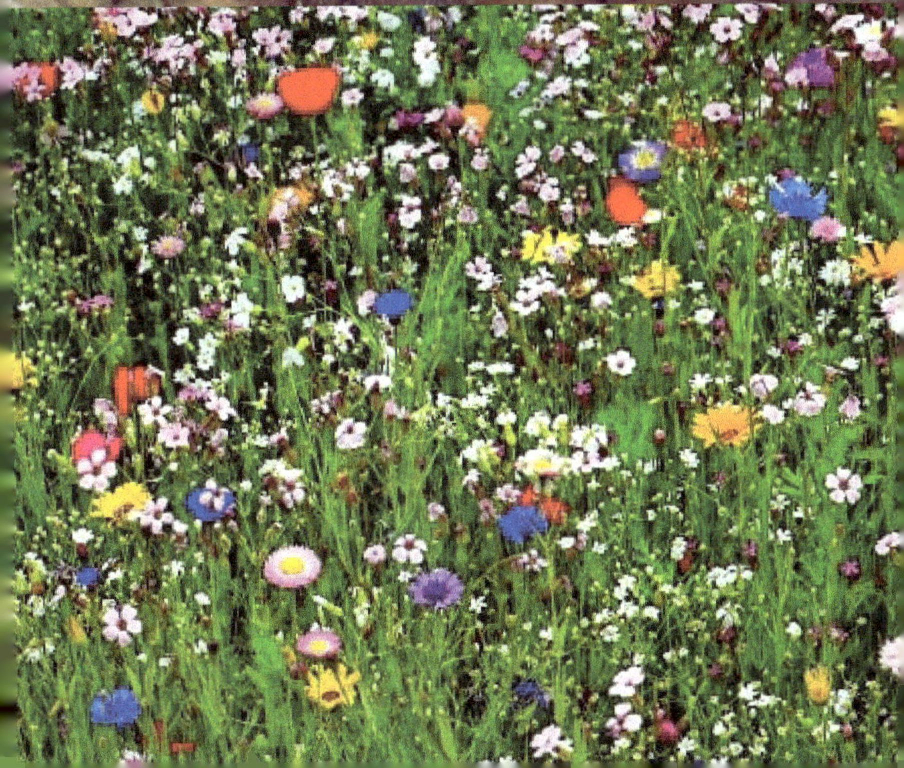

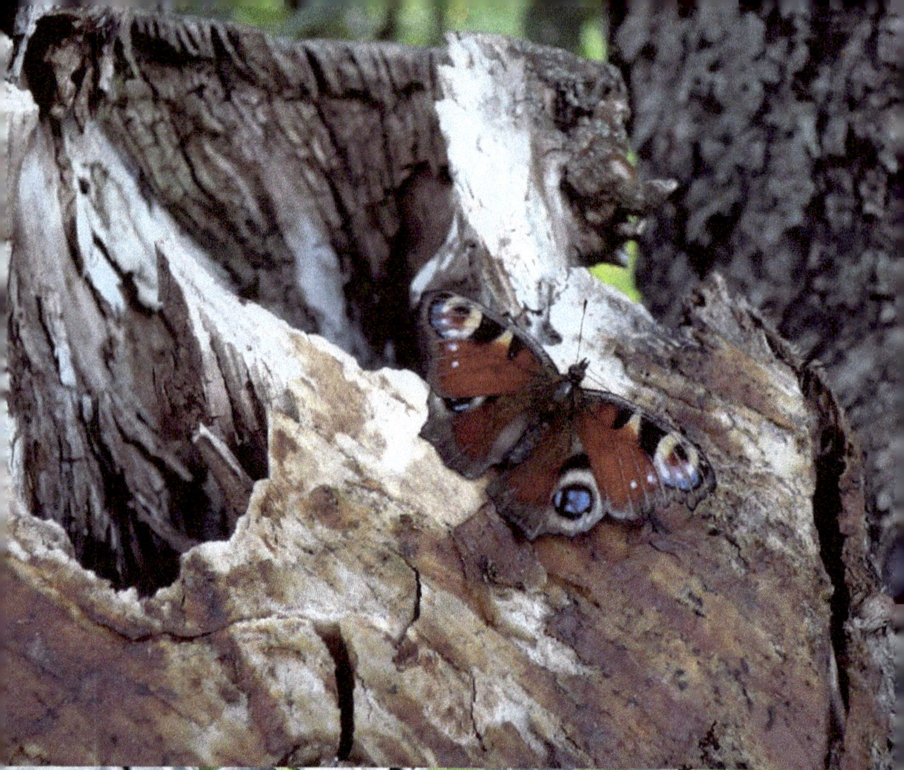
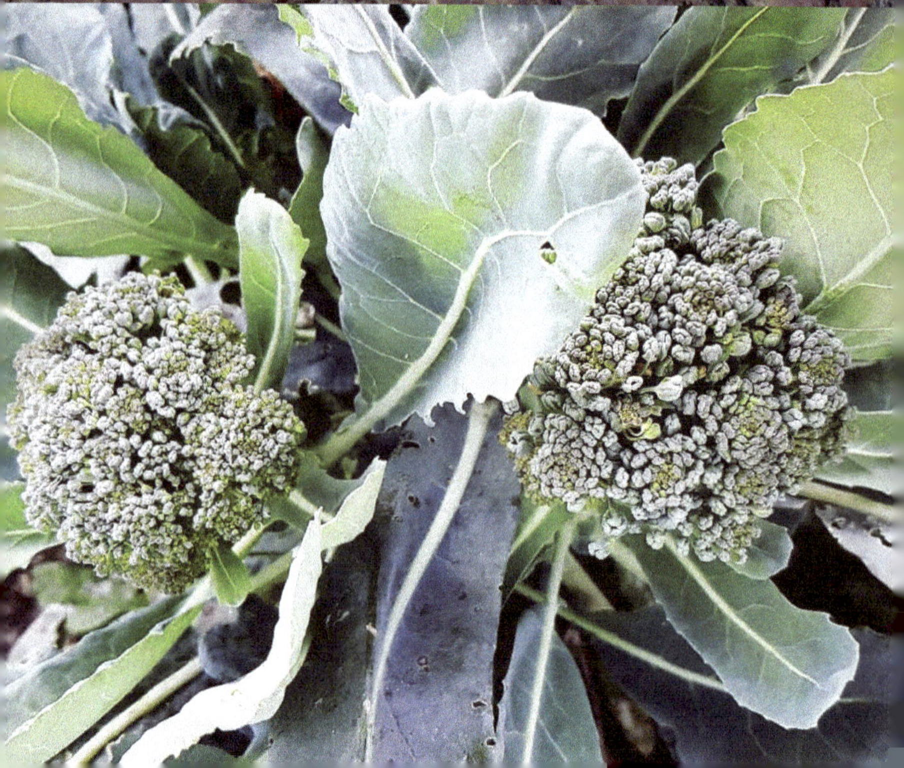

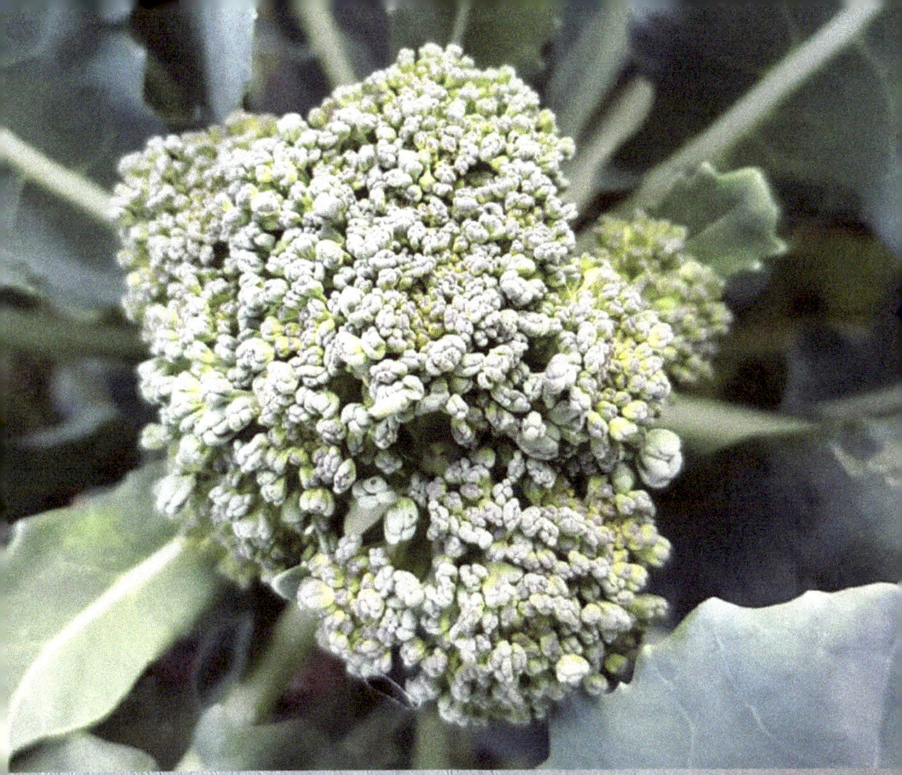

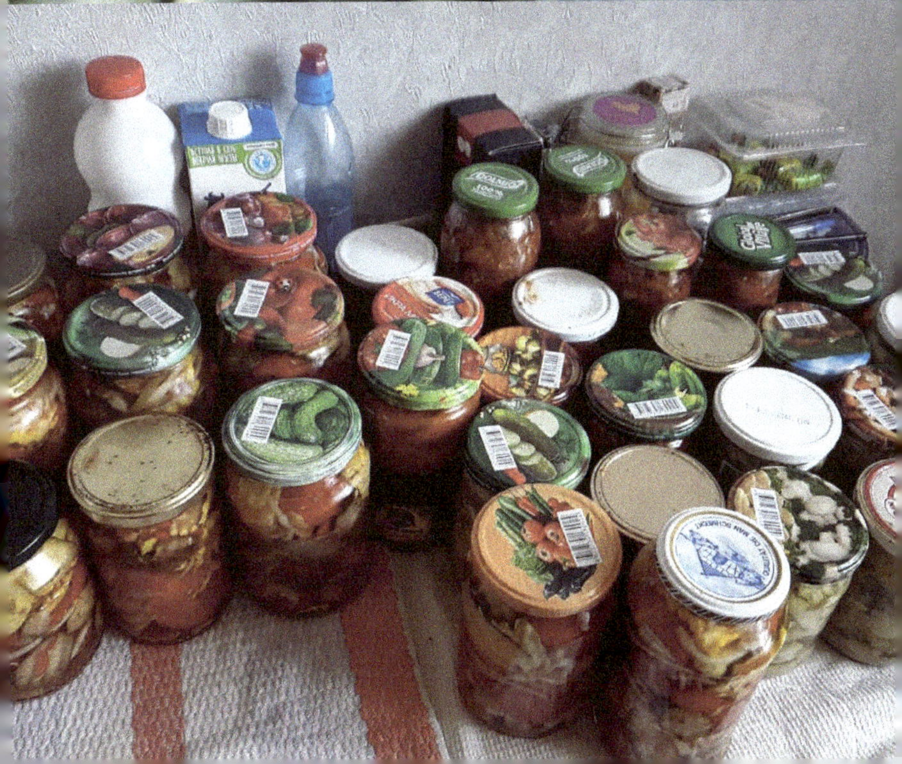
Global Village

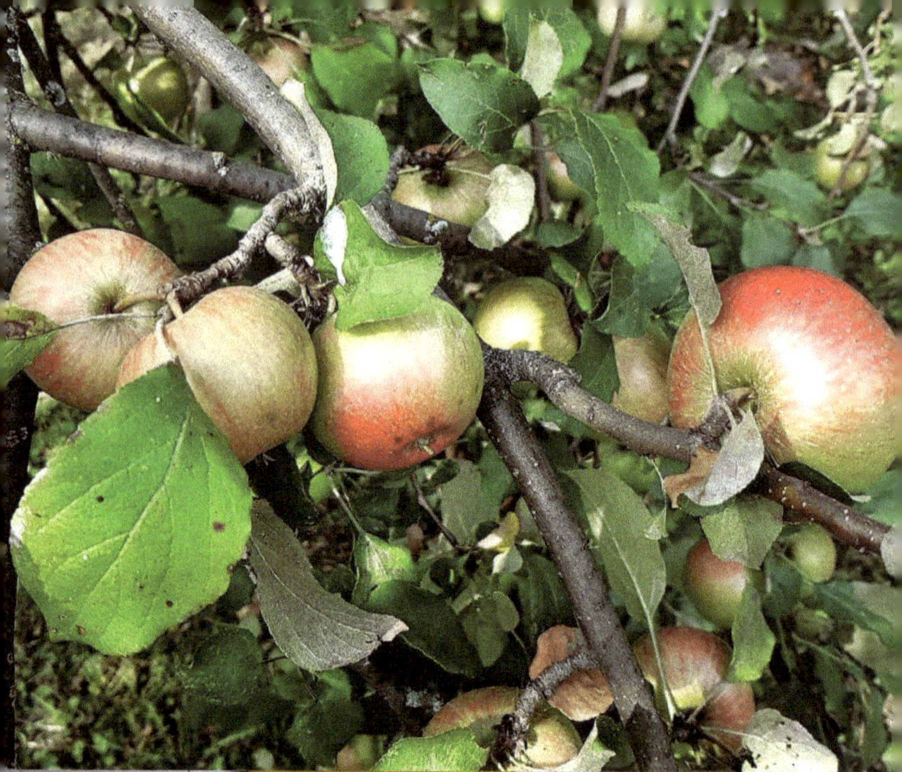

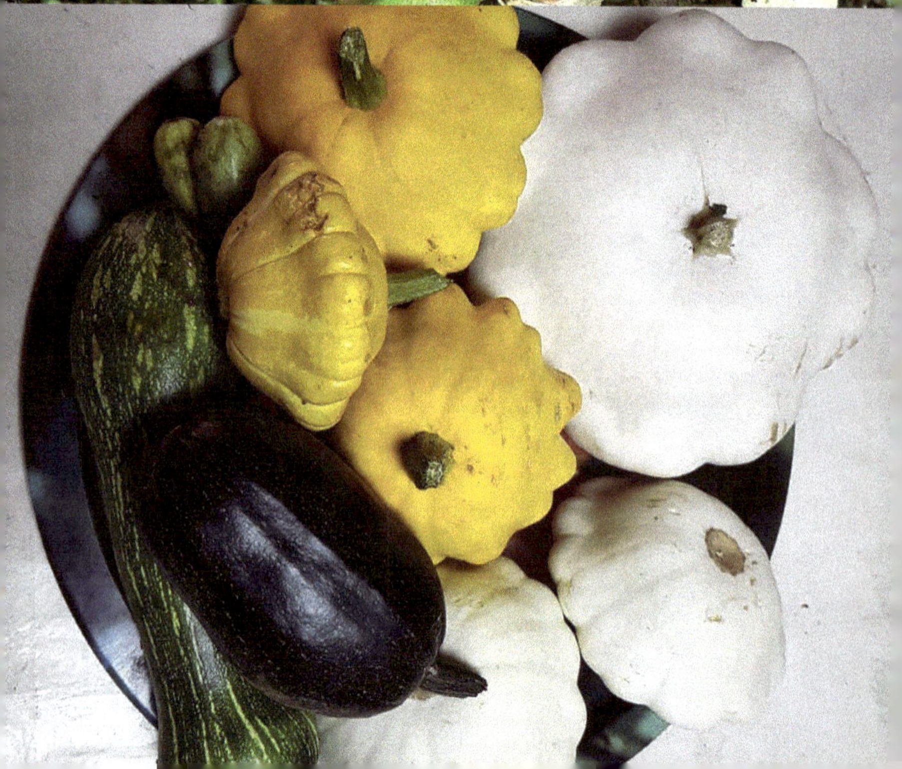

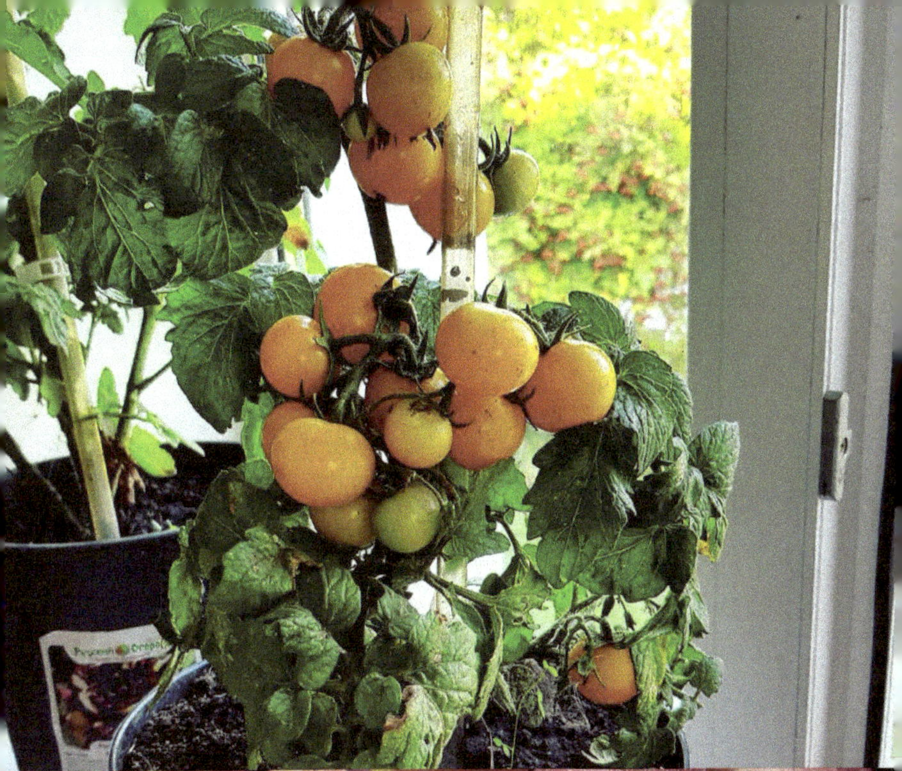

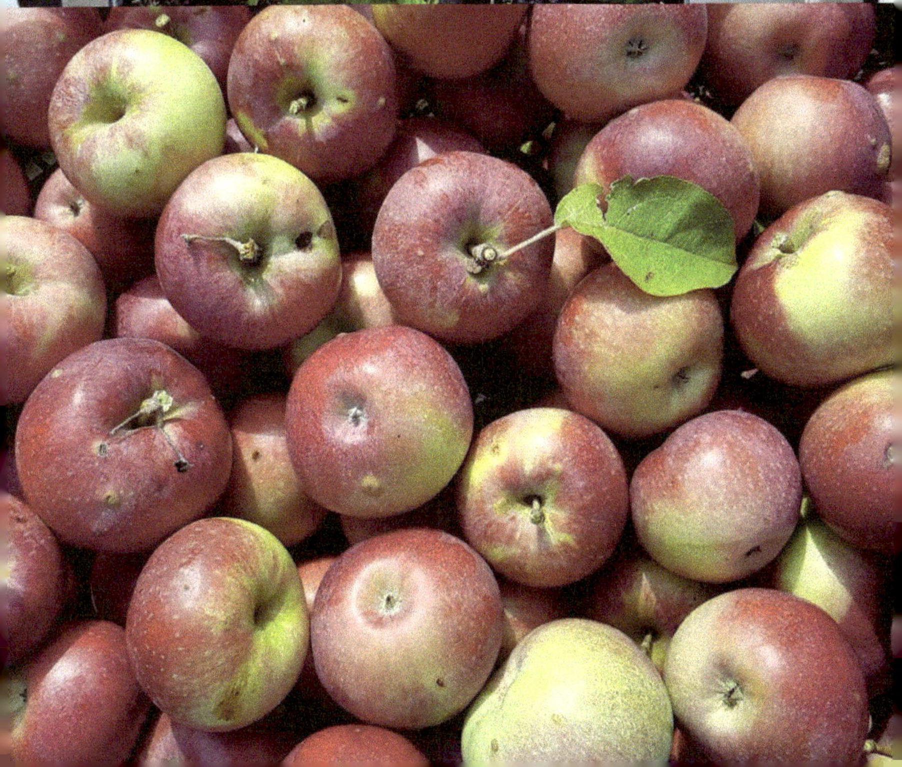

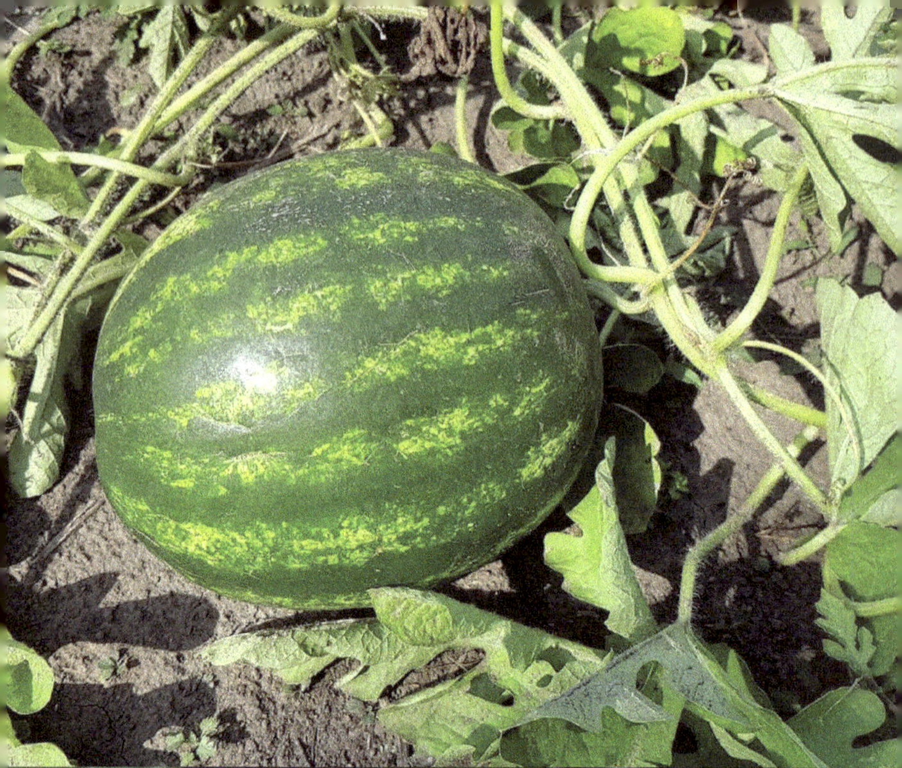

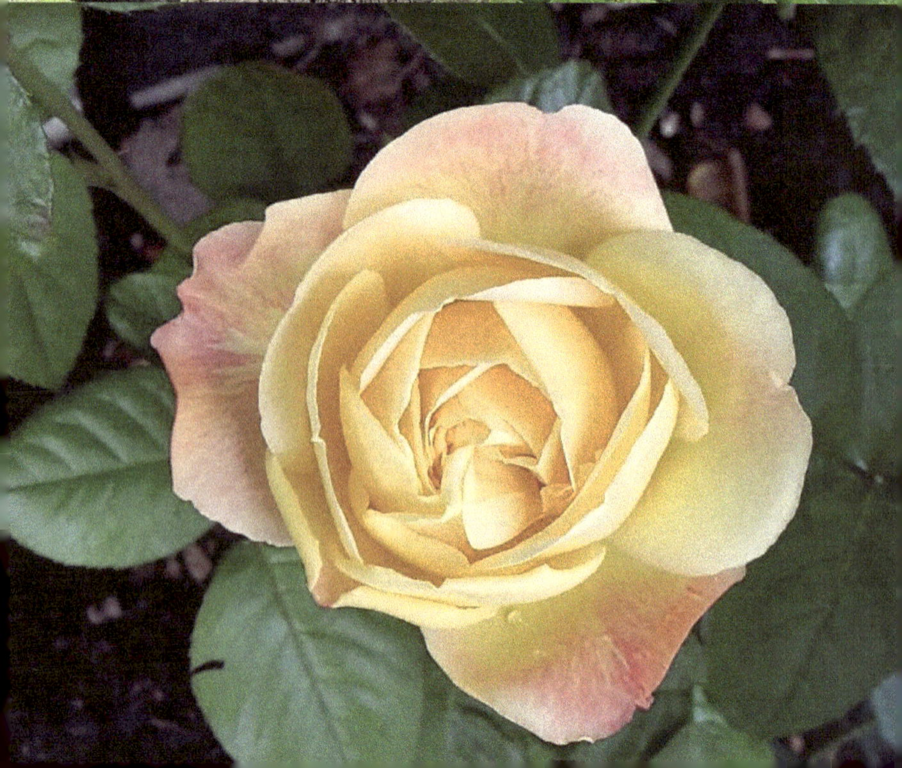

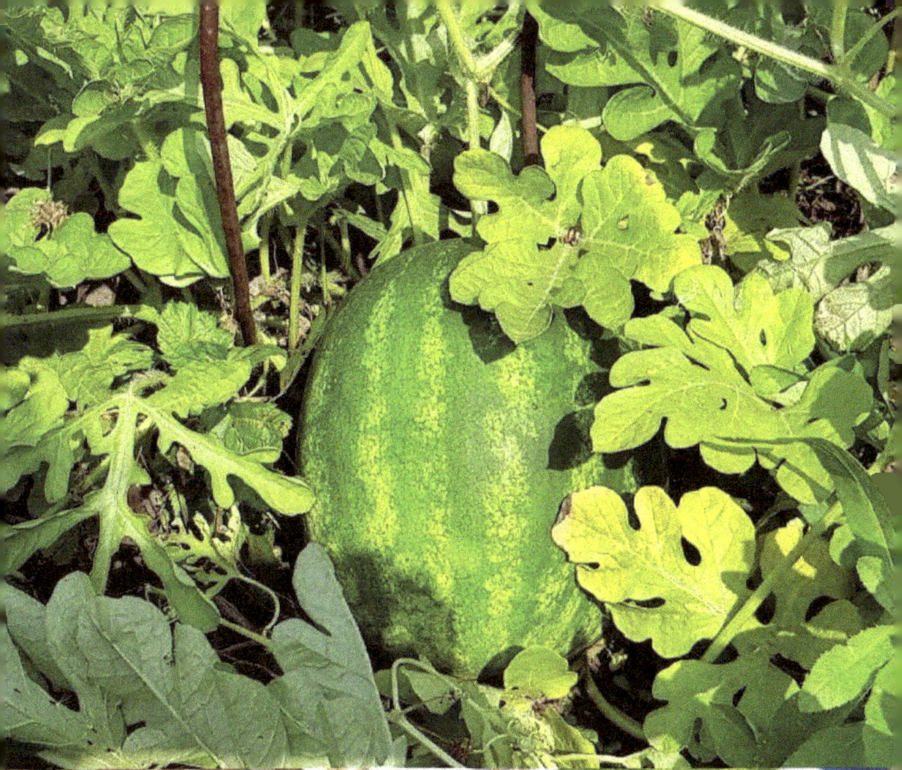

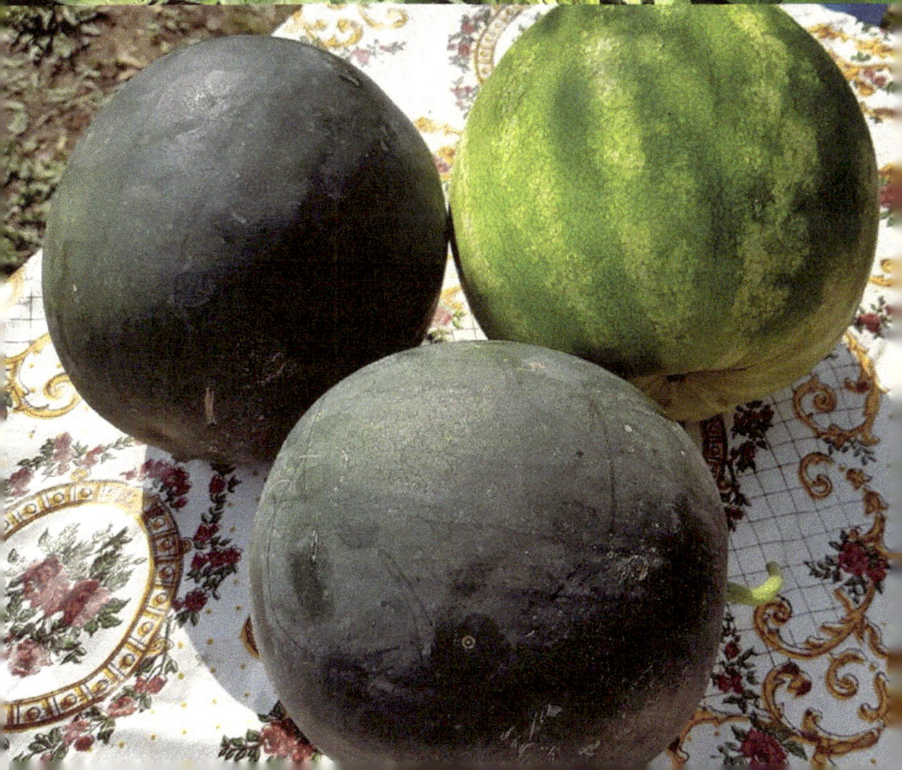

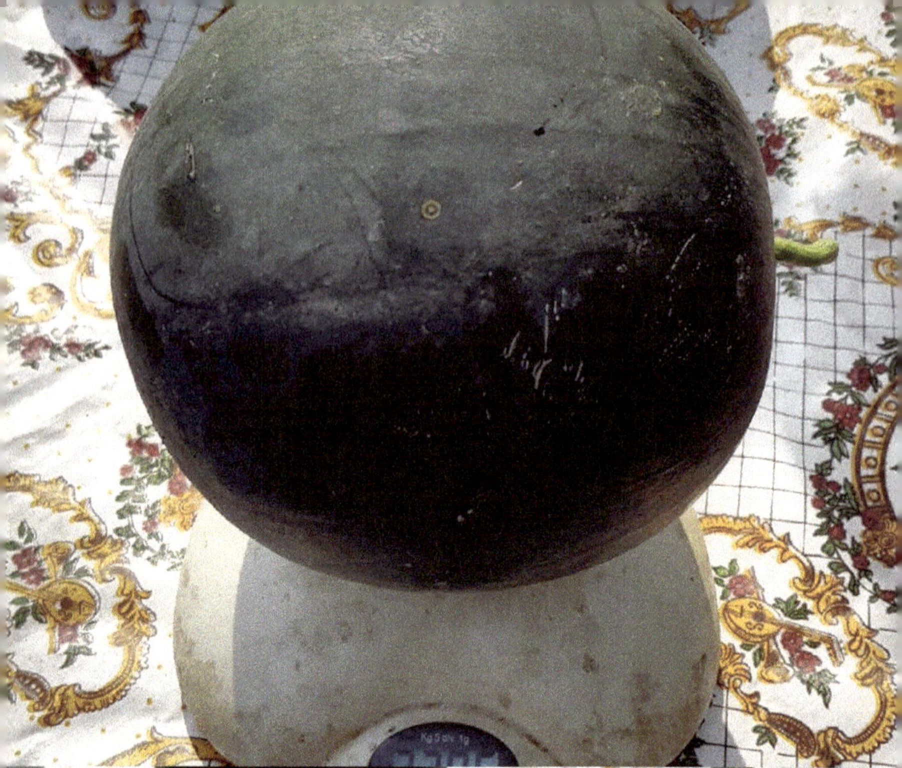

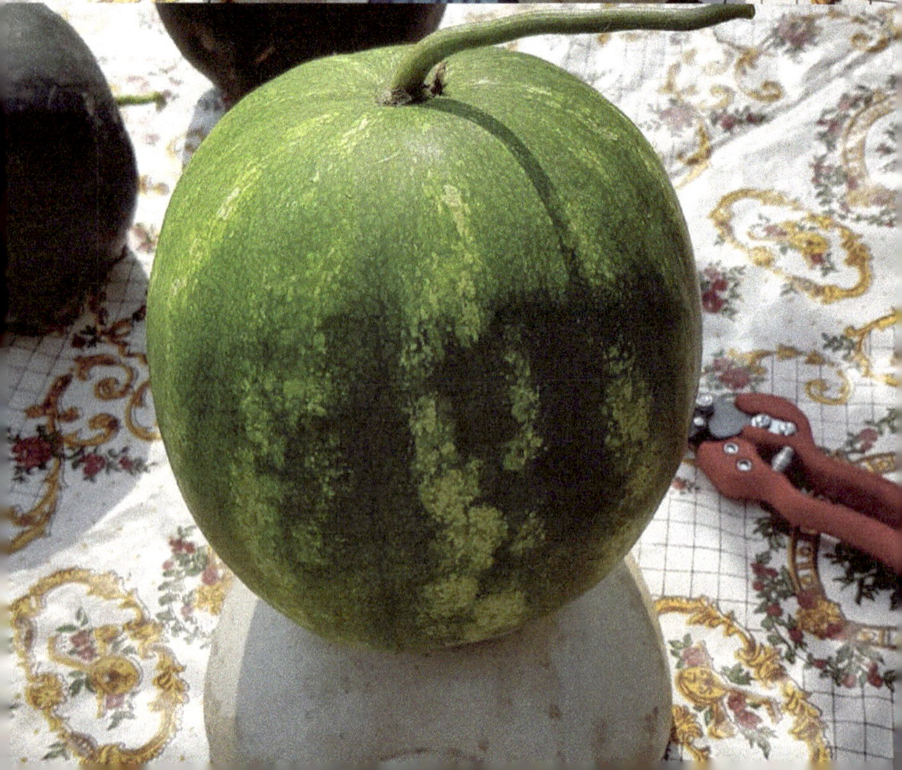

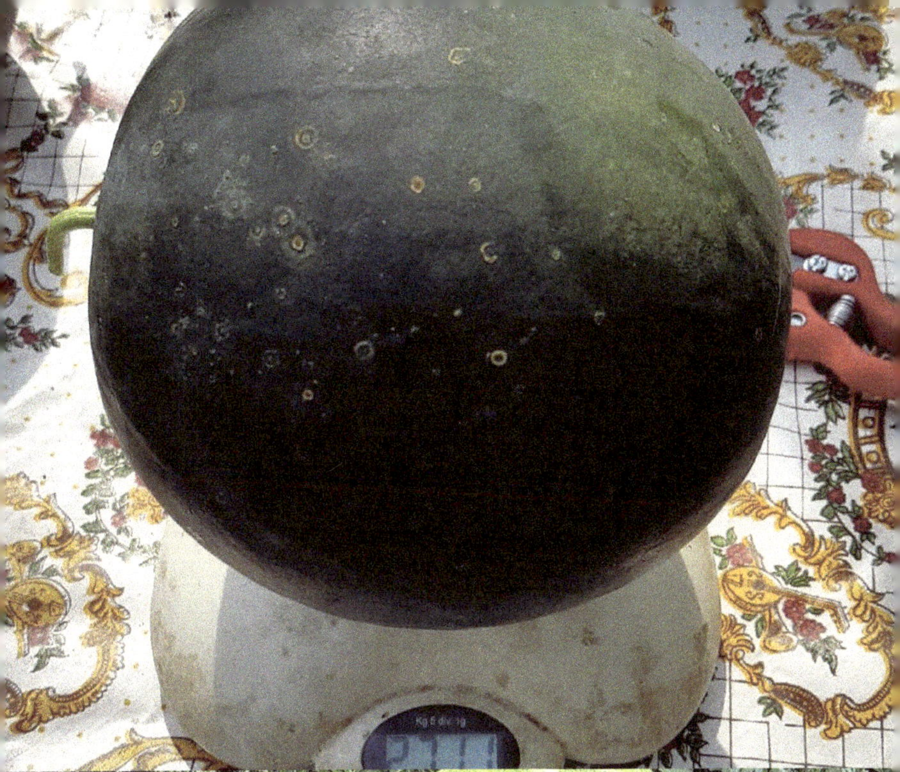

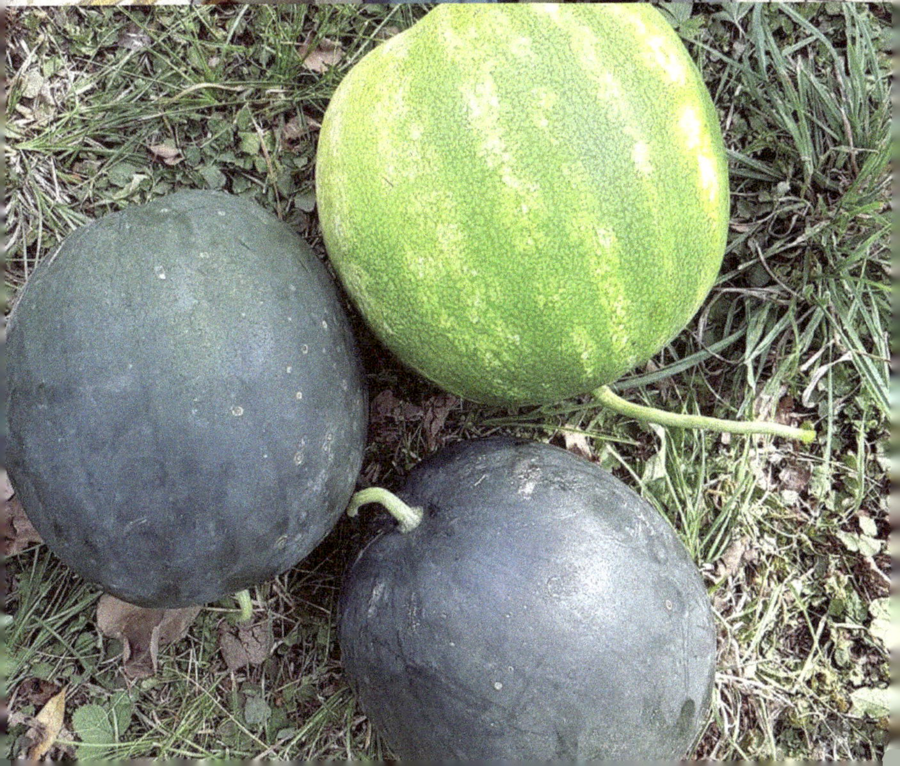

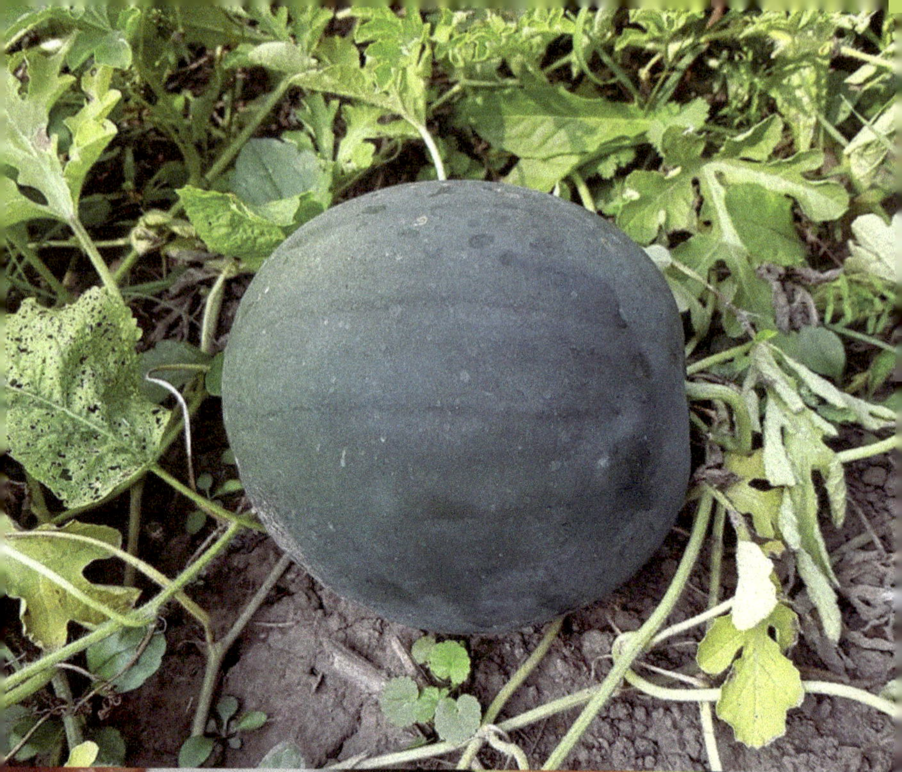

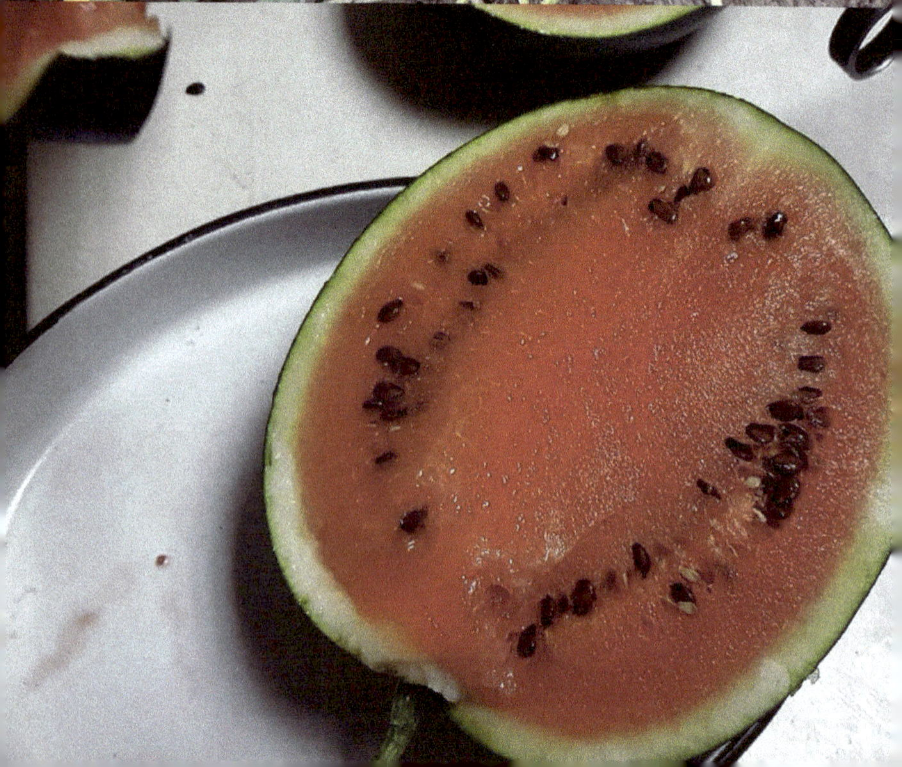

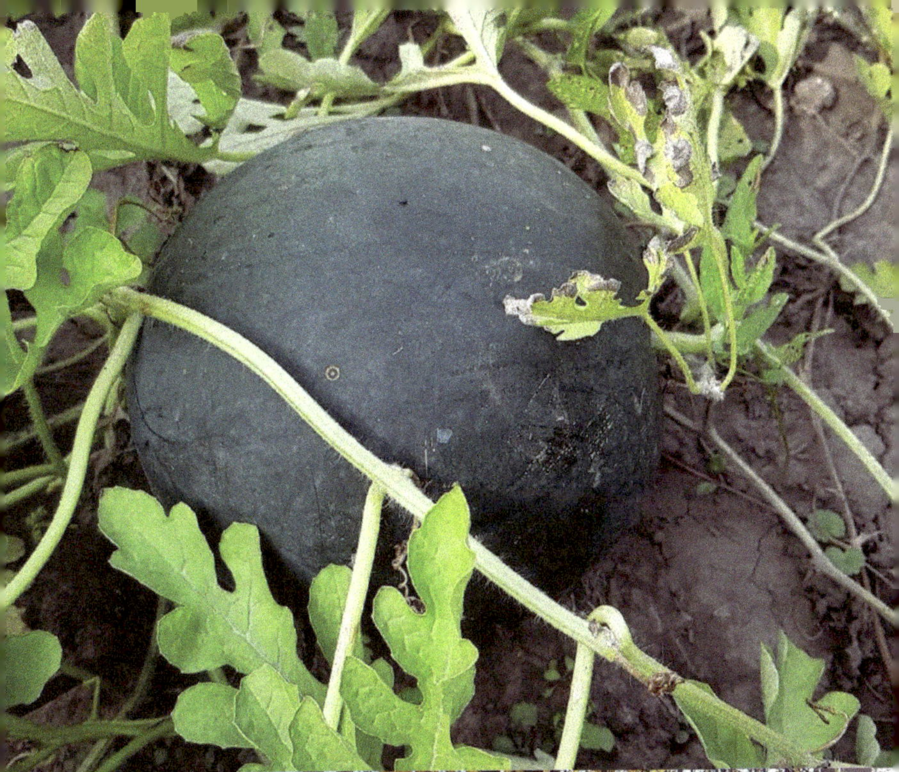

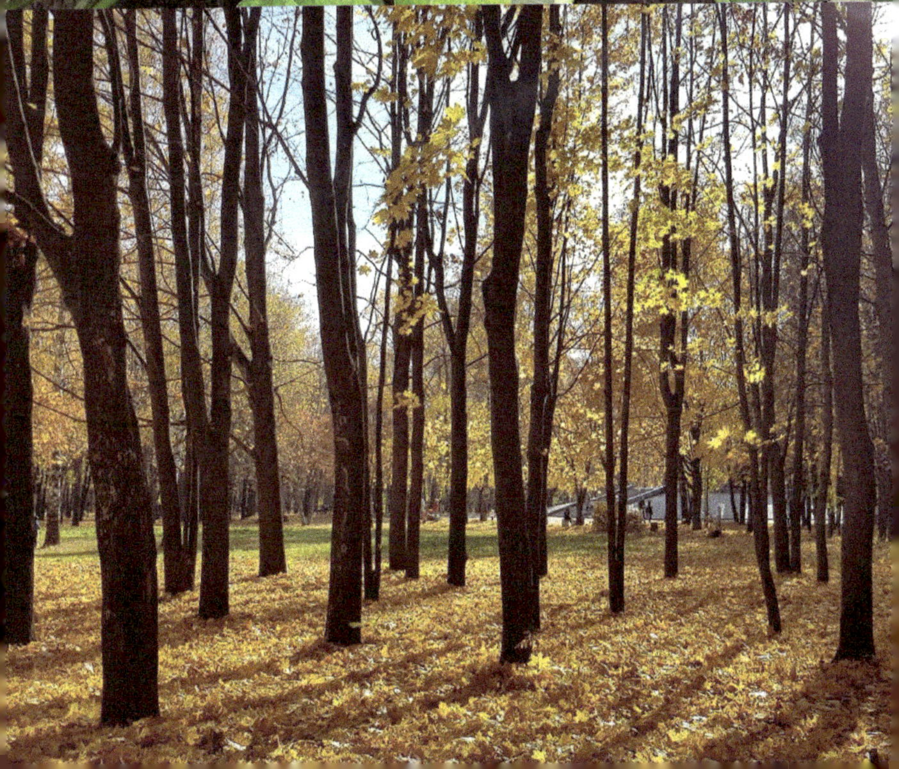

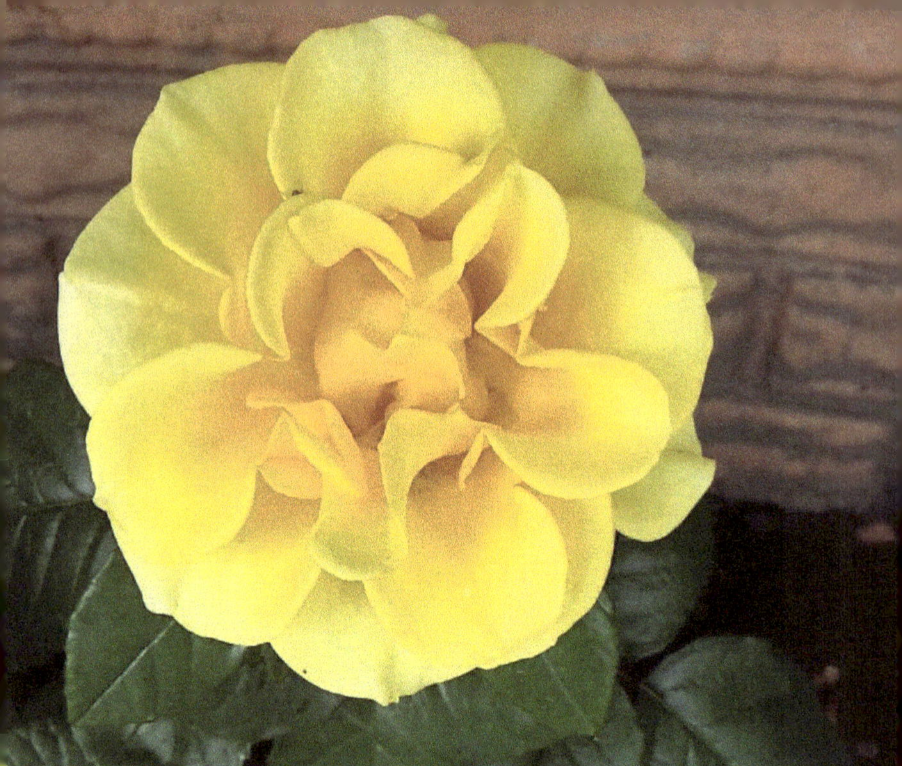

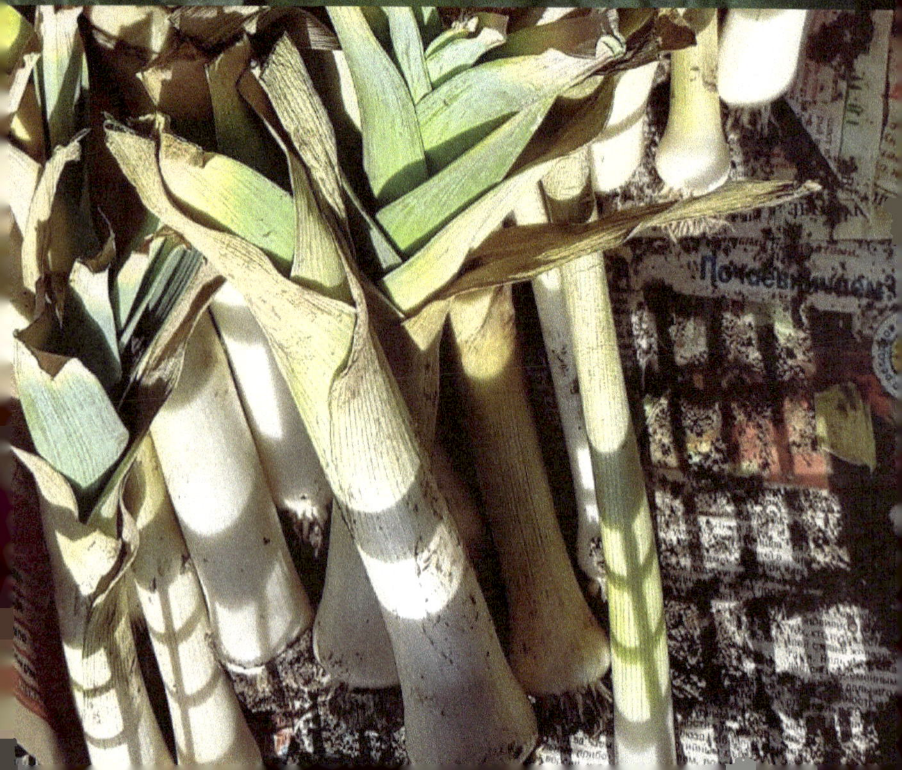

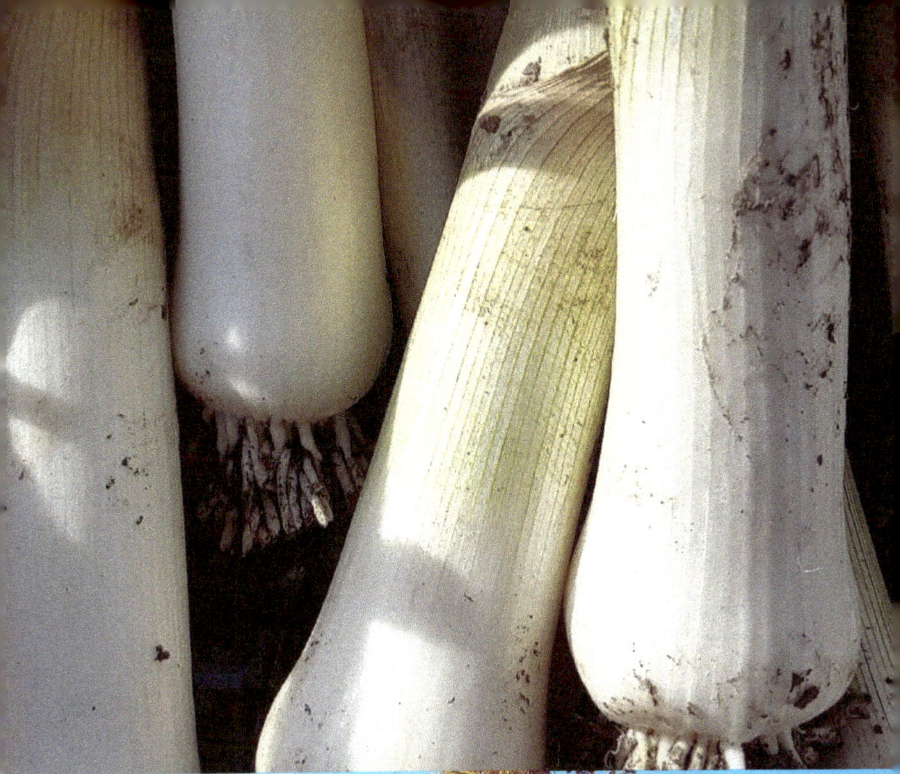

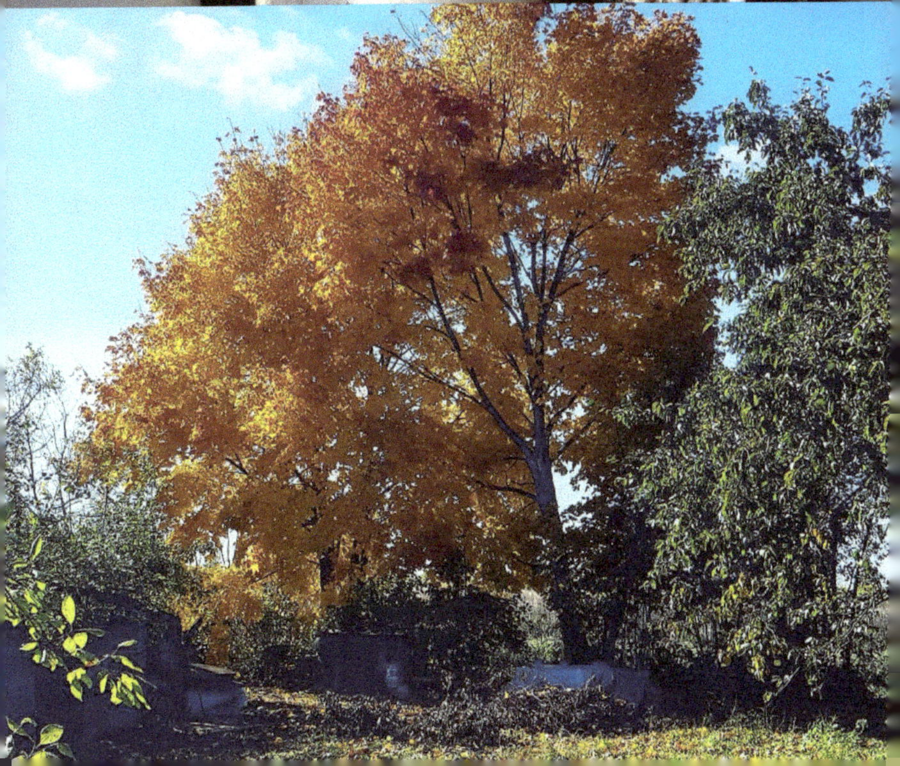

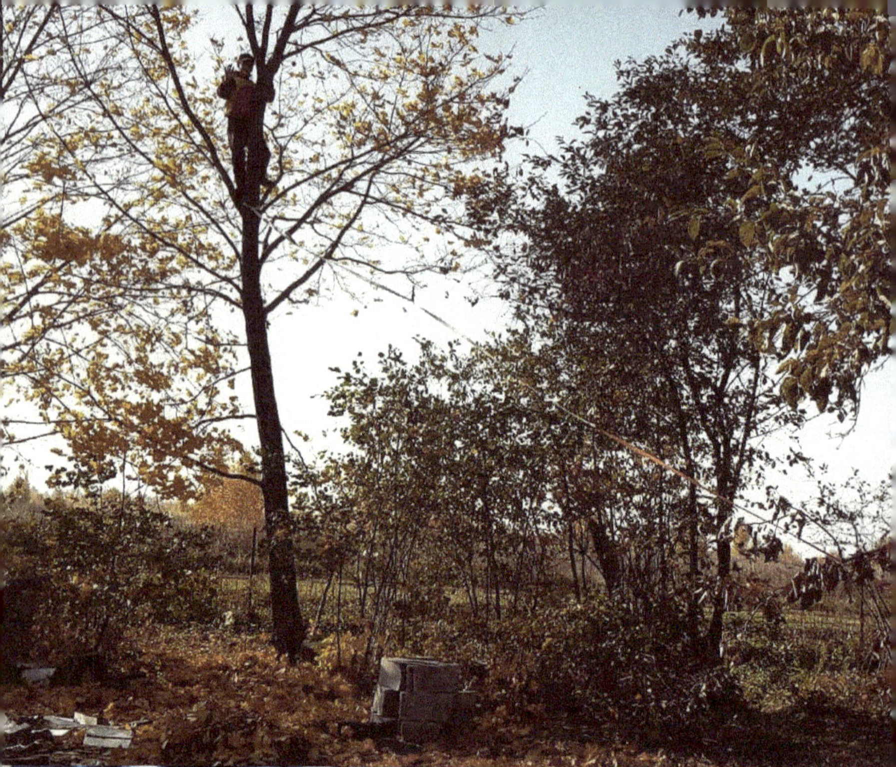
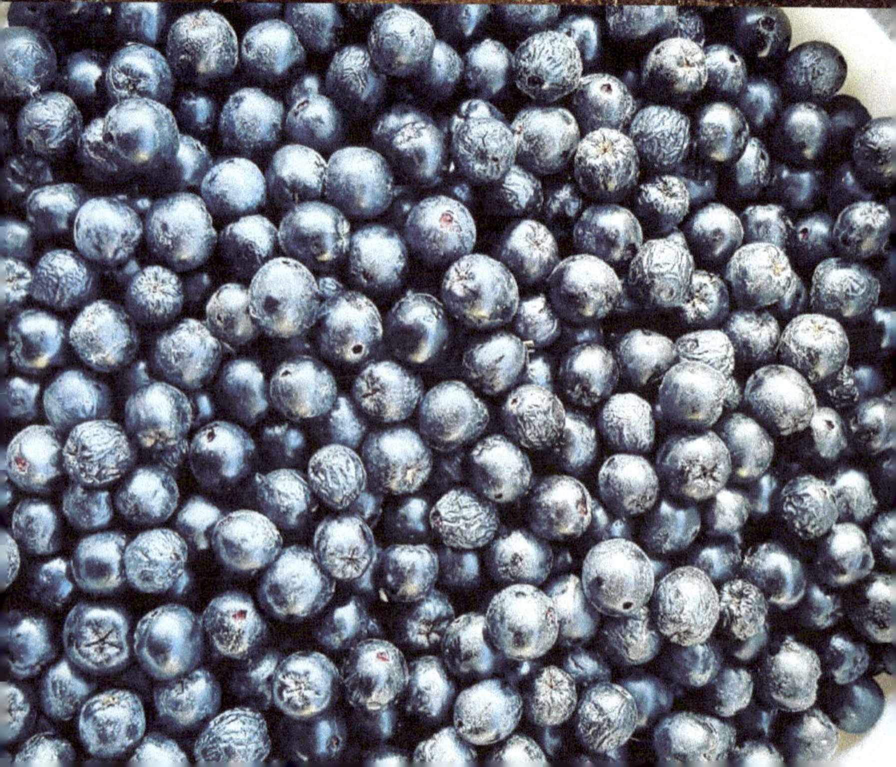

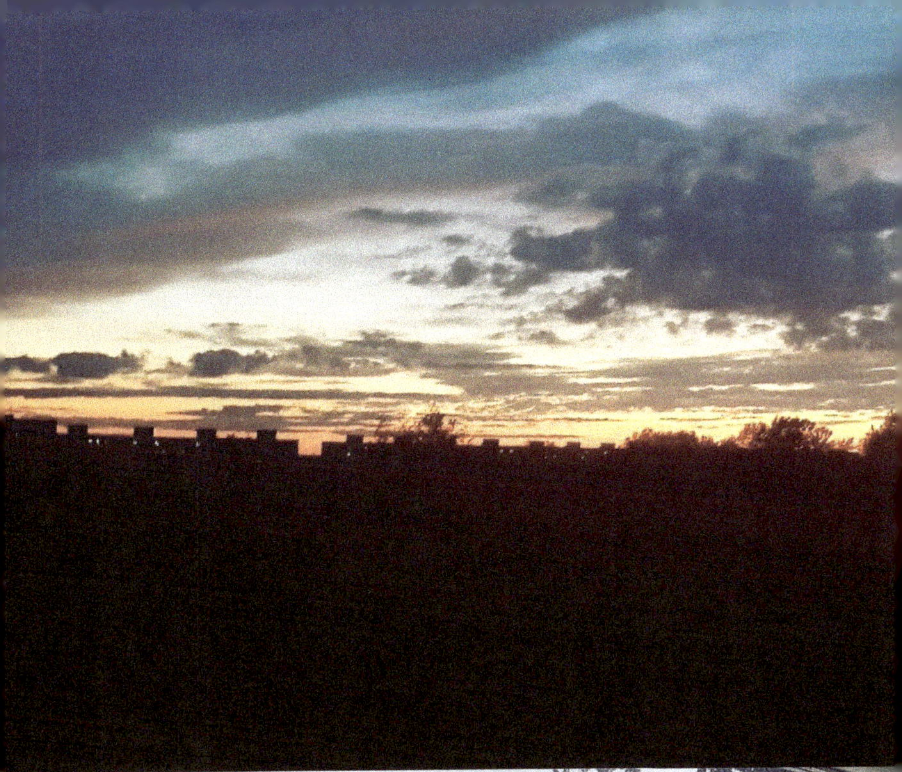

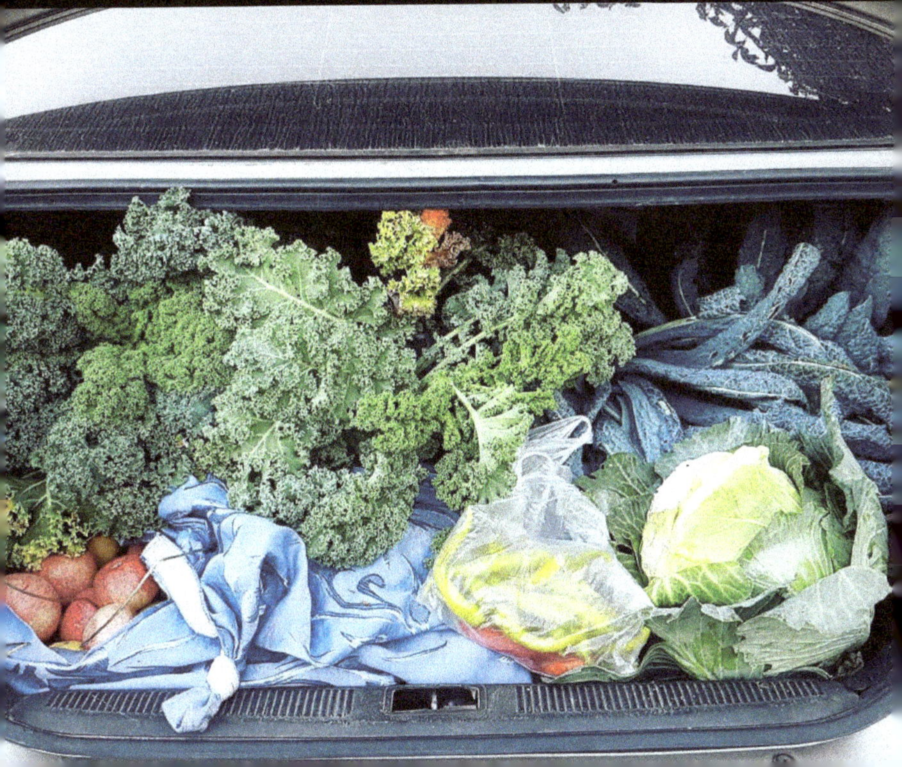

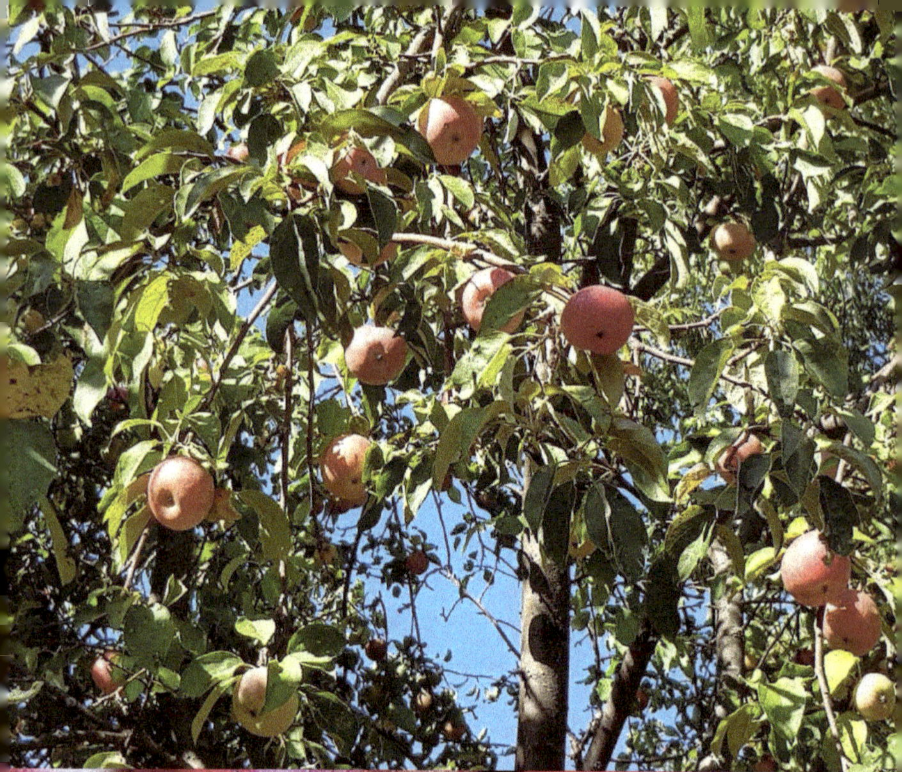
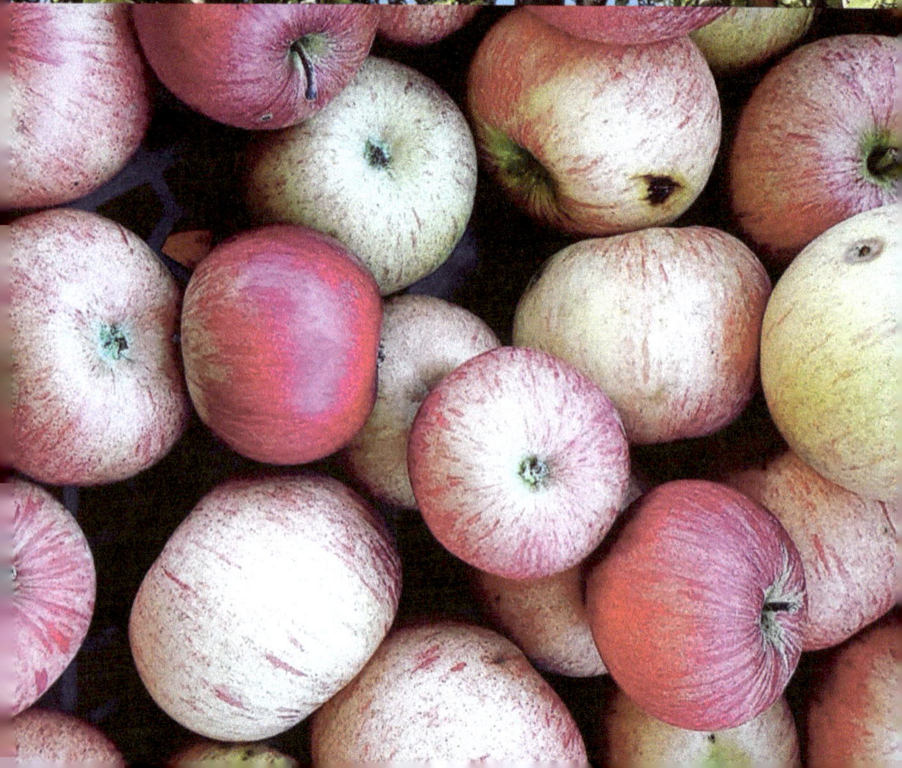

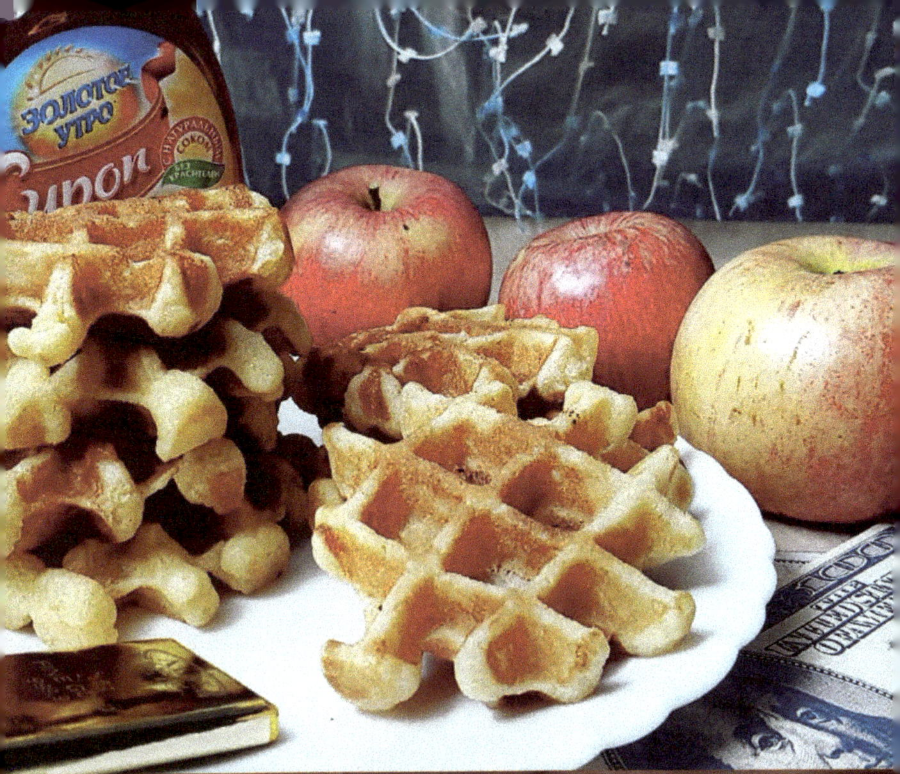
ЗОЛОТОЕ УТРО
Сироп

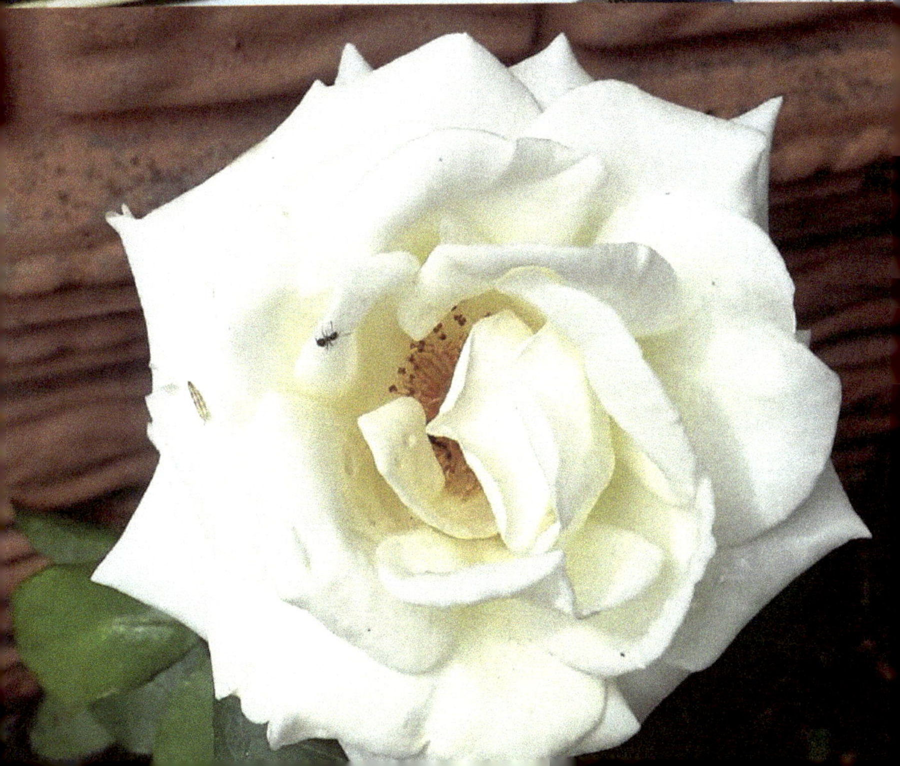

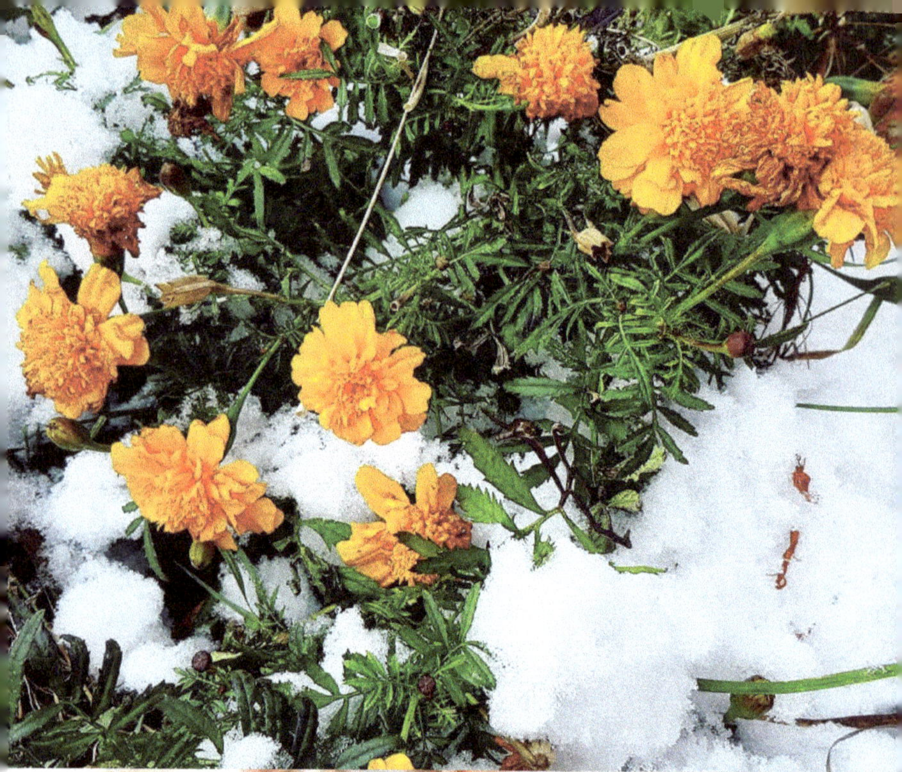

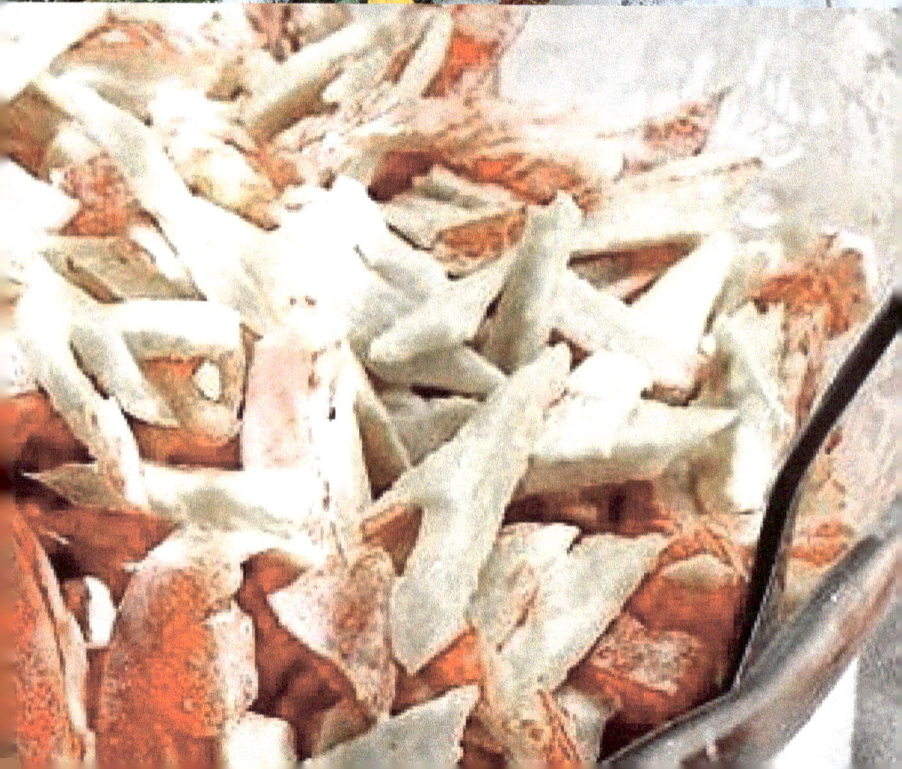

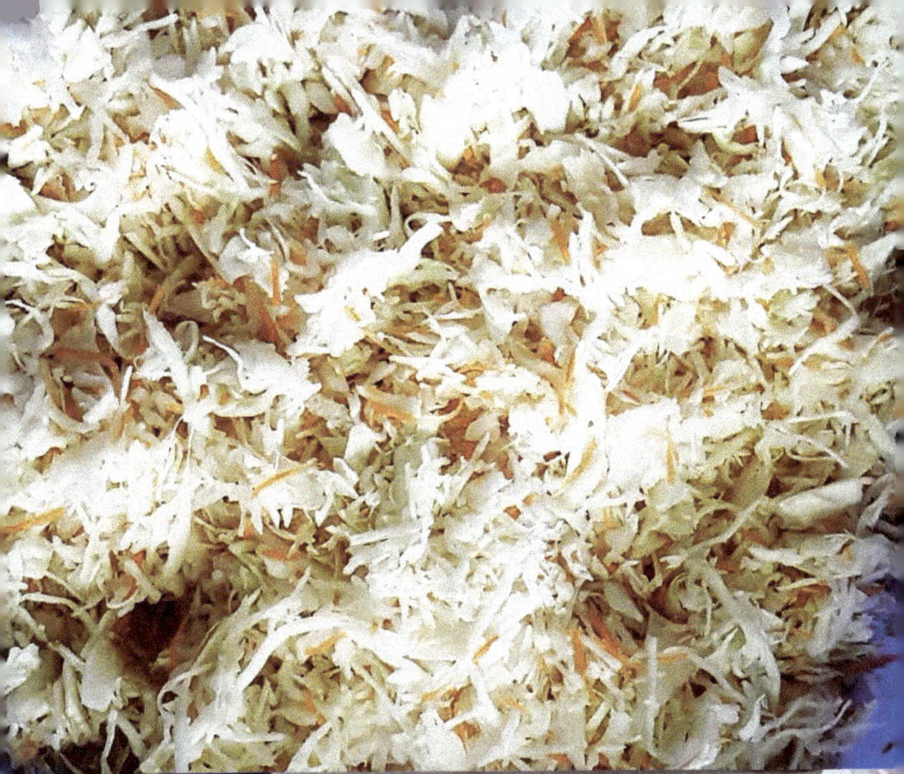

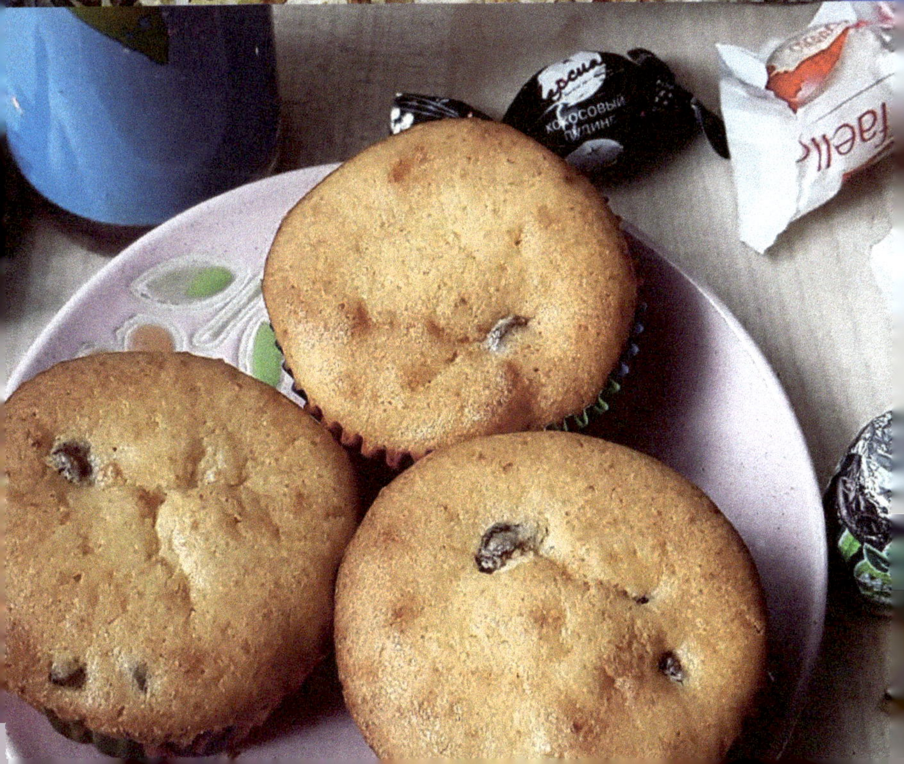
КОКОСОВЫЙ
ПУДИНГ

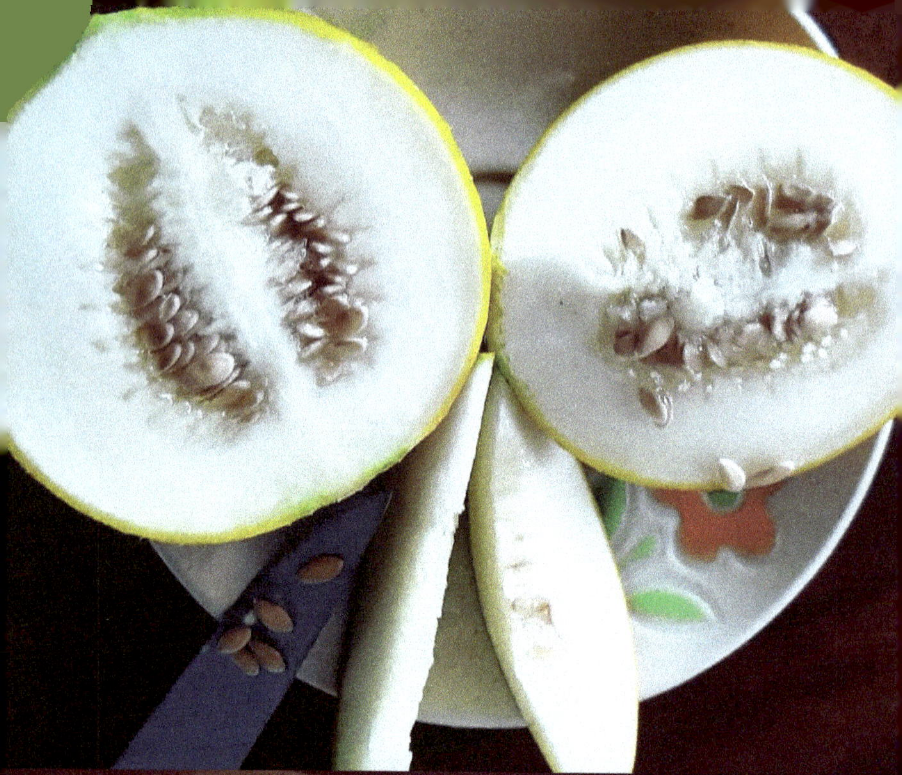

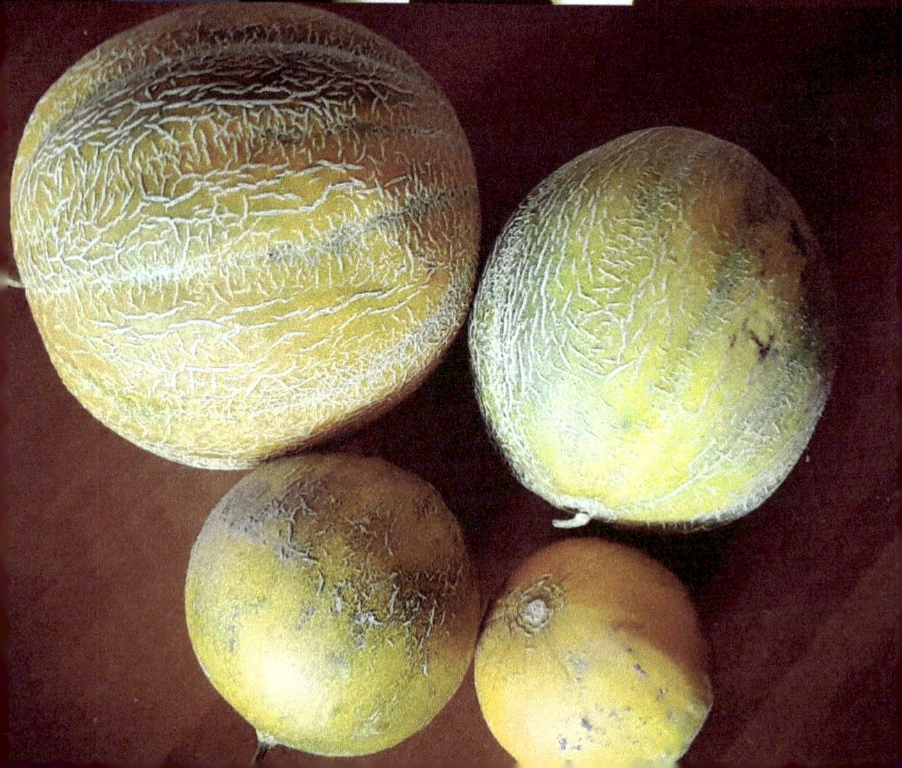

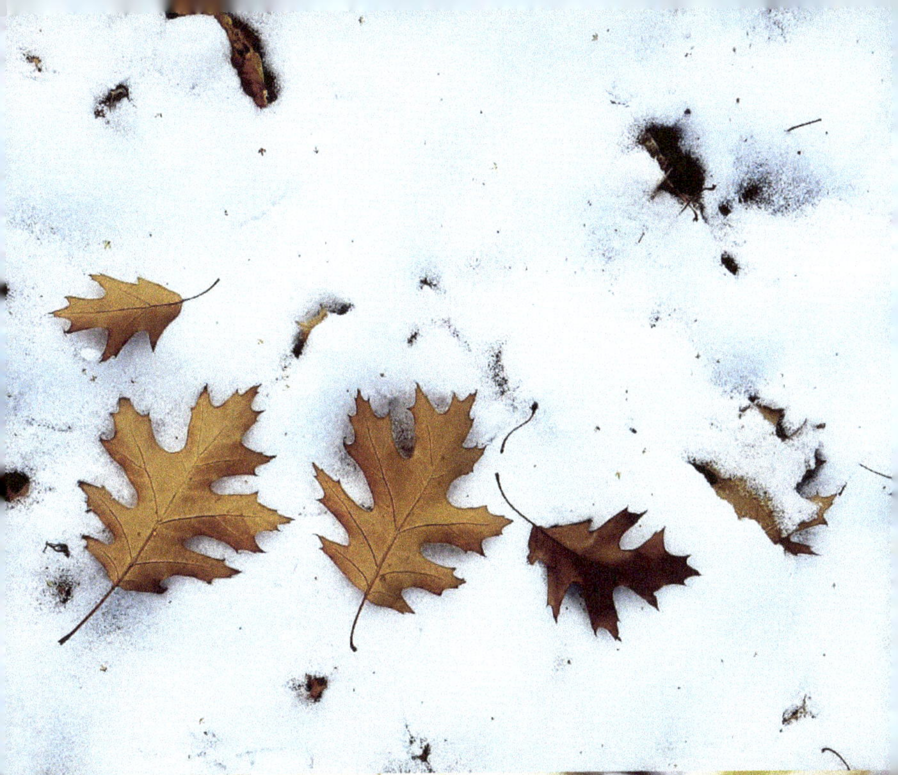

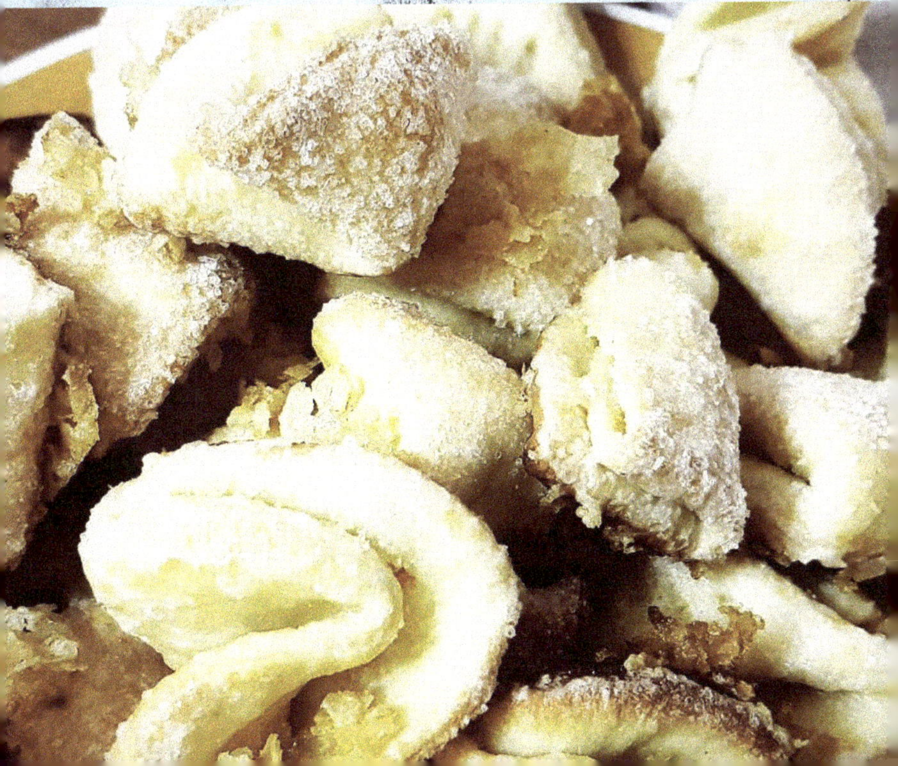

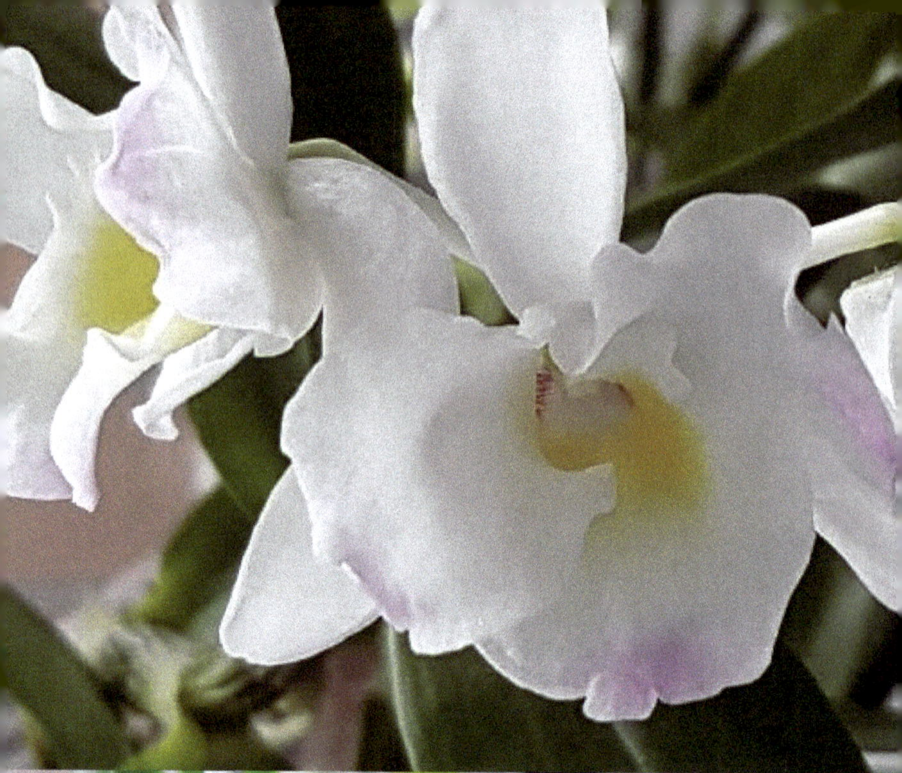
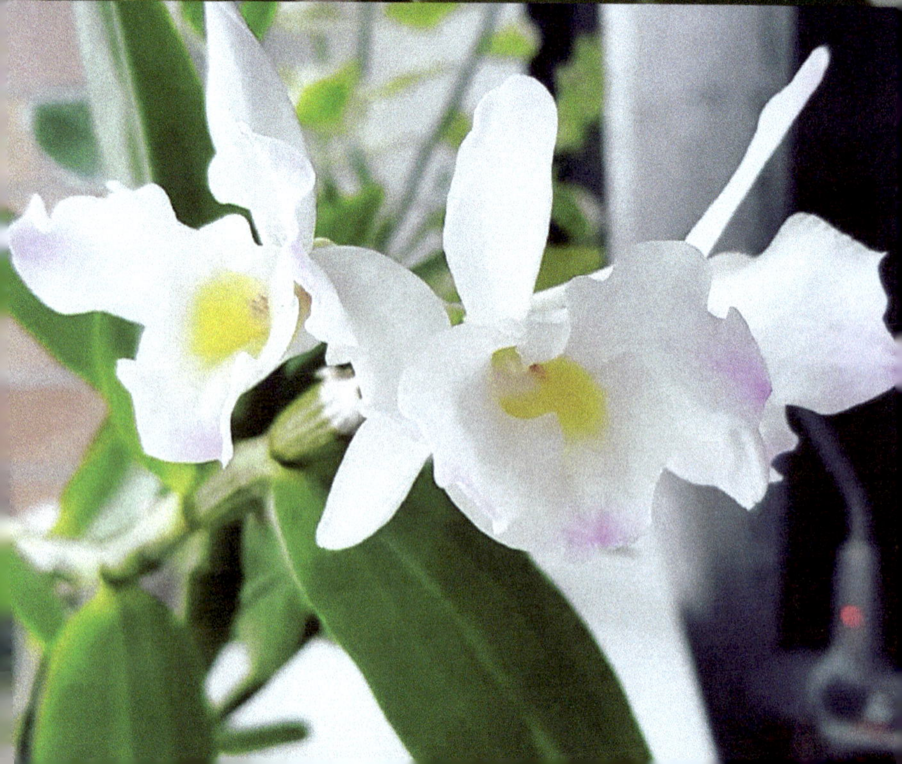

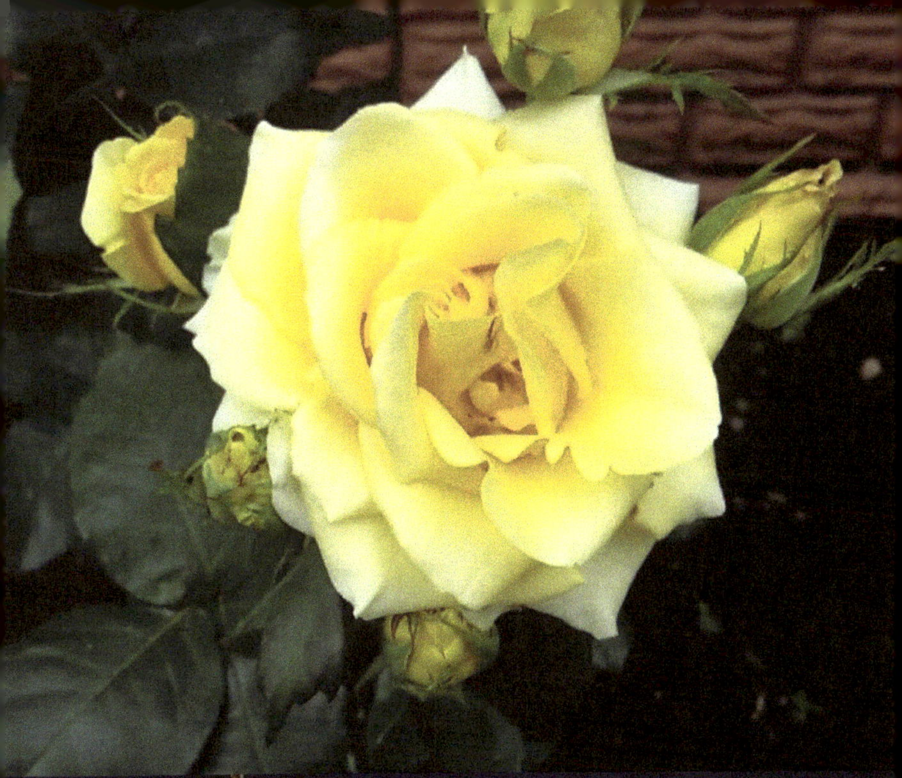

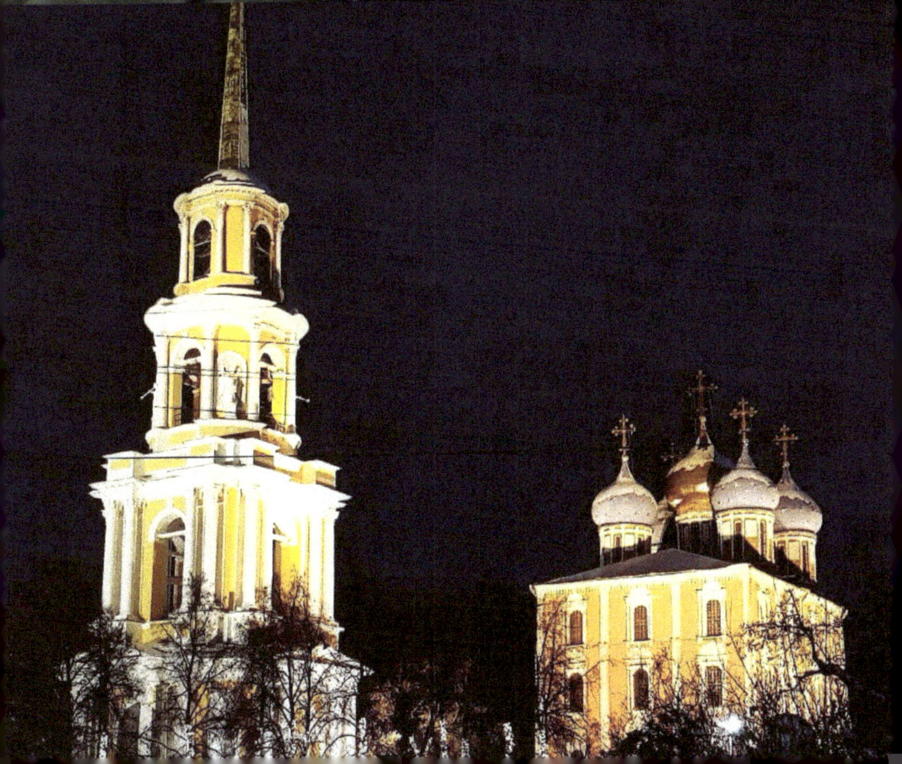

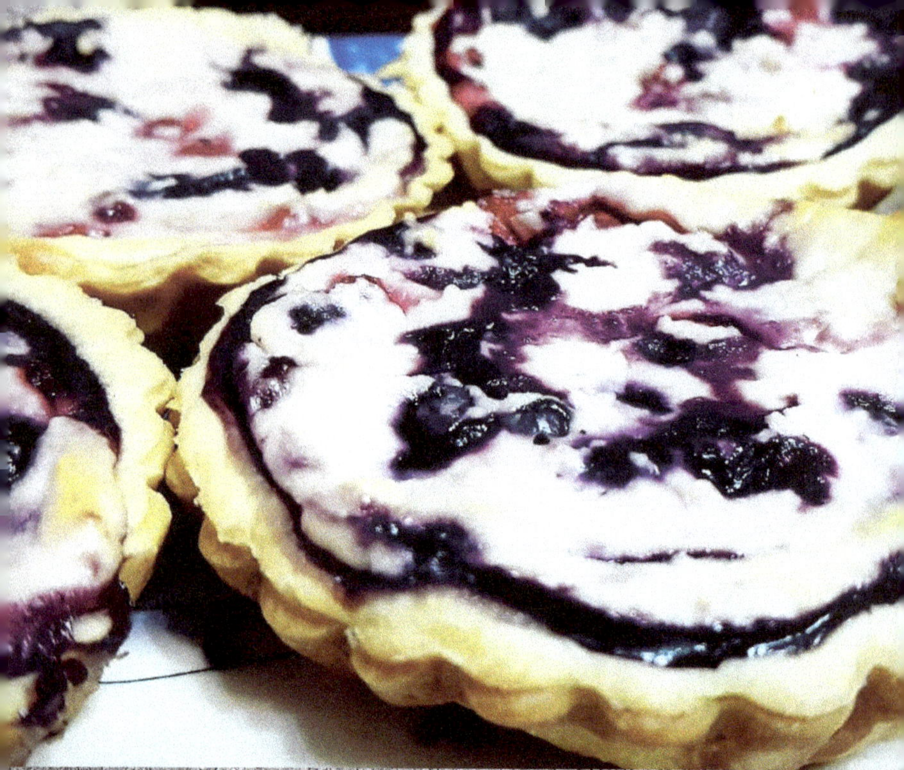

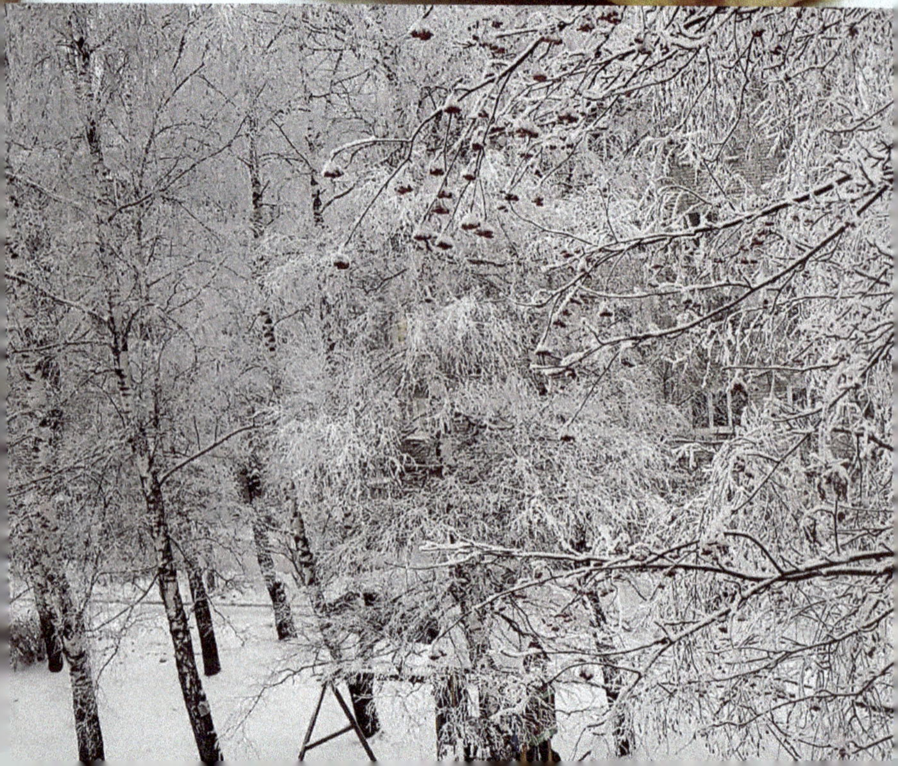

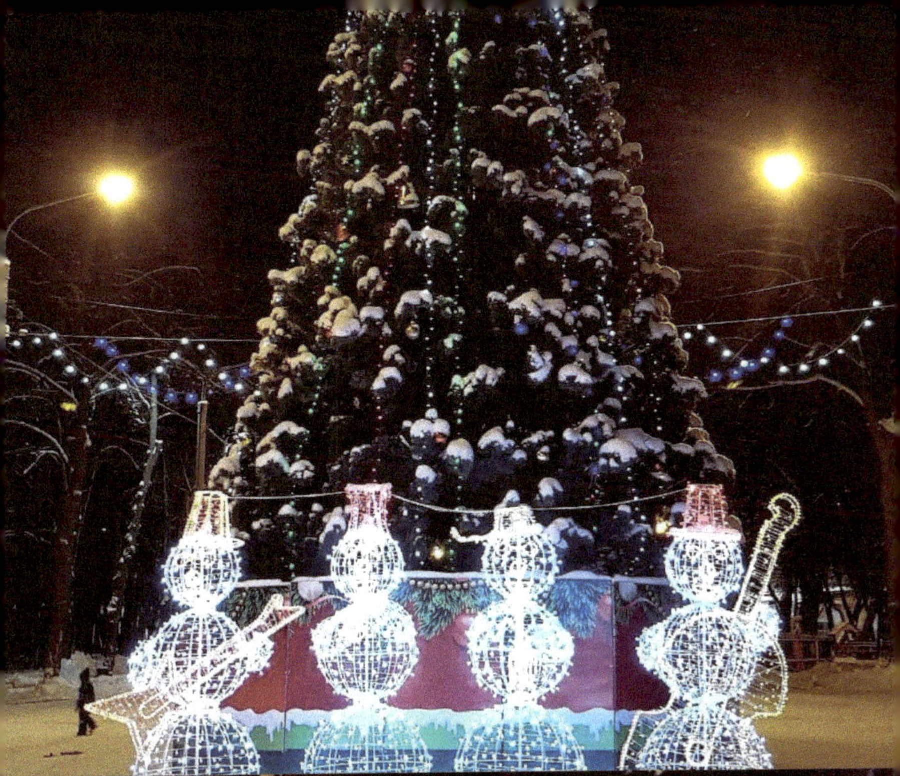
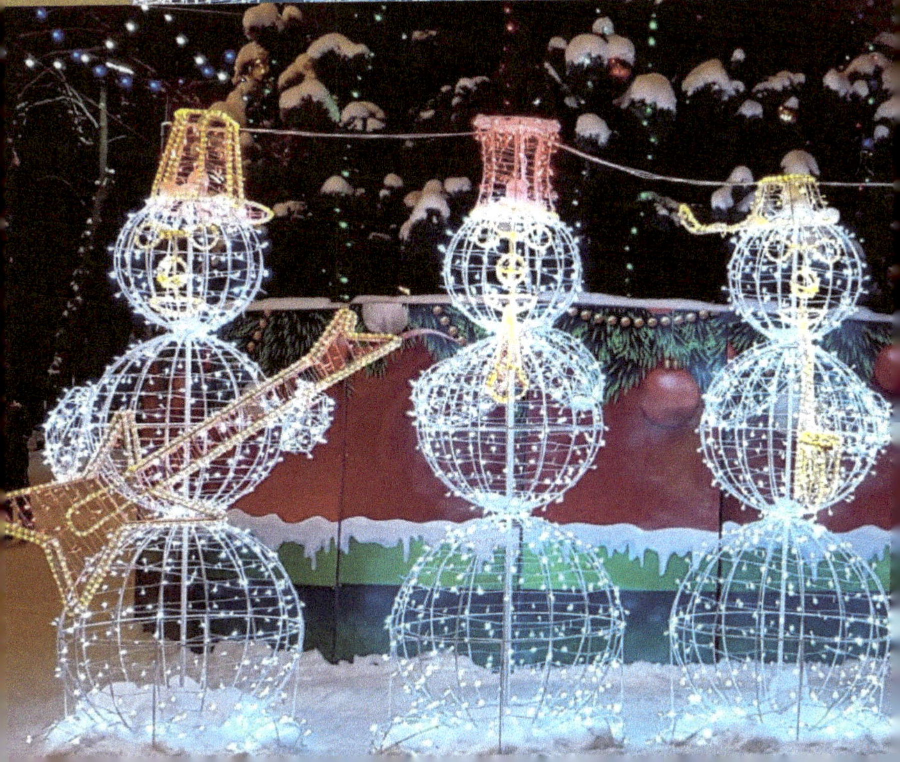

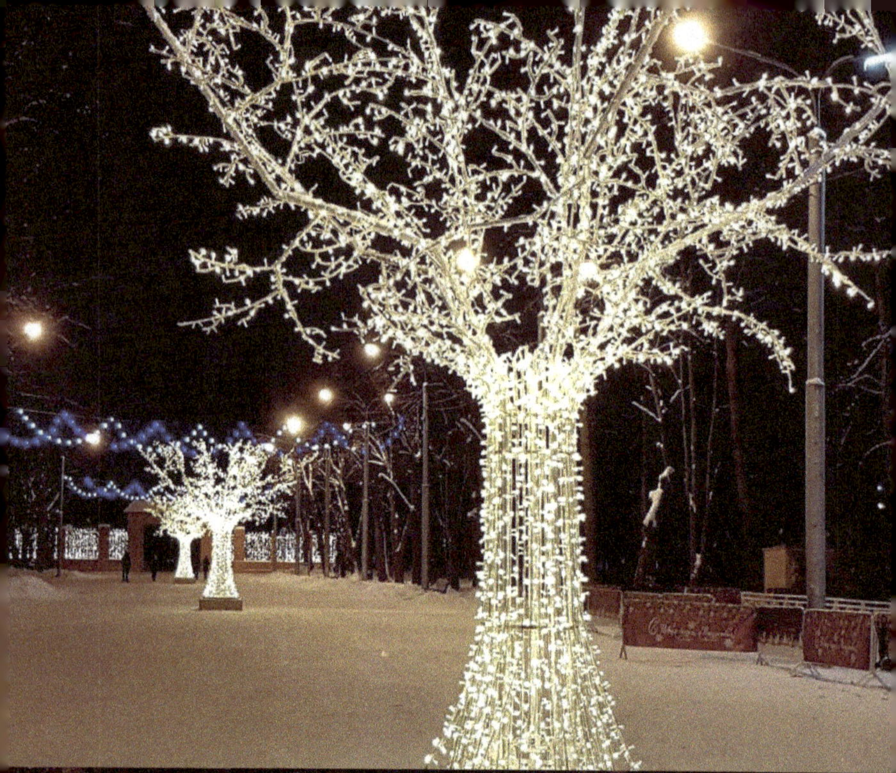

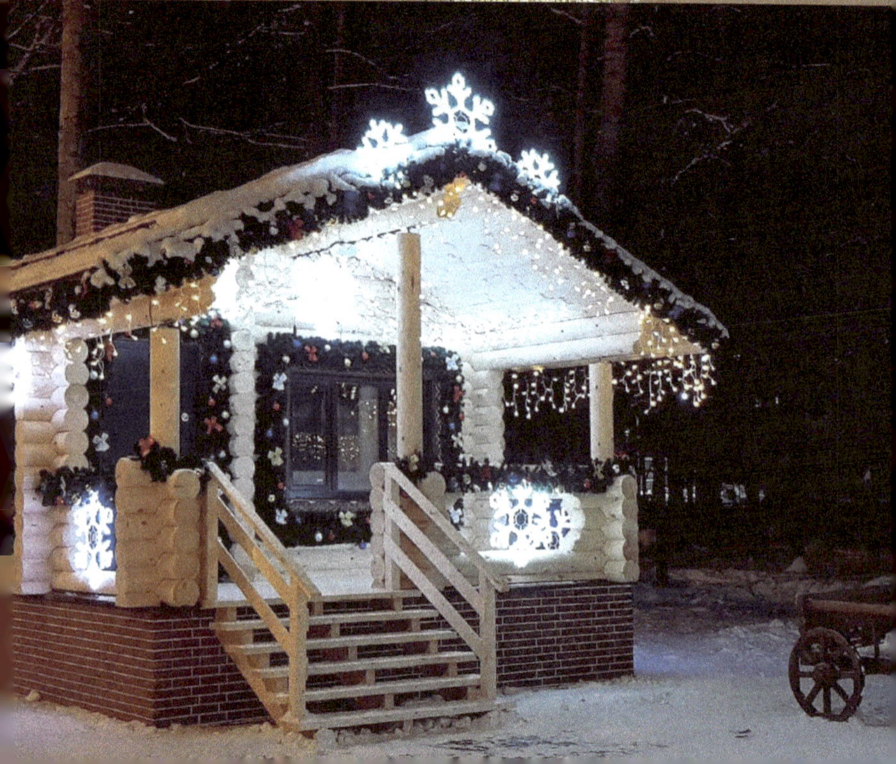

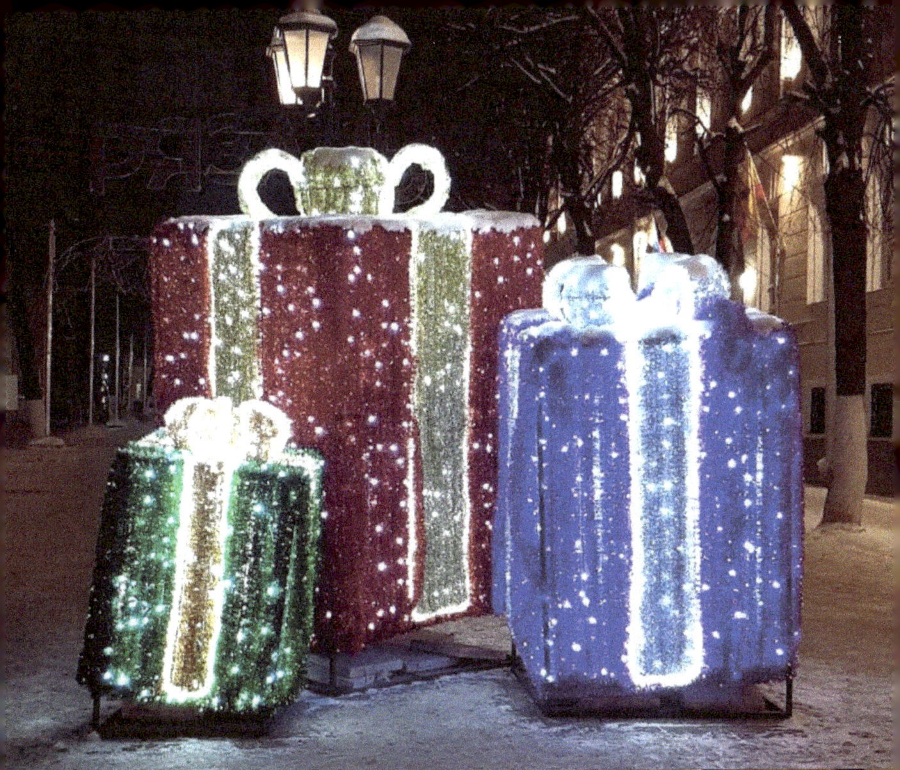

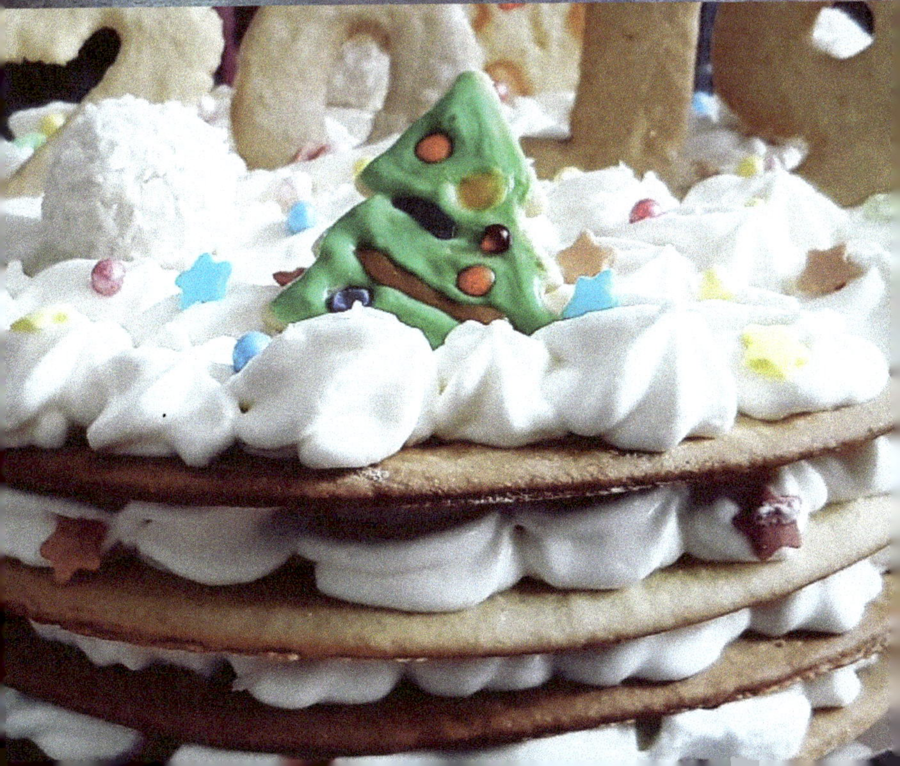

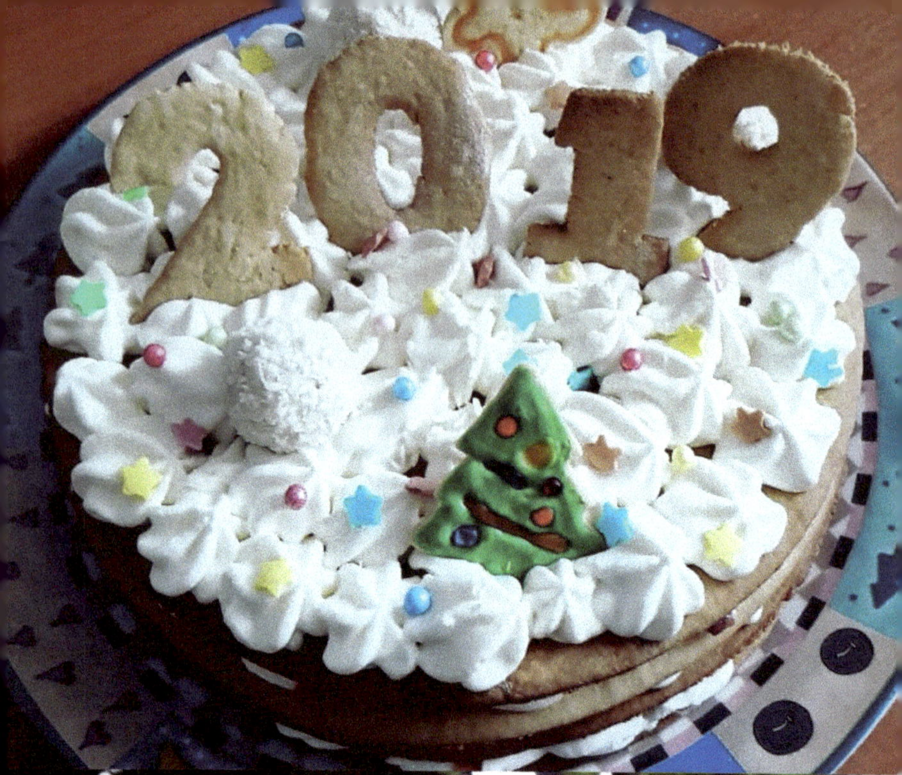
2019

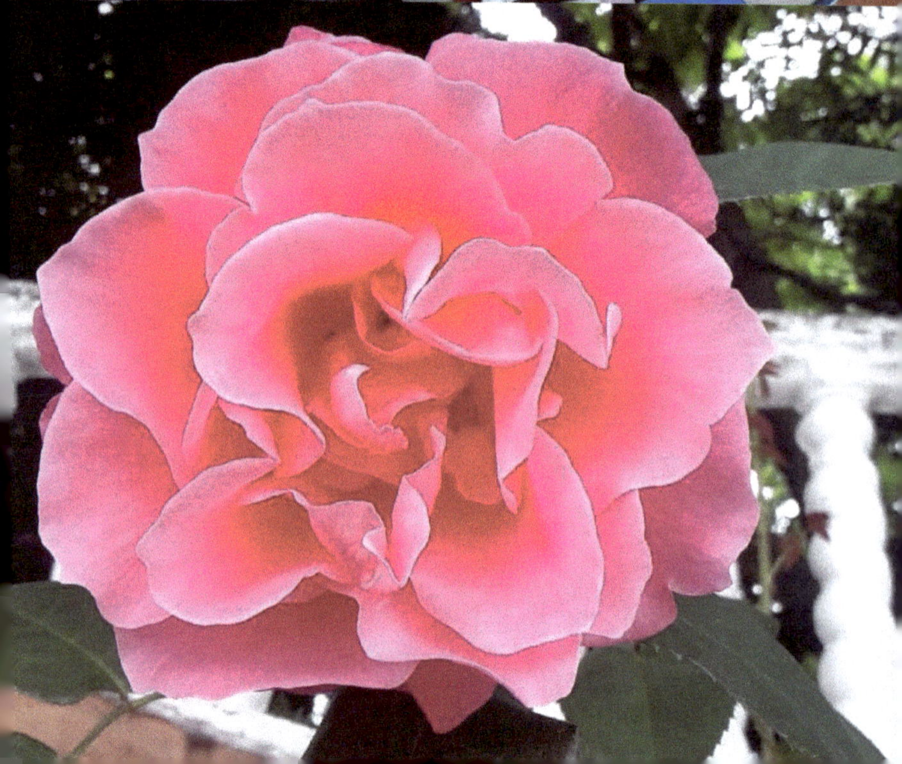

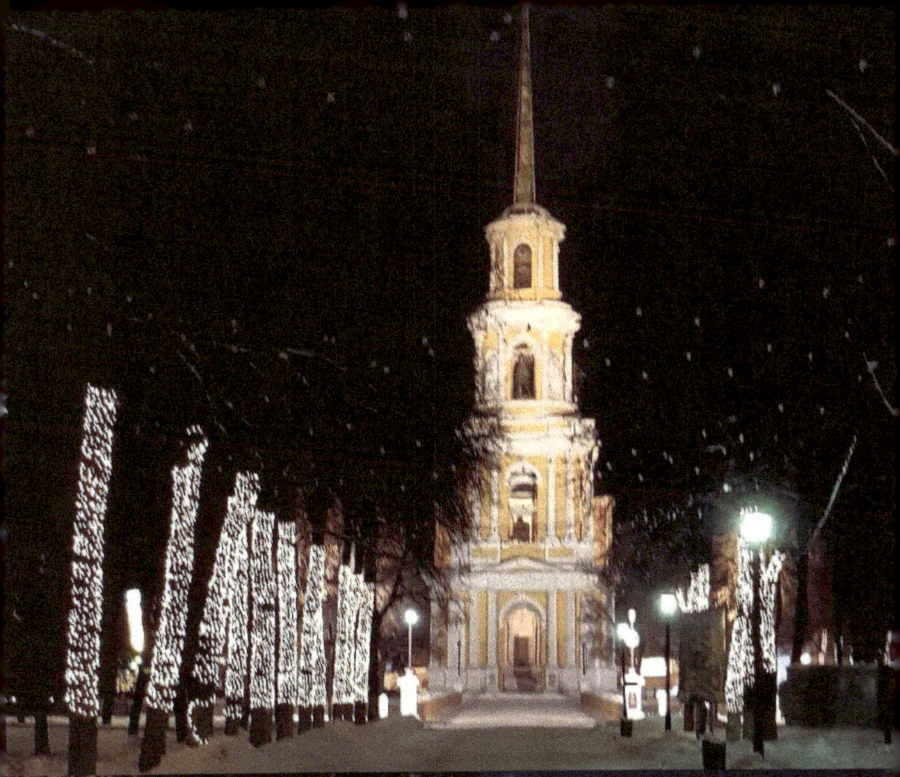
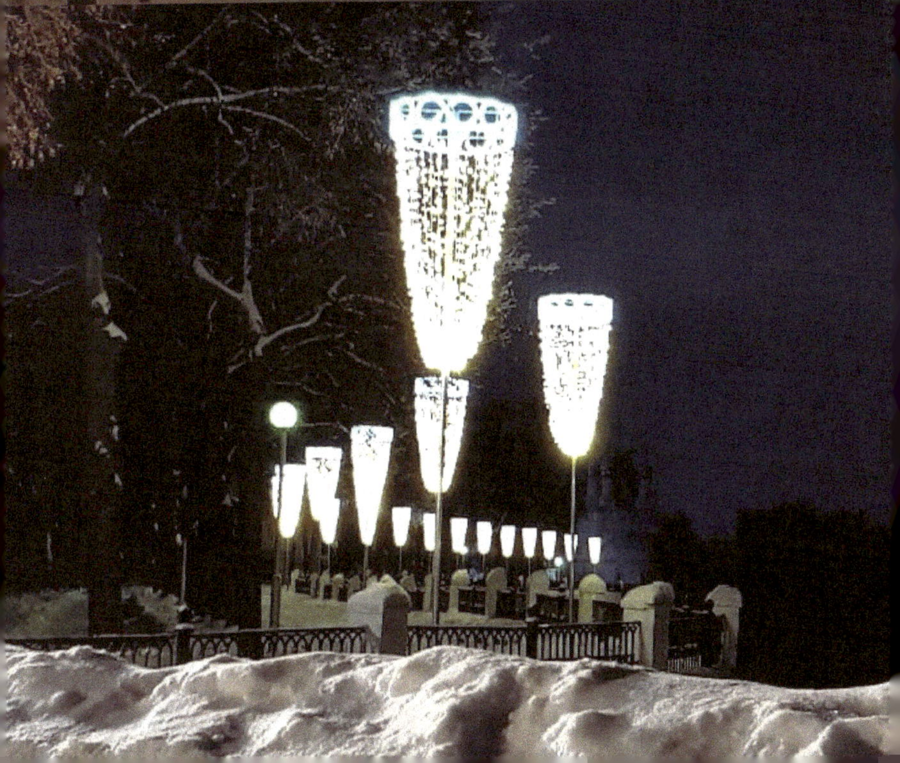

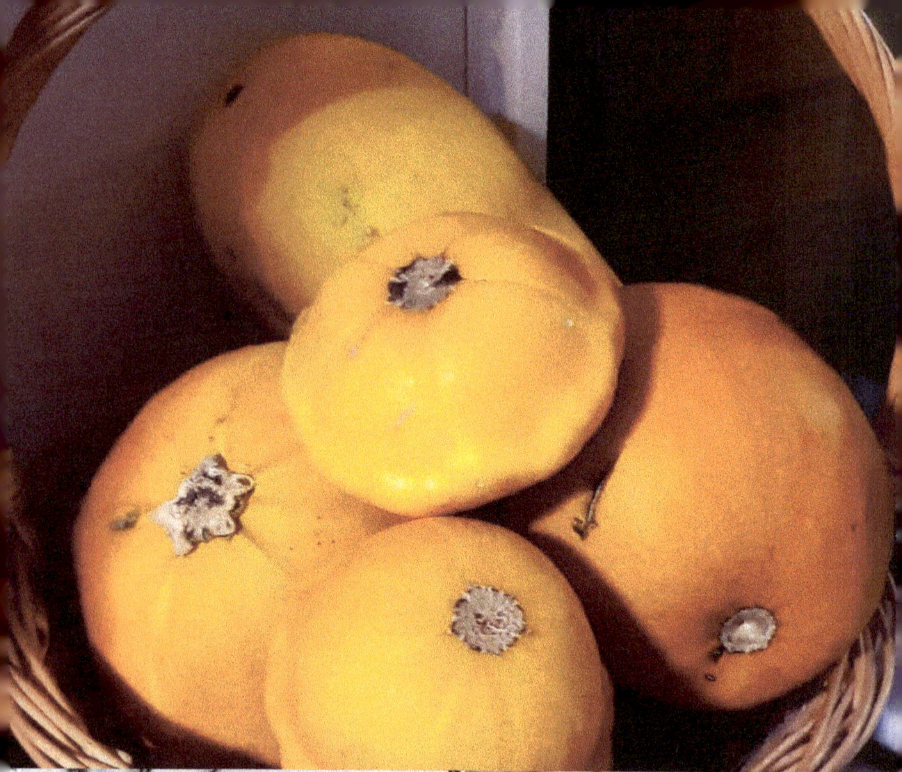
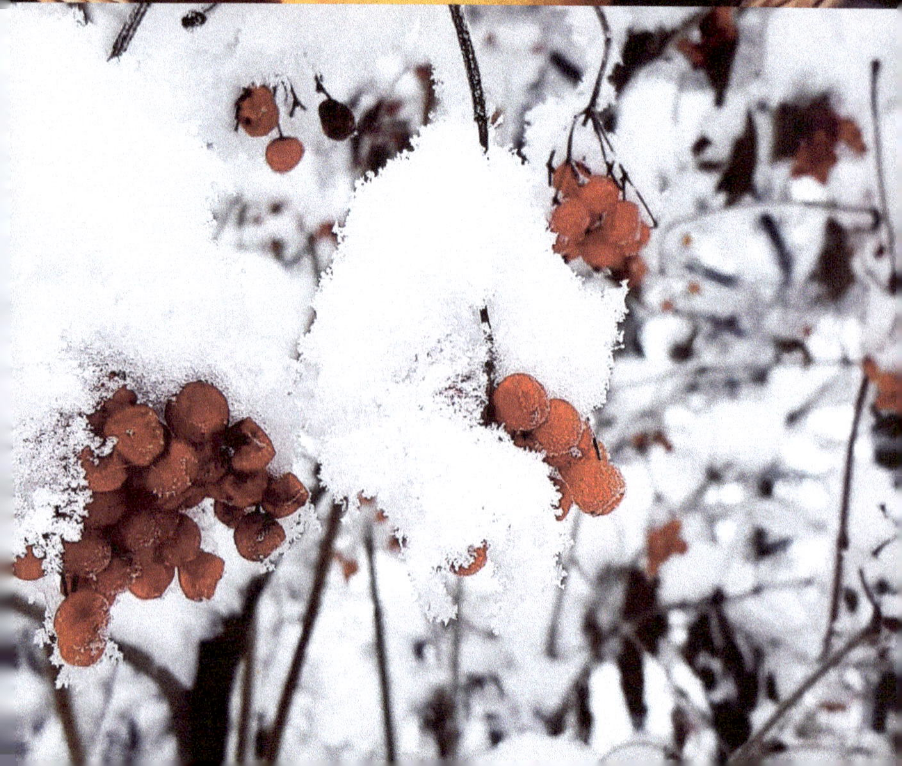

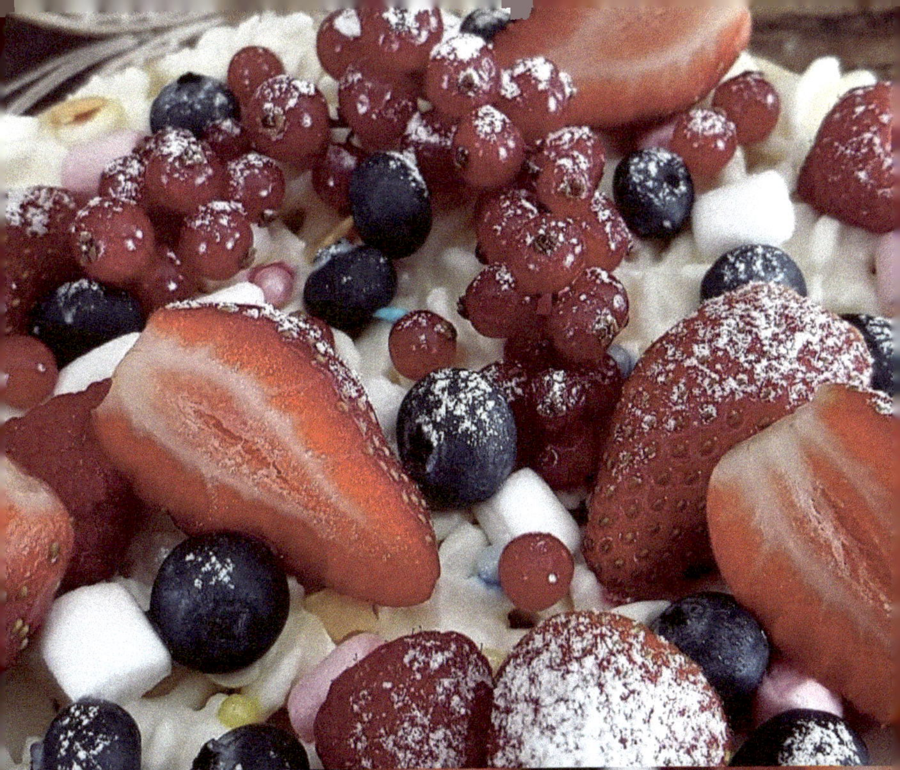
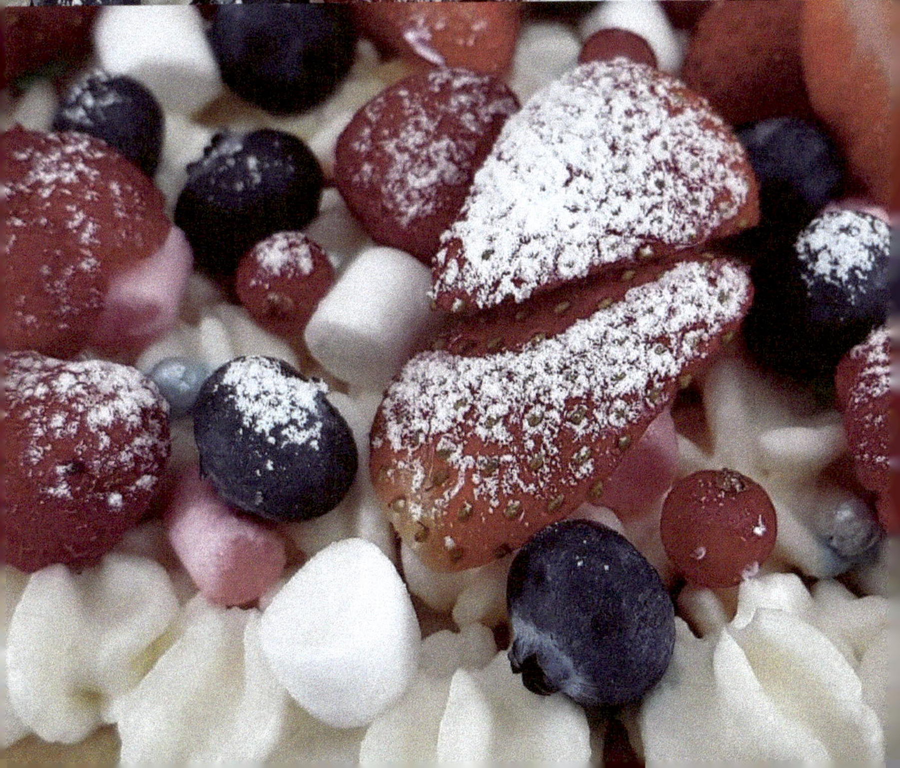

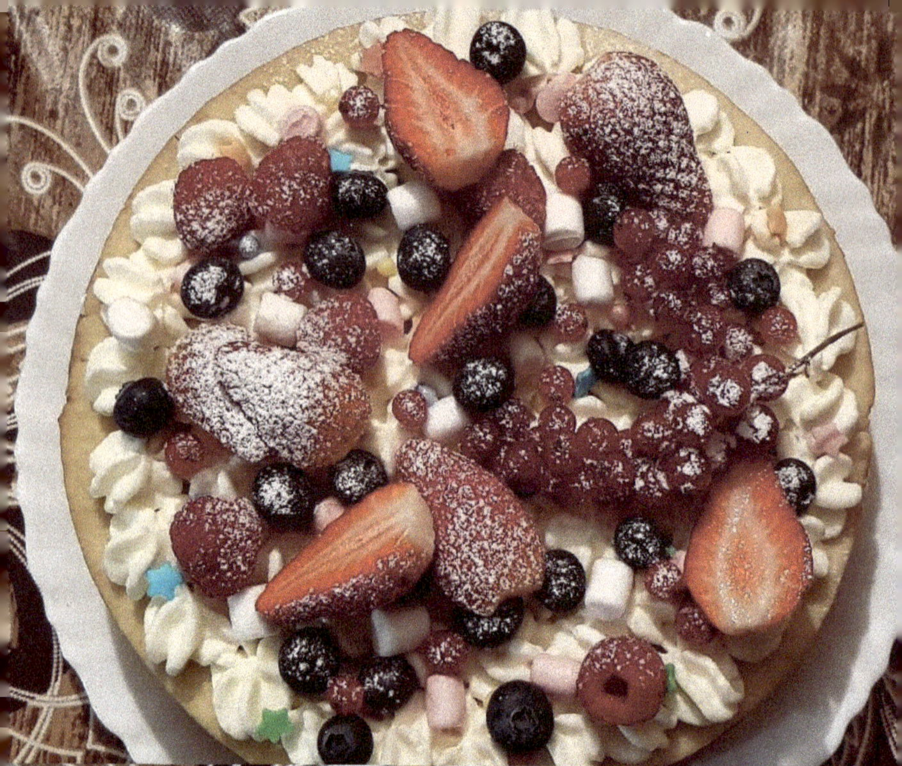

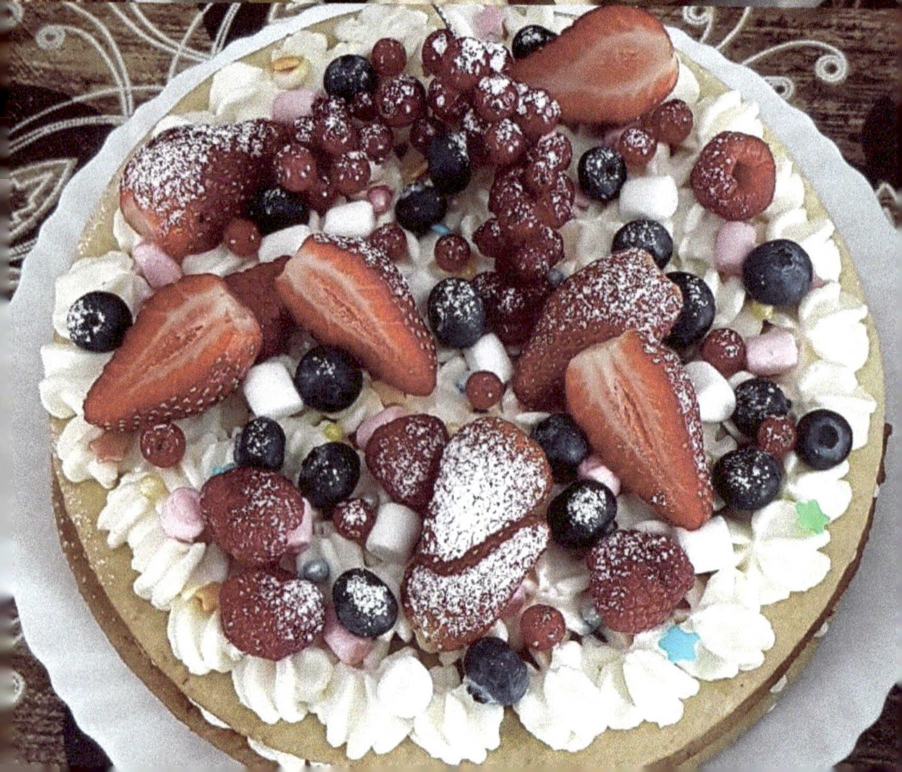

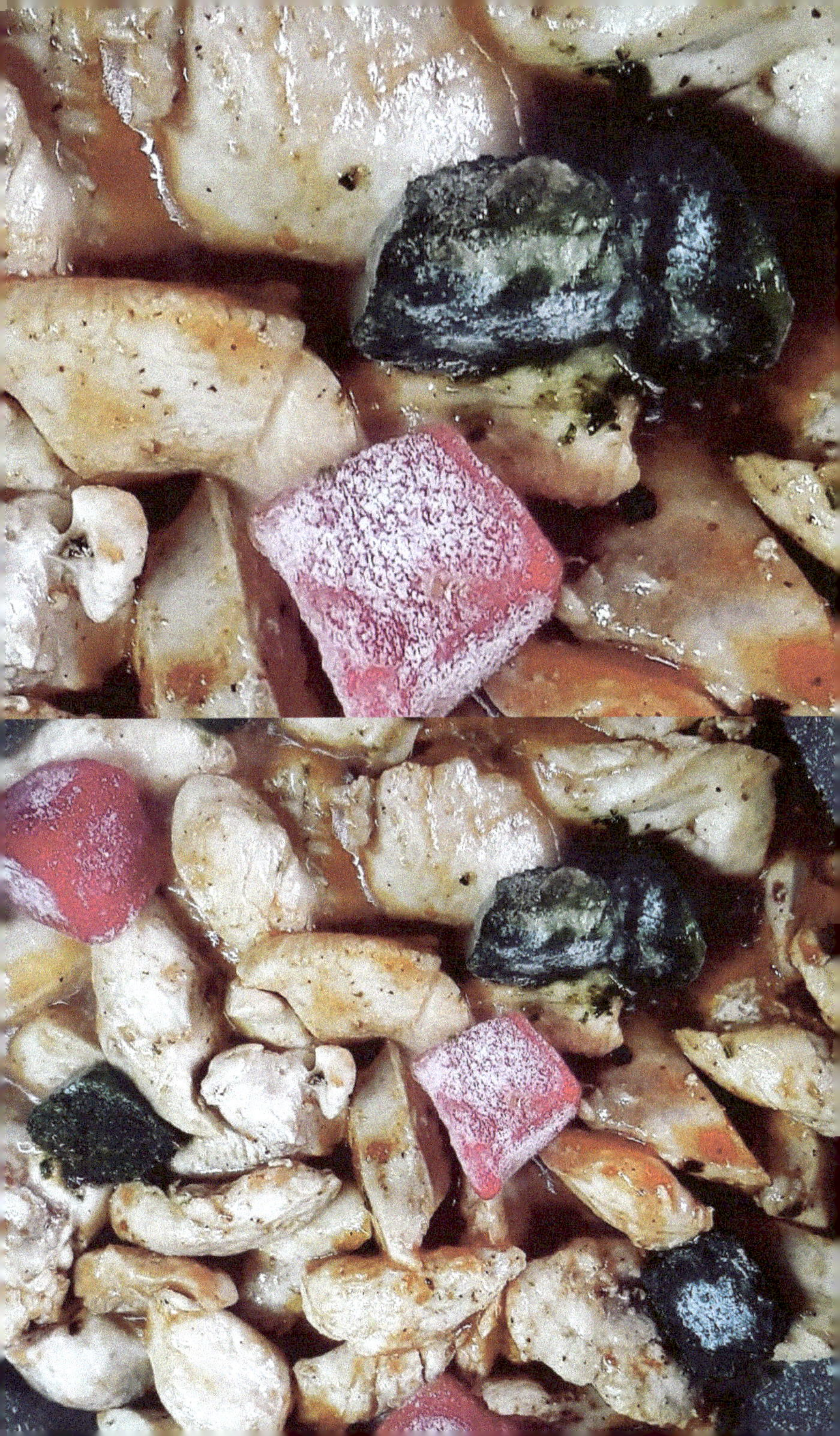

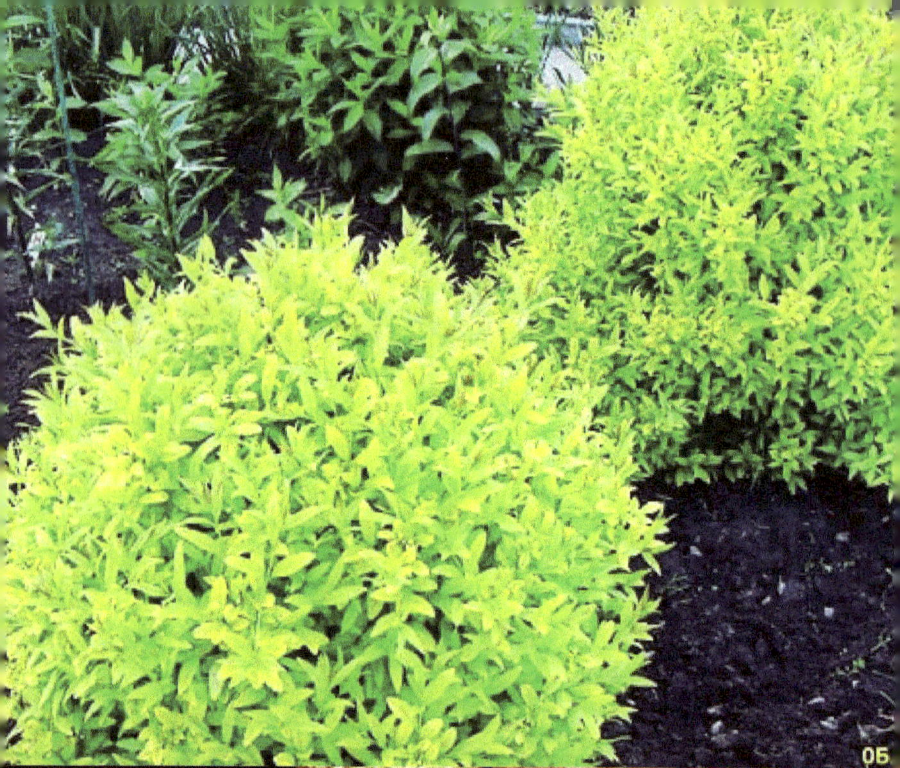
06

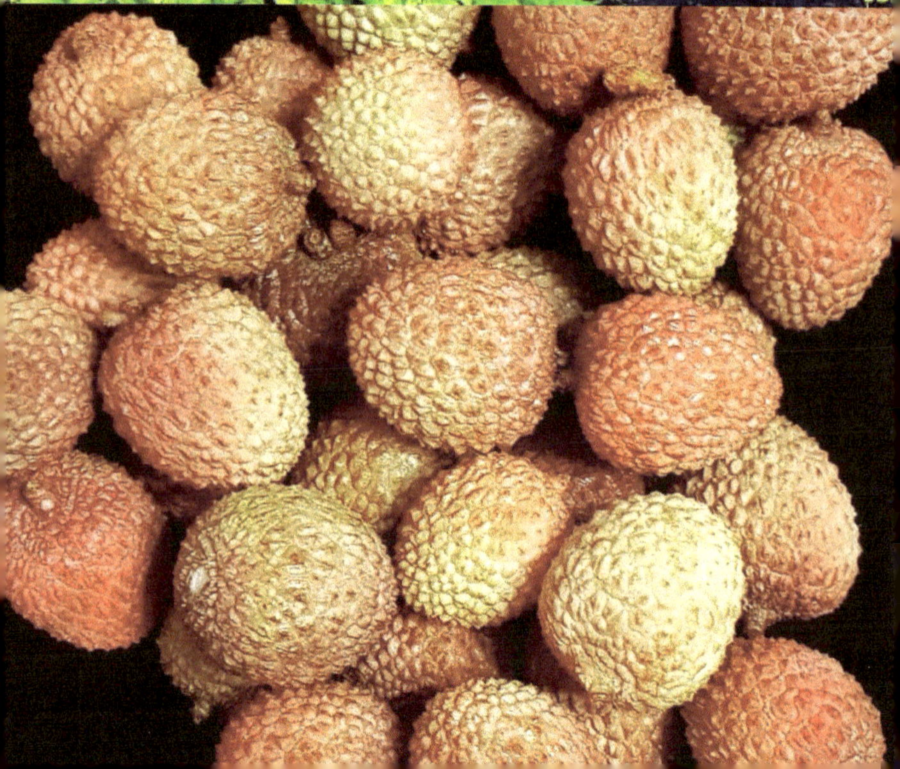